THE SOCIAL ORGANIZATION OF GAY MALES

Joseph Harry
William B. DeVall

THE SOCIAL ORGANIZATION OF GAY MALES

PRAEGER PUBLISHERS
Praeger Special Studies

New York • London • Sydney • Toronto

Library of Congress Cataloging in Publication Data

Harry, Joseph.
The social organization of gay males.

Bibliography: p.
1. Homosexuality, Male—United States. 2. Social interaction. 3. Sex role. 4. Gay Liberation Movement—United States. I. DeVall, Bill, joint author. II. Title.
HQ76.2.U5H37 301.41'57 78-8381

PRAEGER SPECIAL STUDIES
383 Madison Avenue, New York, N.Y., 10017, U.S.A.

Published in the United States of America in 1978
by Praeger Publishers,
A Division of Holt, Rinehart and Winston, CBS, Inc.

89 038 987654321

Printed in the United States of America

CONTENTS

LIST OF TABLES AND FIGURES

INTRODUCTION

Why another book on gay males? Haven't there already been enough? Given the large literature on male homosexuality, these are reasonable questions. Our justification for this book is based on the deficiencies and gaps in the literature. While there are many books and articles on male homosexuality, almost all of them are either purely descriptive or highly impressionistic, deal either with selected aspects of male homosexuality or with selected types of gay males, lack objectivity, or are just plain wrong. The present work is not intended to be simply another description of gay exotica or an ethnography of an institution, such as the gay bar. Rather it is a structural and analytical treatment of important questions for both social theoriests and for those who make public policy.

Although serious analyses of gays and their developing subculture are largely lacking in the literature, the ethnography of gay subcultures is, by now, fairly extensive. Ethnographies of gay life-styles range from Warren's (1974) study of the social circles of middle-class Southern California gays to participant observation studies of gay baths (Weinberg and Williams 1975), gay bars (Achilles 1967), gay neighborhoods (Levine 1977), and social networks (Hooker 1967).

Few works on male homosexuality that rise above the exotic or ethnographic offer adequate data. A few that do include Tripp's *The Homosexual Matrix* (1975), Weinberg and Williams's *Male Homosexuals: Their Problems and Adaptations* (1974), Saghir and Robins's *Male and Female Homosexuality* (1973), and Gagnon and Simon's *Sexual Conduct* (1973). Our book makes frequent reference to their findings while it attempts to assess some of their ideas with new data. At a number of points in our analysis, we found that our statistics were identical to or very similar to those in the above works, and so we can place great confidence in our own samplings and findings. Probably the most significant work in theoretical sociology focusing on homosexuality is Gagnon and Simon (1973). We have frequently attempted to assess some of their hypotheses with our own data, yet at several points, it was necessary to take issue with their views.

Anita Bryant's media blitz and her Save Our Children campaign of 1977 heightened public awareness of male homosexuality in North America more than ever before. Whereas "homosexual scares" occurred in the past, they were all on a local rather than on a national level. These were usually one-sided, since, until recently, homosexuals chose not to fight but to quietly close their "closet doors."

Although we did not anticipate the recent campaigns over human rights for homosexuals when we began our research, the discussions generated by them in the mass media have highlighted the moral differences over the issues of homosexuality and the lack of facts on which to base informed public policy opinions. In the present work, we hope to contribute somewhat more light than heat to these issues.

Our study explored a number of topics about which little or nothing has been written, As deviants, how do gay males perceive and relate to other gay males? Do deviants use and give credence to the labels that the larger society has applied? Do the labels promote negative attitudes among gay males? If so, how are they able to neutralize such negative labels in order to develop more positive relationships among themselves? Chapter 3, Mutual Labeling among the Stigmatized, attempts to answer these questions.

How does the teen-age gay feel about himself, and what sort of identity does he have before he "comes out"? Do teen-age experiences affect the quality of his subsequent gay "career"? Does the timing of coming out affect the quality of that career? We suggest that coming out is largely synchronous with the arrival of adult autonomy and that socialization into how to be gay—as opposed to recognition of one's homosexuality—is deferred until adulthood. The whole coming-out process as it influences the gay career is explored in Chapter 4, Adolescent Experiences and Coming Out.

Conventional wisdom holds that gay males cannot maintain stable, affectionate relationships with each other. But, in Chapter 5, Marriages between Gay Males, we analyze their "marital" relationships and find substantial variations. Gays seem to have developed a version of marriage that is more "open" than traditional heterosexual marriages. Such open marriages among gays appear to be more successful than those where the partners demand fidelity.

How do gays of different ages and social status relate to each other? The conventional assumption is that gay culture is highly youth-oriented and that "no one loves you when you're old and gay." Yet our data indicate that in a large number of instances, older and younger gays are mutually attracted to each other and sometimes form satisfying, nonexploitative "May-December" relationships.

The social ecology of gay communities is explored in Chapter 8, Urbanization and the Development of Homosexual Communities. We argue that in large cities, where gay repression has been minimal, an approximation of "institutional completeness" has developed. In such cities, gays have invented or developed a variety of institutions designed to meet their own needs, such as gay bars and churches and political, leisure, and artistic organizations. Gay ghettoes have, however, developed. In contrast to the gay communities of large cities, those of smaller cities and towns have remained culturally impoverished.

In Chapter 9, Gays and Work: Discrimination and Adaptation, we explore the occupational niches that male homosexuals find for themselves. The conventional assumption is that gay males prefer the occupations of hairdresser, florist, interior decorator, and the like. While there is an element of truth in this observation, we find it much more interesting to analyze the reasons behind the choice of such occupations. Our data indicate, as do all other studies, that gay males are, for the most part, highly educated. Yet probably due to discrimination, they have not been able to translate their education into occupational status and its financial rewards. We offer the, perhaps, brazen suggestion that like blacks in professional sports, those overt gays who are able to achieve occupationally are probably more accomplished than their heterosexual peers. Our rationale for this suggestion is that standards of performance are higher for obvious gays than for heterosexuals in many occupations.

Chapter 10, Gay Liberation: Action and Reaction, analyzes the gay liberation movement and the reactions to it—including Anita Bryant's crusade. The emergence of a serious gay liberation movement at a time when some social and political movements have faded is examined in light of theories of social movements. We also discuss recent surveys on popular attitudes toward homosexuality, especially homophobia.

Finally the concluding chapter, Policy Considerations and the Future: A Place in the Sun?, discusses the advantages and disadvantages for homosexuals of various social-policy alternatives. In the public arena, private problems are considered to be public-policy issues. Prejudice, ideological orthodoxy, and outright ignorance are frequently given greater weight than are the facts. The best service that social scientists can offer is a set of alternative policies and then a rational assessment of their consequences.

A number of questions are not addressed in this book. We have not given great attention to the question of whether gays may be considered mentally ill. Although several recent studies (Seigelman 1972; Saghir and Robins 1973) have found slightly higher rates of psychopathology among gay males than among comparable heterosexuals, the differences in these rates can be attributed to the psychological oppression of individual gays and to the political repression of gay communities and institutions. We also do not consider lesbians, except where the logic of our argument requires it.

A few words about our value premises are in order. The reader will find that in the present work, our sympathies are with the gays and with human rights. We proceed from the conclusion of John Stuart Mill that in the area of self-regarding actions, the freedom of the individual is absolute (except where it infringes on the freedom of others) and may not be abridged by legislatures, popular referenda, or "moralists" of any age, size, or sex.

THE SOCIAL ORGANIZATION OF GAY MALES

1

THEORETICAL PERSPECTIVES ON MALE HOMOSEXUALITY

PSYCHIATRIC THEORIES

From the beginning of the twentieth century through the mid-1950s, the study of homosexuality was almost exclusively done by psychiatrists, with the notable exception of Kinsey and his colleagues (1948). Psychology and sociology contributed in only a minor way to theories of homsexuality current during the first half of the century. Since psychiatric theories, and particularly psychoanalytic (Freudian) theories, became the popular psychology of the literate public at this time, psychiatric interpretations of homsexuality were popularized as well. Hence the public's perception of homosexuals was colored by a combination of popular stereotypes and psychiatric theorizing. Given the similarities between the popular stereotypes and the psychiatric theories, it was relatively easy to view male homosexuals as mentally ill, usually effeminate, fearful of women, and having a feminine gender identity.

Unlike the theories of psychology or sociology, psychiatric theory quickly became dogma with minor alternative variations. Since psychiatrists were practicing professionals licensed by the state, they could not afford the luxury of uncertainty, generally characteristic of academicians. It was an economic necessity to prove to the public and to the licensing agencies that psychiatry was competent to diagnose accurately and to treat effectively psychopathologies. This required a posture of scientific knowledge and certainty that was vastly greater than was actually possessed. Largely lacking a scientific data base, psychiatry—rather than the more empirical and cautious field of psychology—was granted state permission to define, treat, and control those persons viewed by the profession as psychopathological. Psychiatric theory, therefore, became public policy. This historical situation had great impact upon the lives of several generations of homosexuals.

The diagnosing of homosexuality as a pathological condition was also significant for the future of the psychiatric profession. As Tripp (1975, pp. 246-50) has argued, psychiatry and homosexuals have not been good for each other. The former labeled, treated, and institutionalized the latter for the first two-thirds of the century. However, homosexuals have constituted the principal evidence discrediting the scientific credentials of the psychiatric profession. As nonpsychiatric evidence on homosexuality was accumulated from 1948 to the present, it became increasingly clear that almost all the views of psychiatrists on the topic of homosexuality were wrong. Also, during the 1960s and 1970s, members of the gay liberation movement, having realized the theoretical and diagnostic injustice perpetrated upon them by psychiatry, demonstrated against and criticized the profession. In 1973, psychiatry removed homosexuality from its diagnostic manual of mental illnesses. Less known, however, is the fact that the profession recategorized homosexuality as a "sexual disturbance." No one knows whether the profession has in practice come to view homosexuality as nonpathological or whether the 1973 change in the diagnostic manual was simply an expedient relabeling in response to immense criticism. In 1974, the profession held a membership referendum on the above nomenclature change, which was passed by a vote of 58 to 42 percent. Many psychiatrists, such as Albert Ellis (1968), still firmly view homosexuals as pathological, even as psychotic.

In this chapter, we consider the three principal psychological themes that psychiatrists have used historically to interpret male homosexuality: feminine gender identity, dominance-power motivations, and psychopathology. While some authors have emphasized certain of these themes as explanatory mechanisms more than others have, these themes constitute the main elements of the vast majority of psychiatric theory on this topic. Later anthropological and nonpsychoanalytical evidence have shown that the first two elements may be valid in the understanding of homosexuality. At present, however, we focus on the ways in which psychiatric theory has linked the first to elements to that of psychopathology.

Many psychoanalytic theorists have asserted that most male homosexuals have identified with the female gender (Ferenczi 1914; Fenichel 1945; Bieber et al. 1962). There is a prima facie plausibility to this idea. Since male homosexuals have, by definition, eroticized persons of the male gender it seems that they may have also internalized much of the rest of the female gender role. A number of the homosexual patients seen by psychiatrists do report childhood identification with, or a desire to be, like their mother (Bieber et al. 1962, p. 206). Similarly those male homosexuals who are most visible to the general public are the effeminate ones. However, reasons exist for discounting this type of evidence. Seigelman (1972) has found that effeminate homosexuals report the highest rates of psychopathological symptoms. Since such persons would be more likely to find their ways to a psychiatrist's office, it may be that psychiatrists have had contact with a highly selected sample of the population of gay men—namely, those who are both mentally troubled and have a female gender identification. If such a selection process is in operation, then psychiatrists are not in any position to speak of the characteristics of homosexuals due to their highly selective contacts with them. Because masculine homosexuals have remained substantially invisible, most persons outside of gay social circles have seen only those gay men who fulfill the popular or psychiatric stereotypes.

That the samples screened by psychiatry are inadequate to support the contention that male homosexuals have a female gender identity, however, does not disprove this notion. Others (Whitam 1977; Green 1976) have reported that many (nonclinical) male homosexuals had extensive childhood desires to be women. However, even if it were true that many or most gay men have a female gender identity, it does not necessarily follow that this caused them to choose men as erotic objects. It is possible that their choice of men as erotic objects led them to erroneously think that because they desired men, they were, therefore, essentially women. Given that virtually all cultures offer only two "choices" in the area of sexual identity, namely, being male or female, and given that the choice of erotic object is culturally tied to gender identity, gay men might have felt obliged to opt for a female gender identity during childhood.

There are several possible interpretations of the relationship between male homosexuality and female gender identification. The position taken by many psychiatrists is that homosexuality is a corollary of an assumed female gender identity, that is, that female gender identity causes homosexuality in men. A second interpretation is that during childhood, some children eroticized males and then made the unnecessary inference that they were, in essence, women. A third position is that there is no causal nexus between the two phenomena and that the psychiatrists have made the gratuitous assumption that a homosexual erotic object choice implies a female gender identity. A fourth alternative is that both psychiatrists and gay men have made the same inferential error because they are both captives of their culture's view of sex roles.

Some psychiatrists have emphasized dominance and power motivations in the etiology of male homosexuals (Socarides 1968, pp. 135-37; Ovesey 1965). In these interpretations, a homosexual orientation is often seen as a resolution of the Oedipal conflict. Fearing the father and his capacity to castrate him, the male child opts to appease him by symbolically making love to him in the form of other males. Through incorporating the penis, the homosexual acquires both evidence of his father's affection and the symbolic strength of the penis. There is some evidence that dominance motivations do play a role in homosexual behavior. The vast majority of gay men prefer a sexual partner who is quite masculine; few desire one who is effeminate. However, an interest in masculine men need not be explained by involuted theories of Oedipal conflict. Masculinity and dominance are a standard part of the male gender role and are considered erotic and desirable when desired by women. Since dominating behavior, or its appearance, is considered erotic in men in our culture, a desire for that behavior among gay men need not be explained in terms of psychopathology. They seem to have simply internalized their culture's conceptions of what is desirable in men. Hence one need not resort to Oedipal explanations of psychopathology to understand the sexual tastes of gay men.

The major tragedy of psychiatric theory is that psychiatrists utilized plausible explanatory concepts of dominance motivation and a female gender identity as bases for inferring the universal presence of psychopathology in male homosexuals. A desire for dominance or masculinity in sexual partners was viewed as motivated by fears of various sorts rather than simply as eroticization of masculinity. Through viewing homosexual motivations as based on fear of the father, or of women, or of castration, psychiatry fulfilled and extended the popular prejudices against deviations from the cultural sex roles. Believing strongly that only heterosexuality was normal, psychiatrists were blinded to the possibility that homosexuality is learned in ways that are similar to heterosexuality and reinforced through positive, rather than fear-based, motivations and rewards (Tripp 1975, pp. 77–80).

Even if it were true that male homosexuals had internalized a female gender identity, this would not be a sufficient basis for inferring the presence of psychopathology. Although statistically unusual, cross-gender identification is not necessarily pathological. To so argue is to assert that having a female gender identity is intrinsically pathological. For instance, if a couple were to consciously raise their male child as a girl, the result need not necessarily be psychopathological, although one would be tempted to question the mental states of the parents. In practice some parents seem to unintentionally effect a cross-gender identity. While there are substantial social disadvantages to having a cross-gender identity, such an identity is simply statistically unusual, like left-handedness. One may only reasonably infer that the person with a cross-gender identity somehow learned a preference for that gender.

Only after a half-century, during which psychiatric interpretations of male homosexuality held uncontested sway, did some evidence begin to appear that provided grounds for an alternate interpretation. Kinsey's (1948, pp. 625, 650) data showed that homosexual behavior among men was vastly more common than had been believed: roughly a quarter of the male population had had some homosexual erotic experience, and 9 percent were exclusively or predominantly homosexual. However, the Kinsey data did not effectively shake the belief in the pathology of homosexuality, since most of the homosexual behavior reported by Kinsey was confined to the period of adolescence or young adulthood, and this was discounted on the grounds of it being merely a youthful phase undergone by many heterosexual males.

The researches of Hooker (1957, 1965) were the first major blow to the interpretations of homosexuality as being pathological. Comparing nonclinical male homosexuals and heterosexuals on a number of psychological tests, she found no differences in symptomatology. Also, she found no personality differences between the two groups. Her pioneering work gave rise to research comparing the incidence of psychopathology in comparable heterosexuals and homosexuals who were not clinical samples. It also gave rise to two decades of dispute by psychiatrists, who still clung to the notion that homosexuality was necessarily pathological (Stoller et al. 1973; Bieber 1976). (It should be noted that Hooker did not prove that homosexual and heterosexual males are equal in their rates of psychopathology. Her major point was that there are many homosexuals who are free of psychopathology and that homosexuality does not necessarily imply the presence of pathology.)

Findings such as those of Westwood (1960, pp. 130-34) further discredited psychiatric interpretations by showing that most male homosexuals could not be categorized into "active" and "passive" types. The majority of homosexuals appear to be flexible in their sexual activities and freely interchange sexual roles. Simon and Gagnon (1967) and Saghir and Robins (1973) also contributed to the discrediting of psychiatric theory by showing that in many ways, homosexuals are indistinguishable from heterosexuals. They deal with their jobs, friends, and families in conventional ways, as do most heterosexuals. Only in the area of sexual behavior are there marked differences between heterosexuals and homosexuals. By broadening their foci of research beyond the narrowly sexual, later researchers showed that homosexuals and heterosexuals have more similarities than differences. These increasingly evident similarities both undercut most psychiatric theories of homosexuality and blurred the popular dichotomization of people into "normals" and "perverts." By the mid-1970s, the case of homosexuality had done much to contribute to the discrediting of psychiatric theory and made apparent the exhaustion of psychoanalytic theory. While those theories still have some outspoken advocates, such as Socarides (1968), whose views have been approvingly quoted by Anita Bryant, many social scientists no longer rely on psychiatry for interpretations of homosexuality.

A major departure from traditional psychiatric theories of homosexuality is the recent work of Tripp (1975). Using a wide range of cross-cultural evidence, plus unpublished data from the Kinsey Institute, he attempted to overcome the cultural blinders in traditional psychiatric theory. His first major contention was that a homosexual orientation was acquired during childhood through positive motivations and rewarding erotic experiences with same-sex persons rather than being fear-based in origins. Extending his views somewhat, it may be that during their childhoods, gay men came to define physical contacts with other males as erotic. When playing with brothers or other boys or when in physical contact with a father or other adult male relative, the child could have experienced erotic feelings. Sometimes these physical contacts would be intentionally sexual, as when male children engaged in mutual physical exploration. Other times, the child but not the adult may have defined a contact as erotic. While parents do not define their physical contacts with children as erotic, this does not mean that a child may not have experienced them as such. Indeed, the adult assumption that children are substantially free of sexual feelings permits adults to be physically free with caresses, hugs, and playfulness. It is highly unlikely that no children would define such contacts as sexual ones.

Once a child has had such rewarding erotic experiences with same-sex persons, those experiences prove to him that a person of the same sex can be a source of sexual pleasure. Having eroticized same-sex persons, it then becomes extremely difficult to later learn that such persons cannot be sources of sexual pleasure. In contrast, heterosexuals have learned to define same-sex persons as not being sources of physical pleasure. Hence homosexual sex remains puzzling to them and is seen as something that must be motivated by perverse feelings rather than by erotic ones. The homosexual knows otherwise.

Through these extensions of Tripp's ideas, we have suggested some of the possible origins of a same-sex eroticization. We have no convincing explanation of why sexual object choices so often tend to be exclusive. While it is possible for children to eroticize persons of the opposite sex, of the same sex, of both sexes, or of neither sex, they seem to overwhelmingly select only one sex; true bisexuality seems to be quite rare. Tripp attempts to explain the exclusiveness of sexual object choice through a principle of psychological contrasts (1975, pp. 92-93). When one defines a particular sex as erotic, one tends to deny the possible erotic value of the other sex. We suggest that his principle of contrasts may well be the result of the way in which many societies have constructed sex roles, that is, based on a dichotomous model. When a society defines sex roles, and particularly sexual roles, as mutually exclusive, individuals are invited to limit their sexual choices to one sex. Thus the homosexual child may assume that one is allowed to eroticize only one sex.

While erotic experiences with persons of the same sex during childhood are a major start on the road to adult homosexuality, Tripp (1975, pp. 74-75) suggests other cultural conditions that facilitate the development of a full-fledged adult homosexual orientation. He suggests that male homosexuality is most common in societies that strongly idealize masculine values and structure interpersonal relationships between men in a competitive way. Such an idealization of masculinity gives cultural significance to the erotic object choices of homosexual persons. A recent piece of research on homosexual activities between athletes provides some support for Tripp's views. Smith and Garner (1977) found that among several college athletic teams, "25 percent of the questionnaires admitted to homosexuality (homosexual acts) at least twice in the last two years." In one of the teams, 60 percent had been engaged in homosexual fellatio once; 48 percent had experienced it at least twice to the point of orgasm in the last two years. While the availability of substantial opportunity for homosexual acts may have contributed to this rather amazing volume of homosexual acts, the pervasive idealization of masculinity among athletes would also seem to be a likely contributing factor.

If it is true that idealization of masculine values in a culture does contribute to the incidence of homosexuality, we then might expect the currently changing definitions of sex roles to affect future rates of homosexuality. If in the future women will be defined as the equals of men—and thus, if dominance will not be viewed as an exclusively male trait—we might expect fewer male homosexuals.

In the above discussion, we have adopted a consistently negative attitude toward the psychiatric literature on male homosexuality. We believe this is justified, since with the major exception of Tripp, psychiatry has contributed nothing to the understanding of homosexuality. For a half-century, theoretically, it has been in a dead-end. While psychiatry may have had some beneficial influences, such as improving the humaneness of conditions in mental hospitals, its effects in the area of homosexuality have been almost totally malignant. (We can credit psychiatric treatment with serving as an alternative to jail in cases where a judge suspended a convicted homosexual's sentence on the condition that he obtain psychiatric treatment.) The psychiatric professsion has provided several decades of pseudoscientific certification of the truth of popular stereotypes of homosexuals. It has offered to young gays explanations of why they are mentally ill, and many have believed in them. Only within the last decade have gays felt sufficiently self-confident to repudiate the labels offered them by the psychiatric profession. We venture that if a poll were taken today among gays, a majority would opt for the legal decertification of the psychiatric profession.

SEX RESEARCH

A more recent and promising line of research bearing on the etiology of male homosexuality is research into gender, gender identity, and sex role behavior. Of particular importance have been the findings of Money and Tucker (1975), Green (1976), and Whitam (1977), based on groups of adult transsexuals, adult male homosexuals, and effeminate male children. In contrast to the control groups, very large percentages of these three groups of males reported the following behaviors during childhood: desiring to be of the opposite sex, cross-dressing, preference for playing with children of the opposite sex, and avoidance of rough play. Saghir and Robins (1973, pp. 18-31) have replicated these findings for male homosexuals. These data provide substantial support for the idea that gender identity and sexual orientation are established during the first few years of life. Money argues that they are usually fixed by the age of four.

While the data cited here support the notion that gender identity is often determined at an early age, it is not clear from these data whether it is cross-sex gender identification that gives rise to adult homosexuality or whether sexual orientation is partially independent of gender identity. A third of Saghir and

FIGURE 1.1

Gender Identity, Gender Role, and Sexual Orientations of Males

GENDER IDENTITY							
MALE				FEMALE			
GENDER ROLE				GENDER ROLE			
Masculine		Feminine		Masculine		Feminine	
Sexually Oriented to		Sexually Oriented to		Sexually Oriented to		Sexually Oriented to	
Males	Females	Males	Females	Males	Females	Males	Females
Masculine Gays	Masculine Heterosexuals	Effeminate Gays	Effeminate Heterosexuals			Homosexual Transsexuals	Heterosexual Transsexuals (?)
(1)	(2)	(3)	(4)	(5)	(6)	(7)	(8)

Source: Compiled by the authors.

Robins's adult homosexuals reported no childhood behavior indicative of a cross-gender identification. Presumably, these men acquired a homosexual orientation without having also acquired a cross-gender identity. Also, a large majority of adult male homosexuals report a basically masculine gender identity, are quite happy to be male, and would not want it any other way. This calls into question the notion that adult homosexuality is indicative of cross-gender identification. It is possible that many adult homosexuals may have had such an identity during childhood but subsequently changed it, while not changing their sexual orientation. This interpretation also calls into question a presumed close relationship between gender identity and sexual orientation.

In order to more systematically sort out the possible relationships among gender identity, sexual orientation, and sex-role content, we present Figure 1.1. Figure 1.1 depicts only the possible combinations among these variables for males. The definitions of the terms employed in Figure 1.1 are as follows: gender: the physical sex of a person; gender identity: the gender with which the person identifies; sex role or gender role: the cultural content of the gender identity, typically divided into masculine and feminine; and sexual orientation: the gender(s) a person has eroticized. In order to simplify the following discussion, we have omitted bisexuality and asexuality as possible sexual orientations from Figure 1.1.

The first cell of Figure 1.1 provides evidence against the notion that gender identity causes sexual orientation. Persons in this cell are masculine homosexuals, who have no identification with the female gender. Cell two presents no difficulties, since it simply contains heterosexual males who have a male gender identity and play a masculine sex role. Cell three is the case of effeminate gays, who despite their effeminacy, possess a male gender identity. Cell four's inhabitants are heterosexual males with a male gender identity but who are effeminate. Cell seven consists of male transsexuals who have a female gender identity, play a feminine sex role, and who eroticize the male gender.

Cells five, six, and eight are rather problematic and illustrate the difficulties in distinguishing gender identity from sex role. For instance, it is not clear where one should place male heterosexual transvestites. While it seems that they have adopted a feminine sex role, it is uncertain whether they have a male or female gender identity. If they have a male identity, they would belong in cell four with the effeminate heterosexuals. However, is their cross-dressing sufficient grounds for making the inference that their attachment to femininity has gone far enough that we may assume a female gender identity? If so, they would belong in cell eight. A classificatory problem also exists in the rare cases of heterosexual males who have presented themselves for sexual reassignment to the female gender (Barr, Raphael, and Hennessey 1974). It is unclear whether they have a male gender identity, a heterosexual orientation, and a feminine gender role or have a female gender identity, a heterosexual orientation, and a feminine gender role.

Cell five is also a problem, since it may be that some of the masculine homosexuals should be placed here. Those in cell five have a female gender identity, play a masculine sex role, and have eroticized males. However, since the vast majority of masculine male homosexuals profess a strong attachment to a male gender identity, one might be obliged to concede that this cell is empty or argue that their female gender identity is an unconscious one. If one were to introduce the notion of unconscious gender identification in this case, then one would be obliged to similarly consider such a possibility for the effeminate heterosexuals of cell four. Rather than introduce the rather gratuitous concept of unconscious gender identity, our suggested option is that cells five and six are probably empty.

The problem at hand, that of empirically distinguishing gender identity from gender role, arises because most of the evidence for assessing one's gender identity is also the evidence for inferring a gender role. The culturally defined composites of traits that define one's gender role are also the means whereby the individual, or an outside observer, infers his or her core gender identity. Hence it is quite easy to see how gender-deviant individuals can become confused as to what they "really" are. Gender identity is a psychological and cultural inference from gender-role behaviors in the same way that Aristotelian essences are inferences from the composites of traits exhibited by an entity. It seems then that gender identities only need exist when individuals make the culturally prescribed inferences and assume them to exist. While individuals are objectively male or female and masculine or feminine, they only have gender identities by inference.

In discussing the childhood characteristics of adult male homosexuals, Whitam (1977) has introduced the interesting concept of "defeminization." Whitam's defeminization hypothesis suggests that among those with nonheterosexual orientations, gender identity may be a variable rather than the culturally imposed (inferential) constant it seems to be among heterosexuals. For those who have not been psychologically overwhelmed by the fixity of gender roles and gender identities, they may be able to adapt their identities, but not their sexual orientation, to the demands of the adult gay and heterosexual worlds. Such variability in gender identities over time may help to explain the considerable heterogeneity in masculinity-femininity found among gay men. Of course, the interpretation of defeminization as changing gender identity rather than changing gender role is in flat contradiction with Money's claim of the fixity of gender identities. More research, or reconceptualization, is needed to clarify the defeminization process.

He found that although a majority of male homosexuals had engaged in much cross-gender behavior during childhood, by the time they reached adulthood, they had substantially divested themselves of this behavior. During their teen-age years, they apparently became more masculine in their interests and forms of deportment. These findings raise the question of whether the changes they were undergoing were changes of gender identity, of sex-role content, or both. If we subscribe to Money's ideas that gender identity is fixed early in life and that later it is so unchangeable that as in the case of transsexuals, one must change anatomy rather than identity, then it seems likely it is the sex-role content that is changing among teen-aged homosexuals. It would seem that teen-aged homosexuals learn that effeminate behavior, which may be tolerated or appreciated as "cute" during childhood, is increasingly punished as one grows older. Such behavior is frowned on in older male juveniles, because it is increasingly, and accurately, felt to be an indicator of adult homosexuality.

There is some evidence to support the notion that defeminization in male homosexuals does not cease with the beginning of adulthood but continues into mid-life. Observers of the adult gay world (Gagnon and Simon 1973, pp. 147-49) have reported considerable effeminate behavior among gay men who have recently come out. While it has been suggested that such behavior is simply a rather enthusiastic response to the discovery of the adult gay world, it may also be an extension of similar behavior that existed prior to that discovery. It also seems true that after being in the adult gay world for a few years, many gay men discontinue their effeminate behavior. Not only is such behavior punished in the heterosexual world, it is a disadvantage in gay sexual marketplaces, which emphasize not only youth but also masculinity.

The above lines of research and reasoning on gender identity, sex roles, and sexual orientation may constitute a substantial theoretical breakthrough in understanding homosexuality. However, it seems there are a number of instances of homosexual behavior that are not amenable to this approach. Situational homosexuality—homosexual sex in prisons, the military, and other institutions—seems more readily explainable by a lack of heterosexual opportunities. Also, the cases of those males who do not behaviorally express their homosexual interests until mid-life do not fit in well with these lines of reasoning. The cases of bisexuals or heterosexually married homosexual males probably require modification of these theories. Differences between cultures must also be taken into consideration in ideas about the relationships of gender identity, sex roles, and sexual orientations. Carrier (1971, 1977) has reported that in contrast to the Anglo cultures of England and the United States, Hispanic, Greek, and Turkish cultures tie gender identity to sex-role content much more closely. In consequence, it seems that gay men in those cultures fit better into an active/passive or "butch/femme" formulation.

LABELING THEORY

Since approximately 1960, labeling theory has been one of the major perspectives utilized in analyzing the behavior of male homosexuals, as well as many other forms of deviance. Before attempting to evaluate this theory's utility in application to the case of male homosexuals, we will briefly sketch its principal tenets (Becker 1963; Lemert 1967; Schur 1971).

Many persons engage in deviant behavior without major commitment to that behavior and without the intention of making a career of deviance. Some are detected in their deviance and publicly given condemnatory labels, such as "queer," "criminal," or "crazy." The labeling of these individuals may be formal, as in cases of criminal trials or in commitment to a mental hospital, or it may be conducted informally, through gossip about the deviant by friends, acquaintances, co-workers, and neighbors. Subsequent to labeling, conventional persons exclude the labeled person from respectable settings. He may be fired, avoided, court-martialed, not promoted, not hired, excommunicated, or dropped from membership. As access to the rewards of conventional roles is denied to the individual, the exclusionary process makes a career of continuing deviance more likely. He develops associations with other deviants of his particular type. In a deviant group, he finds acceptance. Eventually he also develops a new and deviant self-identity. Because conventional society has denied him the possibility of continuing a conventional career, he develops a deviant one. As such, deviant individuals and groups are cast outs from the respectable world.

Given the research findings on the development of sexual orientation, gender identity, and sex-role content (discussed above), it seems quite unlikely that labeling as "homosexual" and subsequent exclusion could be considered significant contributing factors to the genesis of a homosexual orientation. A homosexual orientation seems to develop quite early in the majority of cases, typically prior to age 14 (Saghir and Robins 1973, pp. 33-35). This orientation seems to precede the times when there could be any significant amount of labeling. Also, many teen-age heterosexuals may not have the label of homosexual in their vocabularies and, thus, would be largely incapable of applying it to their peers. Hence as Plummer (1975, pp. 58-60) has suggested, a homosexual identity seems to arise out of self-labeling rather than as a result of labeling by others.

We would like to qualify our suggestion that labeling is largely irrelevant to the development of a homosexual orientation by noting that labeling processes among children have not been adequately explored. While most children are unfamiliar with the concept "homosexual" or "queer," they do possess the concept "sissy." They apply the sissy concept to their less masculine male peers with considerable vigor and cruelty. If as reported by Whitam (1977), a majority of male homosexuals were effeminate during their childhood, they could have been subjected to substantial labeling, ridicule, and exclusion from boyish activities. For example, physically inept boys are usually the last to be chosen when boys are choosing teams. As a result of such exclusion, homosexual children could be denied the company of other boys and be obliged to associate with girls. Green (1976), Money and Tucker (1975), and Whitam (1977) all reported that their effeminate children spent a lot of time playing with girls.

In such circumstances, girls would be the deviant outgroup into which effeminate boys had been cast.

A second source of childhood labeling can be the parents, and, in particular, the father. Within traditional psychiatric theory, a dominant mother and a cold or rejecting father have often been considered contributory to adult male homosexuality (Bieber et al.1962). It is possible that paternal coldness or rejection is a result of a boy's effeminacy rather than a cause. Many fathers will be disgusted by the effeminacy of their son, give up on him, and leave him largely to his mother's care (Carrier 1971). In this scenario, inappropriate sex-role behavior results in the effeminate boy being consigned to association with females. Although largely unexplored, the processes of childhood labeling may be a fruitful avenue for research and could provide some support for the applicability of labeling theory to the case of homosexuality.

The research shows that adult labeling has a substantial impact on the ways in which an adult homosexual orientation is expressed and elaborated in the course of a deviant career. Before we can assess the impact of such labeling, however, we must estimate the extent to which adult homosexuals are in fact labeled by the heterosexual society. It is also important to know the extent to which the labeling of male homosexuals is formal—as in the forms of arrest, being fired, commitment to a mental hospital, referral to a psychiatrist or psychologist—or whether the labeling occurs informally, through avoidance by heterosexual associates. To what extent are gay men actually harassed and stigmatized, and in what ways? Since firm data on all of the above-mentioned forms of official labeling of gay men are simply not available, we here focus chiefly on arrest.

Saghir and Robins (1973, pp. 165-66) found that 37 percent of the homosexual men they studied had been arrested for reasons related to their homosexuality. The great majority of these arrests had been preceded by public sexual acts, advances to a police officer, or advances from a police officer—entrapment. Other precipitating circumstances were loitering at odd places or at odd hours and vagrancy. Farrell and Hardin (1974) found that only 11 percent of their respondents had been arrested for reasons related to their homosexuality. Weinberg and Williams (1974, p. 185) found that 25 percent of male homosexuals in the United States had been arrested for such reasons. Using Kinsey's data, Gagnon and Simon reported that 23 percent of their respondents had had "trouble with the police" (1973, p. 139).

It seems clear that being arrested for homosexual activities is probably highly related to the way in which the male homosexual pursues his sex life. Those who frequent such high-risk settings as public terminals are much more likely to be arrested. As Humphreys says, "What little data are available indicate that the majority of arrests in the United States on charges related to homosexual behavior are made in the tearoom [public restroom] purlieus" (1970, p. 82). In contrast, those homosexuals who find their sexual partners in the settings of the gay bar, friendship group, or homophile organization are substantially free of risk of arrest. What this implies for labeling theory is that those who are most likely to be labeled through arrest are least likely to be integrated into the gay social world. Those who pursue an extended deviant career in the organized gay world do so without being labeled by prior arrest. While it could be argued that those who have been arrested will later become integrated into the gay world and pursue deviant careers. Humphreys' data do not support this contention. His "gay" respondents who identified with the gay world, as opposed to homosexuals, who engaged in homosexual behavior but did not consider themselves gay—or occasionally, even homosexual—were considerably younger than the latter. The non-gay homosexuals were unintegrated into the gay world, for example, heterosexually married homosexuals.

The above data indicate that roughly a fifth to a fourth of adult male homosexuals have been arrested at some time for their sexual behavior. Since gay men, as a subset of homosexual men, seem considerably less likely to be so arrested, it appears that the vast majority of gay men find their way into the gay world without having acquired any labeling through arrest. Other authors (Weinberg and Williams 1974, p. 186; Farrell and Hardin 1974) have argued that even if larger percentages of gay men had been arrested, this would probably have little effect on their deviant or conventional lives. Such arrests receive little publicity, and hence, other persons cannot use the information for exclusionary purposes.

Turning to psychiatric labeling, the data indicate that substantial percentages of male homosexuals have at some time undertaken some form of psychiatric or psychological treatment. Weinberg and Williams found that 43 percent of their subjects had "visited a psychiatrist regarding homosexuality" (1974, p. 196). In our Detroit sample, 41 percent had "seen a psychiatrist or psychologist." Despite the significant percentages of male homosexuals who have had contact with the psychiatric profession, it seems unlikely that such contacts would have affected their future careers as gay men (beyond whatever changes in life-style are effected through therapy). Except for those few male homosexuals who have been committed to an institution—mostly for reasons not directly related to their homosexuality—contact with the psychiatric profession seems unlikely to give rise to direct public labeling and subsequent exclusion.

INFORMAL LABELING

In contrast to formal labeling, we suggest that informal labeling is more potent in its contribution to a career in male homosexuality. The principal effects of informal labeling consist of social-distancing behaviors, expressed by a homosexual's heterosexual associates. Heterosexuals prefer to keep homosexuals at a distance, because the latter often provoke anxiety in the former.

Hence they exclude the latter from their parties, coffee groups, clubs, and other social settings. Such exclusionary behavior is often perceived by the homosexual, who may then increasingly resort to the company of other homosexuals. In their company, he is able to feel at ease and to know that his sheer existence is not constantly being resented. With them, he does not have to silently endure "queer jokes." Through rewarding experiences with gay peers, he comes to identify with them and see the heterosexual world as an alien place, into which he makes excursions to earn a living and perform other instrumental functions. Farrell and Nelson (1976) have presented data showing a substantial relationship between a homosexual's perceived rejection by heterosexuals and his involvement in the gay world. In response to the perceived rejection, the gay person decides that life is more rewarding among gays and becomes progressively more involved in the world of gay men.

Although most gay men perceive substantial rejection by the heterosexual world, there are limits to the extent they are able, or willing, to forsake that world and repair to the exclusive company of other gay men. Since most must work and pray and shop in heterosexual settings, and since almost all have heterosexual parental families, they are obliged to live dual lives. In some settings, they behave heterosexually; in others, they are gay. The art of "impression management" has been extensively developed among gay men, who daily and constantly select a particular self for a particular audience. Such impression management makes it possible for the gay person to live parallel lives in different worlds, which he hopes, will never intersect.

The ability or necessity to successfully engage in selective self-representation is the principal means employed by gay men for avoiding labeling and its consequences. Through effective impression management, most gay men are able to partially "nullify" labeling theory. Part of the effects of labeling are, as traditionally suggested, exclusion and career deviance. Another large set of effects of anticipated labeling are the devices employed by the deviant to avoid exclusion and labeling. Since this second set of effects of *anticipated* labeling has been often ignored in the labeling theory literature, we now discuss this topic at some length as applied to the case of gays.

Howard Brown, a founder of the National Gay Task Force and author of *Familiar Faces, Hidden Lives: The Story of Homosexual Men in America Today* (1976), has captured the duality of life and feeling experienced by many gay men in their attempt to separate their gay and public lives. The questions, "Who knows I am gay and whom should I tell?" are pervasive in discussions among gay men. These questions are important to them because they are questions about their personal security in relating to the heterosexual world. Control of information about who knows one is gay is difficult, because closure of information channels is usually impossible. Although one can control the admission of gayness to one's associates, one has no security that they will be discreet in whom they tell. From our observations, it appears to be an almost universal norm among gays to respect another gay's degree of "closetedness"—covertness. The norm states that one gay will not reveal another person's gayness to a heterosexual and will not "talk gay" when the other is with a heterosexual, except when one already knows that the heterosexual knows about the other. In settings where a gay associate is with another person, one is to assume the person to be heterosexual until otherwise indicated. These norms, which are also widely used by other deviant groups, that is, devices used to maintain the privacy of the ingroup serve to effectively prevent information flowing from the gay world to that of heterosexuals.

The hidden lives of homosexuals offer a substantial advantage in that since most gay men can avoid being labeled "homosexual" due to "swishiness," or effeminate behavior, they can also avoid much of the stigma that attends the label "gay" in North America. This condition of substantial invisibility is, of course, not unique to gays. Early Christians could also "pass" as Roman, Jewish, or Greek. Unlike those forms of deviance that are defined by visible physical stigmata, for example, dwarfism, deviances of a cultural or psychological nature—for example, alcoholism, prostitution, homosexuality, most drug use, swinging, bestiality, and sexual fetishism—often permit the deviant to pass as normal. (Passing is a technique in which, through taking on the cultural coloring of one's surroundings, one can blend into the normative landscape.) In other situations, such as the gay bar or parks frequented by gays, one can make visible one's cultural gayness through the use of subcultural rituals, subculturally recognized gestures, and verbal thrusts.

The ability of some types of deviants to pass as conventional persons has not gone unnoticed by police authorities attempting to suppress deviant behavior. These authorities have developed at various times and places a number of devices to reduce the deviant's invisibility. A crude invisibility-reducing measure was employed in Nazi Germany, where gays were legally obligated to wear an armband with a pink triangle on it. While this official requirement is not employed in North America, some states have required that if a person has been convicted of a sex offense—sodomy, oral copulation, rape, child molestation—he must register with the police as a sex offender when he moves from one town to another.

The invisibility of some forms of deviance has also meant that when the police are interested in making certain arrests, they must attempt to pass as deviants. Typically this has meant that the police have adopted a number of the cultural symbols and gestures of the deviant group in order to infiltrate it and thereby gain access to incriminating evidence. Classical instances are police decoys in gay bars or public terminals and undercover narcotics agents. In general, to the extent a form of deviance can be carried out with substantial invisibility, effective suppressive efforts must also adopt strategies of invisibility.

The need to live a dual existence requires not only that one be able to perform false self-representations convincingly in many situations but, also, that one be able to ensure that there will be no leakage of information. The most effective means for preventing information leakage has been to be selective about those situations in which one will manifest cultural gayness. Through selecting physically or socially distant settings, one can be assured that no information will filter from one setting to another and that the information possessed about oneself in each setting is only that which one has provided. There have been three principal techniques employed by gay men to protect their informational insulation.

Selecting settings that are quite physically distant from one another appears to be the most effective way of preventing informational leakage. For example, a heterosexually married homosexual will often restrict his sexual encounters to times when he is on business in a distant city. Alternatively he may restrict encounters to anonymous steam bath settings or to public parks and restrooms. Another type of gay man who uses physical distance as his principal device for information control is the one who lives in a small town. Even though there may be one or two settings in that town where other gays may be encountered, the risks of informational leakage are so high that he defers being gay until he can repair to the anonymity of a larger city. In general, the use of physical distance as a protective device seems to be most common among those homosexual men who have the greatest needs for protection—for example, the heterosexually married homosexual—and among those who lack other protective devices.

A second protective device effecting information control has been that of being gay in settings that are socially distant from one's conventional heterosexual settings. A classical instance of this tactic is where a middle-class homosexual frequents only lower-class homosexual bars or steam baths. Since there will be no overlap between the bar's or bath's clientele and one's circle of middle-class associates, one can be assured of informational insulation. This device has also been used by homosexuals to obtain privacy from other homosexuals, such as a lover, or from higher-status homosexuals, who might disapprove of one's "indiscreet" behavior.

A third protective device has been to assume a fabricated separate gay identity, with name, occupation, and even a separate apartment to which one can repair with sexual partners. The use of this device presumes that the person does not frequent a particular gay locale often, since such frequenting increases the likelihood that the assumed identity may be discredited. This device is often used simultaneously with the physical distance tactic and especially by heterosexually married or gay men of high social status.

The segregating of work, heterosexual friends, gay friends, and sexual partners so that the social networks never overlap is theoretically possible but practically difficult. Also, extreme segregation exacts a number of costs. Extreme segregation requires that the individual's gay encounters be quite brief and that they interfere little with the fulfillment of one's obligations in other settings. If such encounters begin to consume much time, heterosexual friends or relatives will often ask, "What do you do when you run into the big city for a weekend?," or "How do you spend your evenings out?" To be truthful could reveal one's gay identity; hence, a cover story is invented or only a partial truth is provided.

Another problem in maintaining segregation of settings is that one often acquires commitments to particular gay settings such that one loses some control over freedom to put on or off one's gayness. One acquires friends and lovers who will make demands on one and not be willing to deny their own existence as a part of one's life. Extreme segregation of settings requires that one forgo friendships, lovers, or commitments to gay political or cultural organizations. Such segregation, however, permits the male homosexual to remain indefinitely in the closet and to maximize his security in the heterosexual community. The adoption of such closeted tactics, however, is often resented by other homosexuals, who feel less need for informational security. The expression, "Don't call me, I'll call you," is not appreciated by gay friends or lovers.

Despite efforts by gays to keep their dual existences segregated, there occur times when the two worlds interpenetrate. These situations can become highly awkward and reveal the individual as the possessor of a discreditable gay self. The most common such situation is one that occurs in a presumptively heterosexual setting and in which there are several gays and heterosexuals present. Harold Brown described how he greeted his lover of many years at an official reception given for him when he was sworn in as the New York City public health commissioner. He shook his lover's hand in the reception line as though he were simply one of the hundreds of other strangers he was meeting that day. He never introduced his lover to anyone at the reception, even as a friend. In this setting of interpenetrating worlds, the norms of gay culture were adequate to maintain the appearance of segregation.

Sometimes the norms are not adequate to the task of maintaining segregation of the two worlds. A breakdown of appearances occurs in settings where the participants are not completely aware of the gay or nongay identities of all parties present. A gay person joining a conversation may erroneously assume that all parties to the conversation are gay. Proceeding on this assumption, he can reveal his own gayness and, possibly, that of other parties. A possible though awkward recovery of appearances can be accomplished through the person who has made the mistaken assumption quickly implying that he is the only gay person present. Through this ploy, he assumes all "guilt" and removes the stigmatic stain from his gay peers.

There occur many instances in the lives of gays in which attempts at information control have not been effective and the gay person's associates are aware or highly suspicious of his gayness. If the associates do not denounce the gay person or exclude him from their company, the most common response is to maintain the appearance of ignorance. Rather than accepting him as gay, they continue to treat him as heterosexual, even though they know otherwise, even though he knows they know otherwise, and, sometimes, even though they know he knows they know. Both gay and heterosexual parties to the relationship work to maintain the appearance of conventionality and conventional identities. This mode of relating between gay and heterosexual persons seems to be very commonly adopted between homosexuals and their parents. Although all parties are knowledgeable about the situation, they simply do not talk about it.

It seems that this conventionalizing of unconventional relationships is done in order to avoid their disruption. Heterosexuals avoid telling the gay person they know in order not to have to choose between rejecting their heterosexual principles and rejecting their gay child or friend. The gay person cooperates with the pretense because he does not want to break up the relationship and is often uncertain whether explicitly saying he is gay would terminate the tie. In some cases, these pretenses continue for years or, even, a lifetime. Out of respect for each other's sensitivities, the parties avoid all conversational reference to homosexuality and never force the issue.

While the invisibility of a form of deviance is a substantial advantage in dealing with conventional persons, it is somewhat of a disadvantage in dealing with other homosexuals. Invisibility makes it very difficult to recognize, and hence become acquainted with, other gays. The most commonly employed means of communicating one's gay identity is to present oneself in a setting that is defined as gay. The setting—such as the gay bar, bath, or homophile organization—serves to define its inhabitants as gay. Such a mode of definition works well, though it is not infallible. Occasionally such settings can also contain intruders, such as vice officers, curious heterosexuals, or heterosexuals intending to exploit gays.

Since there are substantial risks in communicating one's gayness to another person who may or may not be gay, in a conventional setting, certain devices facilitating recognition are employed. One means of communicating one's homosexuality to other homosexuals is through the use of certain subcultural signs, the meanings of which are only known to other gays. Such signs include selected styles of clothing, wearing a certain type of ring, or using certain ingroup expressions in heterosexual settings. Because certain styles of clothing tend to become faddish in gay circles, they often can signify a gay identity to the insider. Of course, clothing styles are not an infallible sign. A number of gay cultural practices, such as wearing a ring of keys at the hip or a denim jacket, have quickly been diffused into the heterosexual culture such that they have lost their utility as communicative signs. Another occasionally employed self-identifying tactic is to use a book of matches from a gay establishment that is not known to be gay except by insiders. Such subcultural hidden means of communicating one's sexual identity tend to be of greater utility in smaller towns, where there are few or no gay settings available.

The problems of keeping one's gay identity private and of leading a dual existence has implications for the political efforts of the gay movement. To the extent that many gay persons feel the need to lead a dual existence, they are substantially unavailable for political mobilization. They are unavailable for demonstrations, letter-writing campaigns, or appearing as a witness at legislative or administrative hearings. Sometimes gays choose not to sign their names to letters to legislators or to be on the mailing lists of gay organizations or sign petitions. Hence although the ability of the gay to hide in a protective closet is, individually, an asset, it is one of the principal liabilities of the gay movement.

With the rise of the gay movement in the last decade, an increasing, though still small, percentage of gays have chosen to come out of the closet and assume the label of "gay" before their heterosexual associates. Howard Brown and David Kopay, the former professional football player, are recent cases in point. The reasons gay persons publicly come out seem to be both personal and political. Kopay states that

> the question (why I publicly came out) seems to bother everybody but me. I'm sure I don't have all the answers but I do know that it had to do with images—the way people see athletes and the way people see homosexuals. Of course I didn't have to talk about my sexual preferences in public. Of course taking on any label is self-limiting and wrong. But that's not the point. Because of my homosexuality I can't get a job as a coach. Unless certain attitudes change there's no way for me to function in this society doing what I want to do. If some of us don't take on the oppressive labels and publicly prove them wrong, we'll stay trapped by the stereotypes for the rest of our lives. . . . Being an athlete does not mean you are a dumb jock. Homosexuals, like athletes, often have little more in common than coffee drinkers do (1977, p. 10).

Kopay's political reasons for publicly coming out appear designed to destroy the popular stereotypes, through providing an example of gay men who are masculine, psychologically fit, and occupationally accomplished. Presumably if sufficient numbers of successful gay persons become publicly visible, the credibility of the popular sterotypes could be eroded. Such goals seem to have been the ones Saint Paul had in mind, as he repeatedly urged Christians to discontinue passing as non-Christians, to come out of their closets to bear witness to Christ.

Whether a number of publicly visible counterexamples to the stereotype of gay men can undermine that stereotype is arguable. Lehne (1976, p. 71) has proposed that the sterotype is largely a weapon used in the everyday status politics among heterosexual men surrounding masculinity. It is a threat used to assure the continuation of male conformation to the masculine role and to discourage the expression of behavior considered feminine in the culture. As such, "stereotypes are not learned from experiences with homosexuals. Homophobia is socially transmitted" (Lehne 1976, p. 71) as part of the subculture of heterosexual males. If homosexuals did not exist the stereotype would be unaffected. Hence, according to this view, homosexuals are simply innocent bystanders to, and occasionally casualties of, status contests among heterosexual males. Also, if Green (1974) and Whitam's (1977) ideas about childhood labeling of pre-gay children are valid, homosexuals may be partially creations of the politics of masculinity during childhood. If this line of reasoning is valid, coming out for the purpose of presenting positive examples of gay men to the heterosexual world will not affect the stereotypes. Such examples would probably be dismissed as exceptions to the stereotype.

There are substantial dangers in publicly coming out, the principal one being loss of occupation. One nationally prominent comedienne was warned by the media that if she came out any further, she would be blacklisted. Such firings largely destroy the political utility of gays presenting counterexamples to the stereotypes in that although the firings generate brief publicity, the fired individuals shortly lapse into public invisibility. Largely through keeping gay persons invisible, it is possible to maintain the credibility of stereotypes.

In the case of the average gay person, we can only say that the consequences of coming out are varied. Some heterosexual associates are accepting, even saying that they have known for a long time. On the other hand, there are recent instances of gay school teachers having publicly come out and being fired as a result. In another recent instance, a gay man and a lesbian spoke at a university class on human sexuality; subsequently, the woman was evicted and the man fired. The reactions of heterosexuals to one's coming out are quite varied and, hence, unpredictable. Given this unpredictability, many gays have assumed the worst and have remained closeted. There is some evidence that the consequences of coming out are, on the average, less negative than many gays imagine. In asking students about their reactions to having learned that certain of their associates or friends were homosexual, Kitsuse (1962) found that their reactions were fairly mild, typically being avoidance or tolerance of the homosexual. Similarly Weinberg and Williams (1974, p. 195) reported that those homosexuals who were more known about by heterosexuals experienced less rejection, anticipated less discrimination, and did not feel most persons were disgusted or repelled by homosexuality. However, it is possible that those who have come out or who are most known about by heterosexuals are so situated that there are few negative consequences of their coming out. Persons in self-employment, in certain gay occupations, and in culturally enlightened places, such as San Francisco or Portland, Oregon, are freer to publicly express their gay identities, because they know they can anticipate little direct discrimination. Hence cultural, occupational, and political atmospheres seem to have much to do with whether gay persons lead dual (closeted) lives or whether they publicly assume the label of "homosexual" and abandon the constant use of information-controlling devices.

It seems that the consequences of labeling as a homosexual are more varied than labeling theorists originally imagined. There appear to be three major processes resulting from societal condemnation of homosexuals. First, since every gay who is not retarded or psychotic has substantial knowledge of what the consequences of being labeled may be, the large majority take protective steps to avoid being so labeled. Through such steps, the gay can substantially "nullify" labeling theory. Second, in those cases where his attempts at information control are ineffective, a number of the classically hypothesized effects of labeling occur. However, most of these effects seem to be the result of informal rather than formal forms of labeling. Third, in still other instances, the gay person may be fortunate enough to be located in a cultural setting where there is little discrimination against deviation. In these settings, many gays publicly come out and escape most of the consequences of labeling. The extent to which each of these three modes is adopted appears to depend on the local political and cultural climate.

2

RESEARCH METHODS AND MEASURES

RESEARCH METHODS

Because of the great difficulties involved in obtaining reasonably representative samples of deviant populations, researchers of deviance must often go to great lengths to devise methods for gaining access to respondents who are not in institutions, have never been arrested for a specific crime, or are not part of clinical caseloads. Sampling methods used by students of male homosexuality have been quite varied. Warren (1974) used friendship networks as the principal means of gaining access to respondents in her participant observation study of gay males. Saghir and Robins (1973) requested volunteers. Humphreys (1970) employed an ingenious combination of participant observation of public restrooms and survey research, although a substantial percentage of his respondents were not exclusively homosexual in orientation. Other researchers have utilized gay bars and homophile organizations as means of obtaining respondents (Weinberg and Williams 1974; Siegelman 1972; Myrick 1974).

All of the sampling methods have advantages and liabilities in terms of representativeness. Bar patrons tend to be a somewhat younger crowd than members of homophile organizations and to be more overt in their sexual lifestyles (Weinberg and Williams 1974, p. 125). It would appear from Warren's research that the members of the particular friendship networks she examined were less overt in their behavior than the usual bar samples, were of fairly high occupational status, and were older than most bar patrons. The "tearoom" (public restroom) participants observed by Humphreys were a very unrepresentative minority of gay men and included a heterogeneous sample of heterosexuals (who occasionally frequent restrooms for purposes of impersonal sex). Given the heterogeneity of gay populations and the variety of social settings in which they may be researched, it is necessary to be aware of the probable selectiveness of sampling that is imposed by any one method.

In gathering our Detroit sample, which serves as the principal source of data for the present work, it was decided to use a variety of methods to gain access to respondents. A 12-page questionnaire was distributed to male homosexuals in the Detroit area during the spring and summer of 1975 in a variety of settings. All questionnaires were returned anonymously by mail to the researchers, who were personally known by very few of the respondents. The principal method of distribution was through three intermediaries. Two of the intermediaries were bartenders at gay bars. These men distributed questionnaires to patrons at eight gay bars, selected for their collective heterogeneity. Since patrons of different gay bars differ substantially in social class, age, and recreational style, these intermediaries were instructed to distribute questionnaires at a variety of types of bars rather than simply at their own places of employment. (Bartenders at gay bars usually are excellent sources of information about persons and events in the gay community because they are often acquainted with hundreds, or even thousands, of gay persons.) The two bartenders were instructed to select persons from a wide variety of ages, life-styles, and occupational background (if they knew the respondent's occupation) as respondents. Utilizing their extensive acquaintance networks, the intermediaries were advised to distribute the questionnaires to potential respondents in a personalized manner. A third intermediary provided assistance to the research by distributing questionnaires among a number of male homosexuals with whom he was acquainted. This person was a distinguished older professional, whose assistance provided access to certain more covert social circles of gay males to whom the researcher might otherwise not have had access.

A further channel for acquiring respondents was through three homophile organizations in the Detroit area. The organizations were a student gay liberation group; Dignity, an organization of gay Catholics; and One of Detroit, an older gay social organization. The student group was composed of persons in their early and middle twenties. This group was highly ideological, suspicious of the motives of the researcher, and provided only a handful (nine) of the returned, completed questionnaires. Dignity and One of Detroit were much more cooperative than the student group. Dignity was largely composed of persons in their twenties and thirties, while most of the members of One of Detroit were from 35 to 55 years of age. The questionnaires to organization members were distributed at their regularly scheduled meetings and were returned anonymously through the mail.

It was planned that through using a variety of methods of distributing questionnaires, an approximation to representativeness might be achieved. Thus distributions took place in a variety of settings: bars, different types of bars, organizations, different types of organizations, and friendship networks. However, it was decided that since representativeness could only be roughly approximated, a more important goal of the sampling process would be to obtain a sample that was collectively heterogeneous with respect to the principal areas of research interest. Such heterogeneity was partially accomplished through using a variety of settings for instrument distribution. It was also accomplished by instructing the intermediaries to attempt to select respondents as widely as possible from the following variables: age, social status, frequency of bar attendance, whether the respondent had a current lover, and apparent masculinity–femininity. Frequency of bar attendance was employed as a selective criterion in the hopes that by not concentrating exclusively on those who attend gay bars frequently, one could avoid a sample consisting primarily of bar patrons.

The total number of returned and usable questionnaires was 243, constituting a 53 percent response rate. While this response rate is a little low when compared with the response rate of the heterosexual population (in those instances when the respondent mails back the questionnaire), it is quite respectable for research done on male homosexuals. By way of comparison, Weinberg (1970, p. 529) had a 30 percent response rate; Siegelman (1972, pp. 11-12) a 49 percent response rate; and Myrick (1974, pp. 81-82), a 66 percent response rate. The obtained distributions of our respondents on pertinent demographic variables were the following: homophile organization members: 26 percent; age: 41 percent from those aged 18 to 29, 39 percent from those aged 30 to 39, 14 percent from those aged 40 to 49, and 6 percent from those aged 50 and over; occupation: 18 percent from upper white-collar respondents, 35 percent from lower white-collar respondents, 24 percent from service occupations, 12 percent from manual workers, the rest being students, unemployed, or "houseboys"; and education: 26 percent with 12th grade or less, 49 percent with some college or B.A., and 25 percent more than a B.A.

So that the reader may be aware of some of the limitations arising from the sampling method used, we comment on a few of the marginal distributions of selected demographic items. Despite our efforts to obtain heterogeneity on age, only 6 percent of the sample was 50 years of age or older. This differs substantially from the 35 percent of the adult (18 and older) white male population in the Detroit area who are 50 and older, as reported by the 1970 census (U. S. Bureau of the Census 1970, p. 648). Although our sample probably underrepresents older gay males, it is difficult for us to estimate the magnitude of underrepresentation, since there are both theoretical and empirical reasons for believing that the incidence of homosexuality declines with age. McIntosh (1968) reanalyzed some of Kinsey's data and reported a decline with age in the percentages who were exclusively or predominantly homosexual. Westwood's (1970) data from Great Britain reported only 16 percent of his sample to be 48 years of age and older. Weinberg (1970) in exploring age-related processes among male gays evidently found it necessary to create a statistical category of the "old" (46 and over), thus suggesting a relative paucity of older gays.

West (1967) has suggested that many older male homosexuals find gay life decreasingly rewarding with age, withdraw from that life, associate more with heterosexuals, and may either attempt a heterosexual marriage or socially retire into a life of grim isolation. Following up on West's suggestion, Weinberg (1970) has documented that older gays do appear to associate more with heterosexuals and less with homosexuals. To the extent that such withdrawal occurs with advancing age, it would seem that gay men may gradually blend into the social world of heterosexuals and, thereby, become less available to researchers. Such withdrawal from the gay world, to the extent it occurs, also seems to create certain definitional problems. When withdrawal is substantial or complete, such individuals might better be described as former homosexuals or, perhaps, even as heterosexuals. In this case, the appellation of "former homosexual" would be similar to that of "former alcoholic," one who no longer engages in a particular behavior even though he may still be motivated to engage in it. As seems to be the case with a number of types of deviance, and sexual deviance in particular, sizable numbers of deviants retire from deviant careers, go straight, or simply "burn out" (Irwin 1970, pp. 202–3; Benjamin and Masters 1964, p. 274). While we are unable to estimate the extent to which our sample underrepresents older gays, we do not think that the degree of underestimation is equal to the full difference between the percentage of our sample who are older and the percentage of the general Detroit population of males who are older. Some part of that difference is likely to have simply "retired."

The occupational and educational distributions of our sample also seem to require some comment, since the sample contains only 12 percent who are manual workers, while containing 69 percent who have at least some college experience. The question we address is whether these percentages in fact underrepresent gays of lower social status or whether they are approximately accurate representations of the educational and occupational distributions of gay males. Lacking any direct way of estimating the accuracy of our sampling on these variables, we must resort to comparisons with the reported results of other students of the homosexual community. Similarity of our results to theirs can provide some assurance of the representativeness of our sample, although such similarity may only mean that most of the studies suffer from similar sampling biases.

Gagnon and Simon (1973, p. 141) found that 70 percent of the male homosexuals studied by the Kinsey Institute had at least some college education and that 77 percent of the exclusively homosexual segment of the Kinsey sample (data gathered between 1940 and 1956) had at least some years of college. The Kinsey data were gathered between 1940 and 1956. Since the percentage of the population with college education was substantially less then than it is today, such a level of education of homosexual subjects is rather striking. These authors do not report data on the occupations of their subjects. While Humphreys (1970) does present data on the occupations of his participants in homosexual activities in public terminals, his sample must be considered grossly unrepresentative of the broader population of gays, since as Gagnon and Simon found, only 16 percent of their respondents "often pick up partners in public terminals" (1973, p. 141).

Weinberg and Williams reported that in their U.S. sample of gay males, 82 percent had at least some college education, while 71 percent were "in the three highest status occupational categories" (1974, p. 95). Their European samples were similarly skewed, but not as grossly as the U.S. sample. Westwood's (1960, pp. 166-67) British sample also contained an overrepresentation of respondents in nonmanual occupations, although 30 percent were in manual occupations. His finding of a higher percentage of gay males in manual jobs than has been reported in U.S. studies may well be due to Great Britain not having developed as large a white-collar labor force. The studies of Siegelman (1972), Warren (1974), and Saghir and Robins (1973, p. 12) all report high educational levels of their homosexual subjects and a strong overrepresentation in nonmanual occupations.

From the consistency of findings reported in the studies of gay males and from our own data, we tentatively infer that our data approximately show the overrepresentation of gay males in nonmanual occupations and, particularly, their very high levels of formal education. It would seem that for a variety of reasons (to be discussed later), gay males may be averse to manual occupations and may pursue their educational careers further than do heterosexuals. However, we caution against the inference from our data that gays have *very* high levels of occupation and income, as opposed to their educational levels. We note that 59 percent of our sample are to be found in the lower white-collar and service occupations. This suggests a substantial clustering of gays just above the manual/nonmanual line. We note that many of these occupations, for example, store clerk, bartender, and typist, are quite low paid, often having wages that are lower than a large percentage of manual jobs.

MEASURING INSTRUMENTS*

The composition of a variety of multiple-item scales employed in succeeding chapters is described at this point. The reader may prefer to postpone the reading of this section until the particular scales are taken up later.

---

*For the reader who may not be familiar with some of the statistical symbols and procedures employed in the present work, Appendix A provides a glossary of definitions. These definitions attempt to translate statistical meanings into more intuitive understandings.

1. Negative attitudes toward gays–This was a five-item Likert scale consisting of the following items: "Too many gays are shallow and uninteresting," and "Homosexuality may best be described as an illness." The measure also included semantic differential responses to the object "gay males" on "powerful-weak," "good-bad," and "friendly-unfriendly" scales. The coefficient alpha reliability of this scale was 0.65 (Nunnally 1967, pp. 196-97). The rationale for the constituent items of this scale was derived from earlier research, which has found that heterosexuals very commonly perceive homosexuals as being "sexually abnormal, perverted, and mentally ill" (Simmons 1965, p. 328), and as being weak and evil on semantic differential scales (MacDonald and Games 1974). Thus, our measure purported to tap the extent to which gay males may have internalized the heterosexual stereotype of gays.

2. Interest in emotional intimacy with other gays–Our emotional intimacy scale was Likert in format, had a coefficient alpha reliability of 0.68, and contained the following items: "Having a steady lover is too confining"; "Living with another guy causes problems in dealing with straights"; "Real love between two gays is very unlikely"; "Gay lovers tend to be unfaithful."

3. Bar cruising (solicitation)–This behavioral measures was the product of two items: "When I go to a gay bar I am usually more interested in cruising than in meeting friends," and "How often do you go to gay bars?" The measure was intended to represent the extent to which the respondent used the gay bar for sexual, rather than social, purposes.

4. Self-esteem–This scale was Likert in format, had a coefficient alpha reliability of 0.78, and included the following items: "I am a fairly self-confident person"; "On the whole I think I am quite a happy person"; "On the whole I am satisfied with myself."

5. Exclusive relationships–As an indicator of the extent to which the respondent had been able to establish enduring sexual liaisons, we employed responses to the question of whether he had ever "gone with" another gay for a period of at least a year, including current liaisons. This item was very similar to the "exclusive relationships" item employed by Weinberg and Williams (1974, pp. 156-57).

6. Homosexual marital status (one)–For our purposes, we needed a definition of homosexual marital status analogous to the definition of heterosexual marital status. Because of the lack of a legal marital status for gays, it was necessary to somewhat arbitrarily impose a set of criteria that would be sufficient to decide whether a given respondent was "married." The logical criteria were continuing sexual availability, time over which a relationship had endured, common domicile, and whether the person saw himself as relatively permanently linked and committed to another male. While all these criteria are highly correlated with each other and with legal marital status among heterosexuals, the lack of such high correlations among gay populations gave rise to definitional problems. Persons defined as "married" when some of these criteria

are used may not be "married" when others are used. Further, when one employs a strict definition of marital status by simultaneously using all of the above-listed criteria, one is left with a rather large category of "semimarried" persons and a different category of "semidivorced."

We somewhat arbitrarily defined the married as those who reported they had a current lover with whom they were living. While this definition excluded length of the relationship as a criterion, 90 percent of the so-defined married had been living with their lover for at least a year. The single were defined as those who were not currently married (as defined) and had never been so married. These two definitions implied the further definition of the divorced, that is, those who had once been but were not currently married. There remained two additional categories: those who had a current lover with whom they were not living (these we labeled "the engaged"), and those who once had a lover with whom they did not live and who did not now have a current lover (these we called "the formerly engaged"). In cases where an individual may have gone through several of these marital statuses, the current classification was used to categorize him.

7. Homosexual marital status (two)–In certain instances, we used an alternative and simpler definition of marital status. This definition had three categories–the married, the single, and the divorced. The married were those who had gone with their current lover for at least a year but might or might not be living with him. The divorced were those who had once gone with a lover for at least a year but did not now have a lover with whom they had been for at least a year. The single were those who had never gone with another male for at least a year. This mode of operationalizing marital status resulted in the exclusion of some seven "newlyweds," who had a current lover but had not gone with him for a full year. The subsequent text indicates which measure of marital status was employed and the rationale for its use.

8. Teen-age heterosexual interest–This two-item Likert scale consisted of the following items: "As a teen-ager how often did you date girls?," and "As a teen-ager were you seriously interested in girls?"

9. Teen-age homosexual interest–This two-item Likert scale consists of the following items: "As a teen-ager did you ever develop crushes on other guys?," and "As a teen-ager did you ever have some sort of sex with other guys?" The response categories for the four items of these scales were four in number, varying from "never" to "often" or "very much."

OTHER DATA SOURCES

Besides the Detroit survey, several other data sources were used. Interviews, ranging from what Schatzman and Strauss (1973) called "extended conversations" to more structured interviews, were conducted in a wide variety of settings in different parts of the United States and Canada. The authors listened to gay discussion groups, attended gay day parades in San Francisco, and observed the street scenes and the acting out of the various gay styles of individual self-representation in New York and San Francisco. We read publications of gay organizations, including the archives of the Society for Individual Rights (SIR), commercial gay publications, including the *Advocate, Newswest, Body Politic* (the major Canadian gay newspaper), and *Bay Area Reporter* (San Francisco). For part of our chapter on urbanization and gay institutions, we analyzed listings of gay bars from the 1972 *Guild Guide*. These listings were integrated with 1970 census data in order to examine the relationships between city size and numbers and types of gay bars. Historical materials, such as those collected by Katz (1976) in his major anthology of gay American history, along with published interviews with major figures in the history of the gay liberation movement in the United States, were utilized in the chapter on gay liberation.

In all of our efforts, we were concerned more with theory than with the description of specific places and times. Unique historical events, of course, shape a particular institution in a specific city or nation, but the sociologist is attempting to generalize more than particularize. The search for social processes and the placing of gay life-styles or typical modes of interaction in historical perspective is limited in this study to North America, with some scattered references to Europe. In analyzing the data, the "grounded field approach," developed as a naturalistic field strategy by Schatzman and Strauss (1973), was utilized to develop hypotheses and test competing ideas against one another. Besides comparing hypotheses with the data, we attempted, where possible, to compare our data with other published works on male homosexuality in North America. As suggested at several points in this book, all the samples and studies of male homosexuality may be biased in as yet unknown ways, but in the absence of a true random sample, replication of findings through different studies is a viable and acceptable research strategy.

3

MUTUAL LABELING AMONG THE STIGMATIZED

Communities of the stigmatized face special problems of maintaining internal cohesiveness and trust with which conforming groups need not deal. Collective and individual morale must be able to counter the condemnation of the conventional world if participants in stigmatized activities are to develop a measure of commitment to the legitimacy of their special world and adequate working relationships. Collective and individual justifications of stigmatized activities serve both internal and external functions for such groups. Externally such justifications serve political functions in dealing with the conventional world and help to reduce social sanctions imposed by that world. Internally they make ingroup relationships more trusting, open, and enduring. Such internal functions are the focus of the present chapter.

Virtually all groups of persons engaged in disapproved activities elaborate justificatory rhetoric about their behavior. Prostitutes point out the socially useful services they render society (Bryan 1966). Con men say that they only fleece persons who are already corrupt by having "larceny in their hearts" (Inciardi 1975, pp. 71-74). Delinquents reduce stigma by arguing that the victim deserved it or that there was, in fact, no real harm done (Sykes and Matza 1957). Game law violators (poachers) variously argue that their poaching is really nonculpable because there is plenty of game, or "we have to get the game before the out-of-staters do," or they need the food to eat. Similarly gays have elaborated many justifications of their behavior.

In those forms of deviance that are achieved through the voluntary actions of the individual, the deviant person will have spent a significant part of his life living in the conventional world and thinking of himself as a conventional person. By the time he enters a deviant group, he will be familiar with many of the negative labels that the conventional culture uses, for example, "drug addict," "alcoholic," "queer," and "lunatic." He may also be specially knowledgeable about the content of the label applied to his own form of unconventionality. Upon entering a deviant group, he must reevaluate or reconstitute that label in order to perceive both himself and his new peers as other than a collection of the unworthy or, as in the case of gays, as other than a company of perceived perverts. But why *must* he reevaluate his label? Although life is certainly pleasanter perceiving onself and one's associates as morally worthy, such a reevaluation need not occur automatically upon entry into the stigmatized group. Many stigmatized individuals spend much of their lives with disvalued self-concepts and associate with persons whom they disvalue. Humphreys (1972, pp. 39–41) has described many—though how many is unknown—male homosexuals as living lives filled with self-hate and loathing for other gays.

Although virtually all stigmatized groups develop justifications for their life-styles, it is not automatic that the group members sincerely internalize those justifications. While group membership provides a structure that facilitates the internalization of those justifications, deviants spend much, often most, of their day-to-day existence associating with conventional persons. Through the latter associations, they continue to have reinforced the views of deviance consistent with the labels of the dominant culture—labels that they themselves probably once believed in. In the case of gays, they are continually exposed to jokes about, and put-downs of, homosexuality in the context of work, school, television, and the church. Thus although coming out most likely serves to soften the extremely negative image adolescent gays have often had of homosexuality, it does not provide a permanently effective justification of that activity. Such neutralization of negative images is a continuing enterprise and, perhaps, a lifelong struggle.

To the extent that a deviant group is not able to effectively neutralize the negative labels, it will encounter problems of distrust among its members, internal friction, and potential disloyalty vis-a-vis nonmembers. When deviant members hold negative attitudes toward each other, they will be especially sensitive to each other's faults and be too willing to interpret each other's behavior as indicative of either mental illness or bad character. We suggest that whether such group members tend to interpret each other's behavior in terms of bad character or mental illness depends on the form of deviance. In criminal groups, trust may be more problematic due to possible infiltration by police or to the fact that when a group member breaks an agreement, the offended party has little recourse other than to violence. Alternatively among such groups as gays, alcoholics, and mental patients, questions of each other's mental competence may be more salient. It is evident that to the extent group members continue to utilize the stereotypes provided by the dominant culture, such stereotypes can readily curtail the development of an enduring or elaborate social organization.

Many deviant groups recognize that not all of the individuals who present themselves for membership possess the desired motivation. Such groups have developed mechanisms for screening out those not properly motivated and for protecting themselves from them. Professional thieves typically use ostracism and occasional violence in instances of betrayal or nonfulfillment of contracts (Inciardi 1975, pp. 71-74). Nudists will expel from the camp persons who engage in behavior considered inappropriate within the culture (Weinberg 1966). Persons involved in drug cultures must be wary of their peers who have become police informers (Skolnick 1966, p. 123). Members of skid row bottle gangs have devised measures to deal with the member who, having received the money to purchase a bottle, does not return with the goods (Rubington 1973).

RELATIONSHIPS AMONG GAY MEN

The culture of gay men has elaborated means for dealing with those who are inappropriately motivated. In gay bars, it is an almost universal custom that individuals introduce themselves, or are introduced, only on a first-name basis. It is considered slightly inappropriate to use a last name in the course of an introduction. This practice serves to protect anonymity. Also, it is considered a breach of ethics to inquire about a person's occupation. More broadly, there exist norms against the soliciting of information about someone that can link him to those particular structures in the heterosexual world to which he is affiliated. Occasionally some gay men will even present themselves to others under a pseudonym and with falsified occupation and place of residence. This pattern of anonymous self-representation appears to have been practiced among gay men for at least several decades. There are some situational exceptions to this practice. At parties of close friends, where the trustworthiness of those present can be assumed, persons unknown to each other may be introduced with full names and other identifying information. Also, a person may make a full introduction when he is close to those being introduced.

It is clear that such a pattern of anonymous self-presentation forestalls the development of closer and more enduring relationships among the members of a group. The development of such relationships *must* violate the group norms. Thus, if a relationship is to be developed, one of the parties must, at some point, decide to violate the norms and either offer information socially identifying himself or solicit it from the other party. Such a norm violation temporarily creates a situational awkwardness in that it is an offer to abandon one set of norms and adopt another set (permitting a closer, and perhaps enduring, relationship to develop). The development of friendship and love relationships among gay men requires the abandonment of norms of anonymous self-presentation. Hence, this part of the culture of gay men is quite ill-suited to the elaboration of nonimpersonal social organization.

The practice of anonymous self-presentation implies a presumed distrust among gay men. To refuse to identify oneself is to assume the nontrivial possibility that the person to whom one is relating may be inappropriately motivated.

He might identify one to one's employer as a homosexual. He might attempt blackmail. If emotionally disturbed, he might intrude himself into one's conventional life in an embarrassingly visible manner, for example, appear at one's home at unwanted times or in unconventional deportment. In order for a close or enduring relationship to develop between gay men, such presumed distrust must be overcome. While the pattern of anonymous self-presentation is sufficient for the negotiation of brief and impersonal sexual encounters, it is an obstacle to the development of more enduring relationships.

There is a basic conflict between the norm of anonymous self-presentation and the development of such forms of social organization as friendship, love relationships, and participation in gay cultural or political associations. Persons participating in gay organizations must be able to contact each other. If only for the purposes of mailing newsletters and information sheets to members, gay organizations must possess lists of names and addresses which are usually highly guarded from outsiders. Members of homophile organizations must be able to trust that membership lists will not fall into heterosexual hands. The potential problems from such an eventuality are evident in the situation where the membership list of a gay student organization got into heterosexual hands and members began receiving obscene and threatening calls. Also, they must be able to trust each other and to assume that delegated tasks will be accomplished. The norm of anonymous self-presentation impedes the development of gay relationships, gay political and cultural organizations, and political consciousness. While most gay men remain "in the closet" to heterosexuals for reasons of self-protection, some remain in the closet to many of their homosexual acquaintances. Such ingroup covertness stands as an obstacle to the development of gay communities, culture, and consciousness beyond the social organizational level of brief and impersonal sexual transactions.

Our principal hypothesis in the present chapter is that because many gay men have not been able to neutralize the condemnations of homosexuality that they learned in their pregay lives, and continue to receive from heterosexual associates through most of their adult lives, they have difficulty in establishing untroubled relationships among themselves. Because they hold negative attitudes toward each other, they are especially sensitive to each other's faults and tend to interpret such faults in the light of popular stereotypes. Such propensities to label or stereotype each other can readily give rise to an unwillingness to commit onself emotionally, as opposed to sexually, to another gay male and to an ephemerality of relationships. If these arguments are true, it follows that friendships within the gay community should also have qualities of fragility and ambivalence, since they also assume a measure of mutual trust and respect.

It has been often reported that the sexual relationships of gay men tend to be brief. Although there is substantial variability in the longevity of such relationships, most are short-lived; the modal form of sexual activity is one of frequent and impersonal sexual encounters. Even more enduring liaisons approximating a marriage are somewhat short-lived, lasting an average of a little less than three years (Saghir and Robins 1973, pp. 56-57). This figure is replicated in our data below. These phenomena of ephemerality of liaisons and large numbers of impersonal sexual encounters (whether or not a gay male has a current liaison) (Warren 1974, pp. 70-76) seem to be among the few findings that have received little dispute in a literature filled with numerous controversies (Hoffman 1968, pp. 164-66; Saghir and Robins 1973, pp. 52-55; Simon and Gagnon 1967; Tripp 1975, pp. 150-70; West 1967, pp. 57-58; Leznoff and Westley 1956). We attribute this pattern of brief sexual relationships to unneutralized mutual labeling among gay men.

In a similar vein to the ideas advanced here, Hoffman (1968, pp. 174-77) has argued that "the problem of paired intimacy" versus promiscuity constitutes "the central problem of the gay world" and is to be explained by gay men having internalized the views of the broader society toward homosexuals as sick, evil, weak, and generally unworthy. He has argued that these internalized stereotypes of gay men are *unconsciously* held by gays in order to exempt the self from such a categorical condemnation. However, we see no compelling reasons why this should be so, since many gay men will quite readily be critical of various aspects of gay communities. Warren (1974, pp. 131-35) and Gagnon and Simon (1973, pp. 151-54) have documented that many gays often feel reluctance or distaste for various activities or subgroups they meet in the broader gay community and consequently establish their own definitions of "deviance." However, such *selective* condemnations of various gay behaviors may not be expressions of the internalized stereotypes to which Hoffman refers, since his argument turns on the assumption that most gay men have internalized a *categorical* view of gays as unworthy of positive affectional commitment. In Hoffman's view, any particular candidate for a gay man's affection is eventually to be rejected not because he is, say, lower class, or dull, or crude but because he is gay.

It might seem unlikely that any significant percentage of gay males would be willing to express such categorical condemnations of other gays. However, we believe that many do have negative views of homosexuality, which they rarely express. There are strong situational prohibitions against the expression of such views in the gay world. Such expressions made to other gays would be socially offensive and strongly counter to the justificatory rhetoric of the gay community. Also, such categorical condemnations would, by implication, be a socially awkward discrediting of the self. Within the rhetoric of the gay world, acknowledged imperfections in gay culture are only admissible when applied to a subset of that culture or when their origins are attributed to oppression by the encompassing heterosexual society. They are not admissible when considered a necessary part of being gay. Accordingly it may be that many gay men hold negative views of other gays and feel reluctant about the gay condition for long periods of their lives without ever finding socially appropriate occasions in the gay world for the expression of such views. If such views ever find expression, it would be more likely to occur in therapeutic situations or to sympathetic heterosexuals, such as researchers, who do not have a strong emotional investment in judging the moral worth of gays or in judging them in states of emotional disarray or drunkenness.

This situation of never-admitted negative feelings about the gay condition is very similar to that described by Matza for juvenile delinquents in the "situation of company" (1964, pp. 50–59). In the presence of such company, admissions of ambivalence about one's deviant activity would provoke strongly negative reactions and identify one as an apostate to the ingroup. Hence one remains silent. We note that this phenomenon of unexpressed regrets or ambivalence is much more broadly operative than in just the worlds of gays and delinquents. How often does a person express to her/his spouse occasionally felt regrets about his/her marriage? How often does one reveal to one's colleagues that one realizes that their mutual firm/school/employer is really third-rate or hopelessly ineffective?

There is some evidence that many gay males are ambivalent about the gay condition. An often-quoted 1963 survey reported that

> 83 percent of a sample of 300 male homosexuals indicated that they would not want a son to follow in their sexual path. Only 2 percent answered in the affirmative, while the remainder said that they would leave the choice up to the hypothetical son. On the other hand, an overwhelming 97 percent of the respondents said they would not want to change their own behavior even if a change were easy to accomplish (Geis 1972, pp. 26–27).*

Also, Saghir and Robins reported that

> at one time or another in their lives 62% of [the male homosexuals] contemplated or desired a change of the homosexual orientation. . . . When the homosexual men were asked if they would consent to a change in sexual orientation if the process was certain, quick, and painless, a majority of them (58%) stated that they would refuse, about one-fourth (22%) answered affirmatively and 20% were receptive to the idea but had their own conditions and doubts (1973, pp. 126–27).

---

*In order to gain firmer documentation for these findings, which were originally published in an article in the *New York Times* (Robert Doty, "Growth of Homosexuality Provokes Wide Concern," December 17, 1973, p. 1ff), we wrote the New York Mattachine Society, the former president of which had conducted the survey. However, that organization no longer exists, and its caretaker had no knowledge of the whereabouts of the former president.

Humphreys has also reported that some gay men, particularly during middle age, may express categorically negative attitudes toward all gays (1972, pp. 118-20). However, we should make clear that the phenomenon to which we are addressing ourselves—How do gays feel about other gays?—is not the same as the self-hate phenomenon that Humphreys describes (1972, pp. 39-41). While Humphreys tends to equate the two, they are logically separate questions; as we shall see later, empirically, they are substantially independent.

It seems clear that some gay men may have enduring reservations about the gay condition. Yet it seems that gay communities are at least partially able to reduce those reservations. As Weinberg and Williams have reported, gay men who are more socially involved in gay communities have fewer psychological problems, feel less rejection by heterosexuals, are more likely to have had an exclusive liaison for at least one year, and have less guilt or shame about their homosexuality (1974, pp. 203-06). Dank (1971) has also reported that gay men often experience a significant reduction of worries about their homosexuality after entering or discovering the gay community. Although such communities are able to eliminate some of the (felt) stigma of being homosexual, the question remains as to whether they are able to mobilize sufficient social and ideological resources to prevent a substantial amount of mutual stereotyping among their members (and a hypothetically consequent instability of interpersonal relationships). It is difficult for the gay community to remove the stigma because that community's rhetoric of justification ("Gay is good") can only be answered with assent, rather than questions, and is principally directed to the company of those already persuaded. Doubts are often responded to with excommunication. Thus, there may be limits to the effectiveness of neutralization when such neutralization will not or cannot provide answers to basic questions.

Having established that a significant, though unknown, percentage of gay men have reservations about the gay condition and that the sexual relationships of gay men are often ephemeral and impersonal, we now face the task of empirically linking such behavior with negative attitudes toward homosexuality. To this end, we have developed a number of attitudinal and behavioral measures. For details about the properties and components of the multiple-item scales here employed, the reader should consult the chapter on methods (Chapter 2). The measures employed here are grouped, for the most part, into three clusters: (1) sexual behavior, items 6, 7, and 8; (2) social integration into the gay community, items 3, 4, and 5; (3) intimate relationships, items 12 and 13.

Scales and Measures

1. Negative attitudes toward other gay men—This largely evaluative scale taps the extent to which the respondent subscribes to the popular stereotypes.

FIGURE 3.1

Hypothesized Zero-Order Relationships

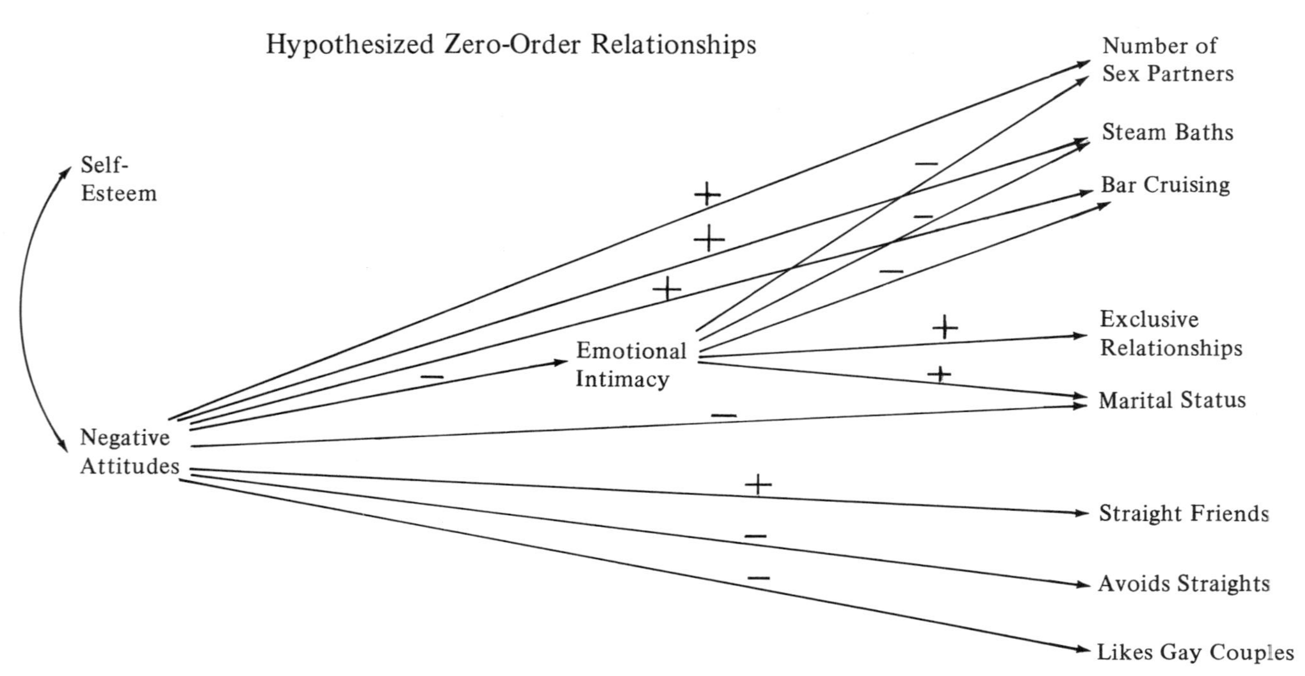

Note: (+) indicates positive hypothesized relationship; (-) indicates negative hypothesized relationship.
Source: Compiled by the authors.

2. Desire for emotional intimacy–This measure reflects the respondent's desire for a long-term romantic relationship with another man.*

3. Straight friends–This measure reflects the extent to which the respondent's friends are heterosexual. This item purports to measure social integration into the gay community.

4. Avoids straights–This measure shows whether the respondent prefers to avoid spending his leisure time with heterosexuals. This item also measures social integration into the gay community.

5. Likes gay couples–This measure reflects the extent to which the respondent likes socializing with gay couples. This item also measures social integration into the gay community. Although the three items ("straight friends," "avoids straights," and "likes gay couples") are mutually correlated in the expected directions, social integration into the gay community is sufficiently multidimensional such that these items do not constitute a single scale of high reliability.

6. Number of sex partners last year–The median of this distribution was slightly less than ten. Because of a very long positive tail (extending to 900 sex partners), we utilized a logarithmic transformation of this item in the analysis below.

7. Cruising–This is a measure of bar solicitation of sexual partners, which is the multiplicative product of responses to the two items, "When I go to a gay bar I am usually more interested in cruising than in meeting friends," and "How often do you go to gay bars?"

8. Frequency of attendance at steam baths–This measures the frequency with which the respondent visits this setting for purposes of brief sexual encounters.

9. Self-Esteem–This multiple-item scale is introduced as a control variable and, also, to explore the extent to which negative attitudes toward other gays is expressive of the self-concept.

10. Age.

11. Years of education.

12. Exclusive relationships–This item indicates whether the respondent has ever "gone with" another man for a period of at least a year. It is an indicator of the extent to which the respondent has been able to establish enduring sexual relationships. It is very similar to the "exclusive relationships" item employed by Weinberg and Williams (1974, pp. 156-57).

---

*We had originally intended to utilize an attitudinal scale measuring a desire for emotional intimacy versus preferring a life-style of impersonal sexual encounters. However, adequate reliability could only be obtained for a scale measuring an interest in emotional intimacy. Neither an intimacy versus impersonal sex scale nor a separate impersonal sex scale were considered to be reliable. Such a lack of reliability reflects the inadequacy of an intimacy versus impersonal sex conceptualization and suggests these may be independent phenomena.

TABLE 3.1

Zero-Order Correlations (r) among Principal Variables

Variable	X_1	X_2	X_3	X_4	X_5	X_6	X_7	X_8	X_9	X_{10}	X_{11}	X_{12}
X_1 Negative attitudes	X[a]	-.31[b]	.14[c]	-.05	-.33[b]	-.03	.15[b]	.03	-.38[b]	.10	.11	-.11
N		214	223	224	226	208	222	225	223	225	223	224
X_2 Emotional intimacy		X	-.30[b]	.00	.39[b]	-.12	-.21[b]	-.05	.20[b]	-.31[b]	-.02	.16[c]
N			225	226	228	208	225	227	226	227	225	226
X_3 Straight friends			X	-.39[b]	-.24[b]	.03	-.06	-.04	-.04	.08	.18[b]	-.11
N				238	239	220	237	240	237	238	236	238
X_4 Avoids straights				X	.14[c]	-.12	.07	.04	.05	.03	-.08	.06
N					240	220	236	240	238	239	237	239
X_5 Likes gay couples					X	-.14[c]	-.16[c]	-.07	.23[b]	.04	-.25[b]	.20[b]
N						221	238	241	239	240	238	240
X_6 Number of sex partners[d]						X	.30[b]	.37[b]	.11	-.09	.15[c]	-.08
N							218	222	219	220	218	220
X_7 Cruising							X	.07	-.06	.08	.03	-.08
N								238	235	236	234	236
X_8 Frequents baths								X	-.01	-.05	-.12	-.12
N									239	240	238	240
X_9 Self-Esteem									X	-.09	-.04	-.01
N										238	236	238
X_{10} Age										X	.03	.18[b]
N											239	239
X_{11} Education											X	-.15[c]
N												237

[a]In this table and all subsequent ones an "X" means that a statistic, if computed, would be meaningless or irrelevant.
[b]Significant at .01 level; two-tailed tests.
[c]Significant at .05 level; two-tailed tests.
[d]The variable "number of sex partners" is actually the log to the base ten of that variable.
Source: Compiled by the authors.

13. Marital status–This measure is an indicator of the respondent's behavioral propensity for paired intimacy. Here, we have utilized the simpler definition of marital status which consists of three states, currently married, never married, and divorced. Marital status is employed below as a dependent variable.

Figure 3.1 depicts our hypothesized pattern of empirical relationships. Rather than having the convenience of a single dependent variable, our form of argument begins with the single independent variable "negative attitudes" and explores its relationships with a variety of indicators of stability and cohesiveness of sexual and interpersonal relationships among gay men. The variables "age" and "years of education" are utilized principally as control variables. The causal status of the self-esteem variable in the analysis below is somewhat unclear, since it may either be causally prior to the negative attitudes measure or an effect of negative attitudes. Later we analyzed the effects of negative attitudes while controlling for self-esteem.

Results

Table 3.1 exhibits the zero-order correlations (r) among all of the above measures, except the marital status variable. As hypothesized, the negative attitudes measure is significantly and negatively related to emotional intimacy, liking gay couples, and to self-esteem. Also as hypothesized, it is significantly and positively related to having mostly heterosexual friends and to bar cruising (solicitation). Contrary to our expectations, it is not related to avoiding heterosexuals in leisure time, number of sex partners, frequency of attendance at the steam baths, or exclusive relationships. However, emotional intimacy is significantly related to not having straight friends, liking gay couples, not cruising, having exclusive relationships, self-esteem, and being younger. It seems that some of the relationships of negative attitudes with the dependent measures are mediated through the emotional intimacy variable, since controlling for emotional intimacy reduces to nonsignificance the correlations of negative attitudes with sexual orientation of friends (0.06) and with cruising (0.08). The correlations of negative attitudes with the rest of its significant zero-order correlates are only slightly reduced when controlling for emotional intimacy. Accordingly it seems that negative attitudes may have both direct and indirect effects, with its indirect effects mediated through emotional intimacy. The set of variables "negative attitudes," "emotional intimacy," "sexual orientation of friends," "gay couples," "cruising," "exclusive relationships," and "self-esteem" constitute a correlational cluster providing some support for our hypotheses.

We note that the two behavioral items, "number of sex partners" and "frequency of attendance at the steam baths," remain very largely unaffected by any of the variables in this cluster, with the exception of the gay couples item.

TABLE 3.2

Principal Variables, by Marital Status

Variable	Marital Status		
	Single	Married	Divorced
Negative attitudes	13.66	12.35	13.34
N	65	88	68
	F = 2.56; df = 2 218; p = ns; eta = 0.15		
Emotional intimacy	11.86	13.63	12.70
N	64	89	70
	F = 4.07; df = 2 220; $p < .05$; eta = 0.19		
Straight friends	2.78	2.61	2.55
N	68	94	73
	F = 1.48; df = 2 232; p = ns; eta = 0.11		
Avoids straights	2.30	2.55	2.35
N	69	93	74
	F = 1.04; df = 2 233; p = ns; eta = 0.09		
Likes gay couples	3.30	3.87	3.54
N	69	94	74
	F = 7.86; df = 2 234; $p < .01$; eta = 0.25		
Number of sex partners*	1.04	0.68	1.27
N	64	89	64
	F = 18.58; df = 2 214; $p < .01$; eta = 0.38		
Cruising	10.87	8.73	11.34
N	67	93	73
	F = 5.33; df = 2 230; $p < .01$; eta = 0.21		
Frequents baths	1.71	1.88	2.07
N	69	95	73
	F = 2.56; df = 2 234; p = ns; eta = 0.15		
Self-Esteem	12.04	12.45	11.70
N	68	94	73
	F = 2.19; df = 2 232; p = ns; eta = 0.14		
Age	30.06	33.20	34.11
N	68	93	74
	F = 3.69; df = 2 232; $p < .05$; eta = 0.18		
Education	15.78	14.19	14.96
N	69	91	74
	F = 3.54; df = 2 231; $p < .05$; eta = 0.17		

*The variable "number of sex partners" is actually the log to the base ten of that variable.

Source: Compiled by the authors.

However, the number of partners-gay couples correlation vanishes when intimacy is controlled (0.10). The lack of any correlations between the two behavioral items most strongly measuring impersonal sex and the basic negative attitudes-intimacy cluster seem to support theoretical formulations of gay behavior that emphasize a notion of paired intimacy versus promiscuity. Within the gay community, it seems that these two dimensions may be roughly independent. Hence formulations attempting to explain the one may not be very suited for explaining the other.

Table 3.2 shows the relationship of marital status to our other measures. While marital status has no significant relationship with negative attitudes, it is significantly related to emotional intimacy, again indicating that the principal link of negative attitudes to the other measures appears to be through intimacy. Marital status is also significantly related to liking gay couples, education, cruising, and number of sex partners. As might be expected, being married serves to depress the annual number of sex partners. However, the finding that being married strongly inhibits bar cruising, while apparently having no significant effect on frequency of attendance at the steam baths, suggests that it is only the more personalized and social sexual relationships negotiated at the bar that marriage inhibits. It seems that engaging in impersonal sexual encounters, such as those at steam baths, may be compatible with a married state. By virtue of their impersonality, such relationships pose little threat to a marriage. As reported in the chapter on gay marriages (Chapter 5), many gay liaisons seem to be "open marriages," in which outside sexual encounters are permitted as long as they remain impersonal. Such impersonality in sexual encounters is also normative among "swinging" couples. Any expressions of endearment are proscribed during swing sessions, since they provoke jealousy and can be threatening to a marriage (Bartell 1971, p. 195).

Table 3.3 presents the first-order partial correlations among the variables of Table 3.1, while controlling for self-esteem and age. (Self-esteem partials are above the diagonal.) The only remarkable characteristic of the self-esteem partials is that there are virtually no differences with the corresponding zero-order correlations, except that emotional intimacy now reveals a modest significant negative relationship with number of sex partners. Our basic negative attitudes-emotional intimacy cluster remains intact after the control for self-esteem. From the data thus far presented, it might seem that both self-esteem and negative attitudes contribute to paired intimacy and social integration in similar but opposite ways. However, the respective partial correlations of self-esteem with emotional intimacy and liking gay couples while controlling for negative attitudes are 0.09 and 0.12, both being nonsignificant. Accordingly to the extent that self-esteem has any effects on our various dependent measures, it would seem that they are mediated through negative attitudes toward other gays.

Turning to the subdiagonal part of Table 3.3, the basic relationships of Table 3.1 are affected by the control for age in only a few instances. Exclusive

TABLE 3.3

First-Order Partial Correlations ($r_{12\cdot3}$), Controlling for Age and Self-Esteem[a]

Variable	X_1	X_2	X_3	X_4	X_5	X_6	X_7	X_8	X_9	X_{10}	X_{11}	X_{12}
Negative attitudes	X	-.26[b]	.14[c]	-.04	-.27[b]	.02	.14[c]	.03	X	.07	.10	-.12
N	–	211	220	220	220	205	219	220	–	220	220	220
Emotional intimacy	-.29[b]	X	-.30	.00	.36[b]	-.14	-.20[b]	-.05	X	-.30[b]	-.01	.16[c]
N	211	–	222	223	223	205	222	223	–	223	222	223
Straight friends	.14[c]	-.30[b]	X	-.39[b]	-.24[b]	.03	-.07	-.04	X	.07	.18[b]	-.11
N	220	222	–	234	235	216	232	234	–	234	233	234
Avoids straights	-.06	.02	-.39[b]	X	.14[c]	-.13	.07	.04	X	.03	-.08	-.06
N	221	223	235	–	235	216	232	235	–	235	233	235
Likes gay couples	-.33[b]	.42[b]	-.25[b]	.14[c]	X	-.17[b]	-.15[c]	-.07	X	.06	-.25[b]	.20[c]
N	222	224	235	236	–	216	232	236	–	235	233	235
Number of sex partners[d]	-.01	-.16[c]	.04	-.12	-.14[c]	X	.31[b]	.37[b]	X	-.08	.15[c]	-.08
N	205	205	217	217	217	–	215	216	–	216	215	216

Cruising	.14[c]	-.20[b]	-.07	.06	-.17[c]	.31[b]	X	.07	X	.07	.03	-.08
N	219	220	233	233	233	210	–	232	–	232	231	232
Frequents baths	.03	-.07	-.04	.04	-.07	.37[b]	.07	X	X	.05	-.12	.12
N	224	224	235	236	237	210	228	–	–	235	233	235
Self-Esteem	-.39[b]	.18[b]	.03	.05	.23[b]	.10	-.05	-.02	X	X	X	X
N	220	223	234	235	235	216	232	235	–	–	–	–
Age	X	X	X	X	X	X	X	X	X	–	.03	.18[b]
N	–	–	–	–	–	–	–	–	–	–	233	235
Education	.11	-.01	.18[c]	-.09	-.25[b]	.15[c]	.03	-.12	-.04	X	–	-.15[c]
N	220	222	235	235	236	215	233	236	234	–	–	228
Exclusive relationships	-.13[c]	.22[b]	-.13[c]	.06	.20[b]	-.06	-.09	.13[c]	.03	X	-.16[c]	X
N	221	223	235	236	236	217	233	236	236	–	235	–

[a]Partials for self-esteem are above the diagonal; partials for age are below.
[b]Significant at .01 level; two-tailed tests.
[c]Significant at .05 level; two-tailed tests.
[d]The variable "number of sex partners" is actually the log to the base ten of that variable.
Source: Compiled by the authors.

TABLE 3.4

Emotional Intimacy, Number of Sex Partners, Attendance at Baths, and Cruising, by Marital Status and Age

	Emotional Intimacy			Number of Sex Partners*		
Age	Single N	Married N	Divorced N	Single N	Married N	Divorced N
18–29	13.30 33	14.30 33	14.25 24	1.06 35	-0.71 33	1.41 23
30–39	11.67 24	13.64 39	12.16 25	0.99 22	0.73 37	1.24 24
40 and Over	5.71 7	12.38 16	11.57 21	1.12 7	0.58 17	1.14 17

Sources of Variation	SS	df	Mean Square	F	p	SS	df	Mean Square	F	p
Main effects	435.74	4	108.94	8.24	.01	13.42	4	3.36	9.16	.01
Marital status	167.92	2	83.96	6.35	.01	12.98	2	6.49	17.71	.01
Age	313.78	2	156.89	11.87	.01	0.53	2	0.26	0.72	ns
Interaction	60.13	4	15.03	1.14	ns	0.57	4	0.14	1.39	ns
Residual	2814.29	213	13.21	–	–	75.47	206	0.37	–	–
Total	3310.16	221	–	–	–	89.47	214	–	–	–

Age	Attendance at Baths: Single N	Attendance at Baths: Married N	Attendance at Baths: Divorced N	Cruising: Single N	Cruising: Married N	Cruising: Divorced N
18–29	1.71 38	1.97 34	2.04 26	9.97 36	8.68 34	10.31 26
30–39	1.62 24	1.93 41	2.19 26	12.00 24	8.49 39	12.65 26
40 and Over	2.00 7	1.61 18	1.95 21	11.57 7	9.44 18	11.00 21

Sources of Variation	SS	df	Mean Square	F	p	SS	df	Mean Square	F	p
Main effects	5.35	4	1.34	1.47	ns	389.34	4	97.33	3.15	.02
Marital status	5.06	2	2.53	2.76	ns	333.61	2	166.80	5.40	.01
Age	0.78	2	0.39	0.43	ns	72.39	2	36.19	1.17	ns
Interaction	0.68	4	0.17	0.18	ns	77.29	4	19.32	0.62	ns
Residual	207.10	226	0.92	–	–	6859.74	222	30.90	–	–
Total	213.12	234	–	–	–	7326.36	230	–	–	–

*The variable "number of sex partners" is actually the log to the base ten of that variable.
Source: Compiled by the authors.

relationships now exhibit several significant and strengthened correlations that were not visible in the zero-order relationships. Exclusive relationships now joins our basic negative attitudes–intimacy cluster through its significant links with negative attitudes, intimacy, sexual orientation of friends, liking gay couples, and cruising. The emergence of these relationships when age is controlled for seems to add some additional support to our original hypotheses. We should note that age, unlike self-esteem, does not lose its link with emotional intimacy when negative attitudes is controlled, the partial correlation being a significant 0.30. Thus age seems to exert an independent depressing influence on intimacy, while at the same time, obscuring the correlations of exclusive relationships with our basic correlational cluster.

Table 3.4 attempts to sort out the respective contributions of age and marital status to variation in emotional intimacy and the sexual behavior items. It is evident that both age and marital status are related to emotional intimacy, with age being the somewhat stronger correlate. Age is associated with a deromanticization of attitudes toward sexual relationships; this is particularly so among the single gays. We suggest that this process is similar to the deromanticization of affectional relationships that occurs among heterosexuals in or out of marriage (Blood and Wolfe 1960, pp. 263-66). With experience, the idealization of love relationships is transformed into a more "practical" approach. However, Table 3.4 suggests that the decay of romanticism occurs faster among the never-married. It seems highly likely that there is substantial self-selection occurring in Table 3.4 such that those who never were interested in romantic relationships remain never-married; this gives rise to the very low intimacy score of the older never-marrieds. To argue the contrary, that marital status causes rather than reflects differences in emotional intimacy, would be to argue that gay males get married regardless of their level of interest in an emotionally intimate relationship, that is, it just happens to them. This is unlikely.

Turning to the measures of sexual behavior, it is apparent that marital status inhibits bar cruising and the number of sex partners but is without effect on steam baths attendance. Age has no significant relationship with any of the sexual behavior items. Extending our earlier interpretations, it would seem that being married decreases the number of sex partners, chiefly through inhibiting the more personalized sexual relationships negotiated in the bar setting. Thus the interest in emotional intimacy manifested by the married does not extend to a ban on such impersonal sexual encounters as those at the steam bath. It would thus seem that within gay culture, impersonal sex is widely condoned and not thought incompatible with more intimate relationships.

Implications

The causal status of the self-esteem variable in the above data remains unclear. It was evident that controlling for self-esteem made no appreciable difference in the pattern of correlations of Table 3.1. Also, self-esteem had no direct link with emotional intimacy after controlling for negative attitudes, since its partial correlation with intimacy was nonsignificant. However, the partial correlation of self-esteem and negative attitudes with intimacy controlled is a significant -0.34. This suggests that self-esteem may be either causally prior to negative attitudes or be an effect of negative attitudes. We must remain mute on this question of the direction of causality between these two variables, while noting that whichever is true, negative attitudes retains links with our other variables independently of self-esteem.

The findings that negative attitudes toward a deviant group of which one is obviously a member has effects, or at least correlates, which are independent of one's self-evaluation raises certain interesting questions about the effects of labeling by the broader society on self-concept. It seems that the techniques for neutralizing the negative aspects of a label that is applied to one's membership group may be different from those for neutralizing that label when applied to oneself. In particular, the technique of "special justification," in which one continues to negatively evaluate one's deviant peers while excusing oneself, may be widely used among homosexuals (Lofland 1969, pp. 88-93). Such a separation of self and peer evaluations could serve to explain the earlier reported survey of gays, in which the vast majority would not want their son to be gay. Presumably this may reflect a categorical disapproval of homosexuality. The respondents were also disinclined to change their own sexual orientation, even if it could be easily changed. This may reflect a justification of homosexuality for self.

Such a separation of self and peer evaluation criteria may imply a weak or ambivalent identification with one's deviant peers. To the extent gay males do not identify with each other, they seem reluctant to enter into emotionally intimate relationships, have many gay friends, or associate with gay couples. A similar lack of social cohesiveness has been reported among juvenile delinquents by Hirschi, who describes their interpersonal relationships as "cold and brittle" (1969, pp. 159-61). Also, Perrucci has reported that patients in a mental hospital often prefer not to associate with other patients because they are believed to be untrustworthy and unreliable sources of information (1974, pp. 57-58). Thus to the extent that the individual deviant is unable to effectively repudiate conventional values and their derivative labels, is he placed in a state of "drift" between conventional and deviant values, during which he repeatedly engages in deviant behavior without commitment to it (Matza 1964, pp. 27-30)? We believe our data suggest an affirmative answer for a segment of the gay community. Like the drifting delinquent, many gay males remain unconvinced by the justificatory rhetoric of the gay community and are ambivalent and tentative about their social commitments to that community. We note the correlation of 0.10 between age and negative attitudes, suggesting that negative views of one's deviant peers undergo no decline over time.

Of course, delinquent gangs and the gay community differ in their degrees of ideological sophistication and, hence, in the degree to which they may be able to effectively neutralize their respective labels. As Matza (1964, pp. 132-33) suggests, delinquent groups have only a very primitively developed ideology and are certainly lacking such mechanisms as newspapers, books, and lobbies, which help justify the gay life-style to the world and to the gay community. Yet despite the presence of great social and cultural resources within the gay community, and particularly within gay communities of larger cities, it still seems that the attitudes of many gays toward their peers remain immune to neutralization. Again we point to the lack of a significant relationship between age and negative attitudes.

One quite reasonable objection that our theories must deal with is that the interpersonal behavior of lesbians differs substantially from that of gay men, although the former are equally stigmatized. If internalized negative attitudes give rise to a lessened interest in emotional intimacy and an unwillingness to enter into enduring paired relationships, why do lesbians not also exhibit similar behavior? The research literature rather uniformly reports that lesbians differ from gay men in that they much more often and enduringly enter intimate relationships and are much more sexually faithful in those relationships (Saghir and Robins 1973, p. 229; Gagnon and Simon 1973, pp. 275-77; Tripp 1975, pp. 150-70).

Our answer to this problem is that lesbians do not internalize negative attitudes toward other lesbians nearly as much as do gay men. Negative stereotypes differ not only in emotional intensity but, also, in their degree of salience. Research suggests that lesbians and gay men are either equally intensely disapproved of by the general public (Lubeck and Bengston 1977) or that the former are somewhat more disapproved of by the general public (MacDonald and Games 1974). However, we suggest that the lesbian stereotype is less salient in the popular mind. Lesbians are simply less on the popular mind than are male homosexuals. Our evidence for this is largely impressionistic, but it is both extensive and compelling.

1. The frequency of references to male homosexuality in popular discourse is vastly more common than are references to lesbianism. While there are hundreds of "queer jokes," they are virtually all about gay men rather than about lesbians.

2. Playful imputations of homosexual intent are quite common in male heterosexual behavior but relatively rare among heterosexual females.

3. Serious imputation of homosexuality is more common among heterosexual males than among heterosexual females, particularly when the person whose sexual orientation is in question is unmarried and older. Thus while the status of "old maid" is largely devoid of suspicion, that of "old bachelor" is not.

4. It seems that the symptoms of potential homosexuality in a male child are more anxiety producing to parents than are such symptoms in a girl (Maccoby and Jacklin 1974, p. 339).

5. In final support of our point, we cite the well-known fact that the English Parliament never passed a law proscribing homosexual acts among women, because it never occurred to them that any woman might engage in such practices.

When a label, even though quite negative, is not salient, individuals to whom that label would apply will not experience it on a daily basis. They are, therefore, not encouraged to make invidious comparisons between themselves and conventional persons and, thus, do not strongly internalize the label.

We have seen that some gay men hold negative attitudes about other gays and that holding such attitudes is related to the ways in which they relate to their homosexual peers. Such attitudes seem to give rise to a reluctance to become socially integrated into gay networks. As such, they remain outsiders in a community of outsiders. This outsider status would seem to deprive them of the psychic and social support that are the main benefits the gay community can bestow on its members in their lifelong struggle to maintain views of themselves as morally worthy. Such gay men are in the community of male homosexuals but not of it, because they hold at a distance other gays as a reference group. In further support of this interpretation, we note that those who identify themselves as "exclusively homosexual" or "predominantly homosexual-only incidentally heterosexual," compared with those claiming greater admixtures of heterosexuality in their sexual orientations are more interested in emotional intimacy ($t = 3.61$; df = 1,223; $p < .01$). These two groups are also barely nonsignificantly different in the suggested direction on negative attitudes ($t = 1.79$; df = 1,221; p = ns).

We have argued that negative attitudes toward other gay men gave rise to a disinterest in paired intimacy and to a pattern of many impersonal sexual encounters. While we did find negative attitudes and emotional intimacy to be related in the anticipated direction, the relationships between negative attitudes and the measures of sexual behavior proved to be either indirect (through emotional intimacy), or weak, or both. Moreover emotional intimacy was found to be unrelated to number of sex partners. Very little of the variation in the measures of sexual behavior was found to be associated with the attitudinal measures. This strongly suggests that variation in these measures is better explained by considerations other than those explaining a desire for emotional intimacy. It would appear that within the cultural world of gay men, emotional intimacy and impersonal sex have not been structured as the nearly polar opposites found in the heterosexual world.

SEX-ROLE EXPLANATIONS

A variety of authors have suggested that the intimate liaisons of gay men tend to be short-lived because both parties to the relationships were socialized as males. Cavan (1966, p. 192) and Hoffman (1968, p. 183) have claimed that the question of who is to be the more dominant partner of a gay couple is culturally indeterminate. Both parties to the relationship, because of their socialization as males, expect to be dominant. If this were the case, it could readily lead to much conflict and to termination of the relationship. Trip argues that empirically, dominance problems are not great in the pairing of male homesexuals: "Such matters as who is to fix the screen door, or do the cooking, or feed the cat as well as which partner is to wield the most influence in social or in household decisions all seem to fall into place as if by magic" (1975, pp. 162-63). Saghir and Robins seem to have reported the only nonimpressionistic data on this point (1973, p. 56). They say that the most common reason for the breakup of liaisons which had lasted at least one year was that one of the parties had to move away for job- or school-related reasons. The next most common reasons, in order, were involvement of one of the parties with a new person and, then, jealousy and fights. However, it is quite possible that among Saghir and Robins's couples, dominance problems had surfaced before the lapse of a year and, hence, had either been largely solved or had already led to the termination of the relationship.

The dominance question is rather complicated. Although dominance is clearly emphasized as an aspect of masculinity in heterosexual culture and is broadly desired by men, males are not socialized to be dominant in all situations. They learn that vis-a-vis an employer, instructor, or parent, they are not expected to be dominant. Similarly in friendship situations, questions of dominance are considered largely, though not completely, irrelevant to the relationship. Indeed the case of friendships between males, heterosexual or homosexual, is the principal empirical obstacle to the hypothesis that conflicting dominance expectations disrupt homosexual liaisons. If males generally expected to be dominant in their relationships with other males, heterosexual friendships would be substantially unworkable. This not being the case, an application of an unqualified dominance-disruption hypothesis to the pairings of gay men has questionable validity.

A further reason for doubting the validity of an unqualified dominance hypothesis as applied to the pairings of gay men is that to the extent that a relationship is intimate or has the potential of becoming intimate, both parties will inhibit attempts to dominate (Maccoby and Jacklin 1974, pp. 273-74). Such attempts are largely alienating and can readily lessen commitment to the relationship. Also, since it is difficult or impossible to force affection from another person through aggressive or dominating behavior, such behavior must be largely excluded from intimate relationships. Persuasion and the expression of affection become the chief means of achieving influence with the other party. Alternatively dominating behaviors may be more appropriate with strangers or acquaintances but are inherently incompatible with affectional relationships.

Dominating, and hence alienating, behavior does occur in intimate pairings, both heterosexual and homosexual. Persons using such behavior to an inappropriate degree may have internalized to inappropriate excess the youthful norms of masculine dominance and hence remained committed to those norms beyond the years when overt displays of macho behavior are felt appropriate. Among heterosexual males, such a commitment often gives rise to divorce. Similarly we anticipate that excessive commitment to norms of masculine dominance could give rise to a brevity of relationships or, more likely, an unwillingness to enter into relationships in which one's autonomy or dominance would be compromised. The dominance-disruption hypothesis concerning the pairings of gay men implies that they may have strongly internalized and retained into adulthood commitments to masculinity and its norms of dominance. Although many traits have been attributed to male homosexuals, excessive masculinity has not been one of them.

We cannot within our data attempt a complete assessment of the dominance-disruption hypothesis. We show below that a commitment to dominance does seem to be related to the sexual behavior and attitudes of gay men and that it is negatively related to a desire for emotional intimacy. Subsequently we also assess the relative contributions of negative attitudes toward other gays and of dominance to variations in our respondents' attitudes and behavior. Our measure of commitment to dominance consists of responses to the item, "If I lived with a lover (or do live with) I would probably make most of the decisions." Since a belief in his ability to dominate or control his immediate environment seems to be the principal component of a man's conception of masculinity (Maccoby and Jacklin 1974, p. 157), our item could, with some degree of generalization, be alternatively conceived of as a measure of self-perceived masculinity. Yet since this item measures desired dominance more directly than it measures masculinity, we limit our interpretation of this measure to the narrower and more secure concept of dominance. In the data below, we also utilize the respondent's self-reported degree of homosexuality-heterosexuality. Our present hypotheses are that dominance expectations should be negatively related to emotional intimacy and that to the extent a homosexual includes in his sexual identity a significant component of heterosexuality, his social integration into the gay community will be limited. Table 3.5 provides the particular question and response categories (taken from Weinberg and Williams 1974, p. 303) and the percentage distribution of our respondents with respect to degree of heterosexuality-homosexuality.

Data on Dominance and Heterosexual Identity

Table 3.6 provides the correlations of dominance and heterosexual orientation and the attitudinal and behavioral measures utilized earlier in this chapter.

TABLE 3.5

Self-Reported Degree of Homosexuality–Heterosexuality (percent)

Do You Think of Yourself As:	Percent
Exclusively Homosexual	49
Predominantly Homosexual, Incidentally Heterosexual	27
Predominantly Homosexual, Significantly Heterosexual	14
Equally Homosexual and Heterosexual	5
Predominantly Heterosexual, Significantly Homosexual	2
Predominantly Heterosexual, Incidentally Homosexual	3
N = 238	

Source: Compiled by the authors.

The pattern of correlations of dominance with the other variables seems to provide some support for the dominance hypothesis. Dominance is negatively related to emotional intimacy and positively related to number of sex partners, bar cruising, and frequenting of baths. However, the lack of correlation of dominance with exclusive relationships suggests that even though persons with a penchant for interpersonal dominance may be less motivated toward entering intimate relationships, they somehow find their way into them. When we examine the relationship between marital status and dominance, we also find no significant differences ($F = 0.87$; $df = 2{,}230$; $p = ns$). A possible explanation of the lack of relationship between dominance and exclusive relationships is that although those with dominance needs are somewhat less motivated toward intimacy, their greater volume of sexual encounters provides them increased opportunity to enter intimate relationships, that is, they select among a wider pool of eligible partners.

While the data of Table 3.6 offer some support for the dominance hypothesis, the results of other research do not. Siegelman (1972, p. 15) found the male homosexuals he studied to rank higher on submissiveness than his heterosexual controls. Myrick (1974) found homosexual males to have less "personal competence—a feeling of mastery over the self and environment." Thus it seems that the emotional and sexual behavior of gay men cannot readily be explained as a result of their need for dominance as being greater than, or even equal to, that of heterosexual men. In the light of our data, it would seem that their overall lack of dominance needs may be an asset in intimate relationships. Needs for dominance are a liability in both heterosexual and homosexual pairings. As Blood and Wolfe have reported, marital satisfaction (of wives) is higher in those marriages where one partner is not dominant in decision making (1960, pp. 252-58).

Turning to an examination of the correlates of a heterosexual self-identification, we had anticipated a significant positive association between this variable and negative attitudes. It is plausible that those persons who engage in homosexual activities but who retain a self-concept as significantly heterosexual

TABLE 3.6

Correlations of Dominance and Heterosexuality with Attitudinal and Behavioral Measures

Variable	Dominance[a]	Heterosexuality
Negative attitudes	.05	.11
N	224	224
Emotional intimacy	-.28[b]	-.25[b]
N	226	227
Straight friends	.04	.22[b]
N	237	239
Avoids straights	.01	-.17[b]
N	237	239
Likes gay couples	-.02	-.19[b]
N	239	240
Number of sex partners[c]	.15[d]	-.05
N	217	219
Cruising	.18[b]	-.03
N	236	238
Frequents baths	.13[d]	-.05
N	238	235
Self-esteem	-.10	-.11
N	236	238
Age	.13[d]	.04
N	237	239
Education	-.02	.04
N	235	233
Exclusive relationships	.00	-.09
N	236	238

[a]The correlation between dominance and heterosexuality is 0.02 (N = 232).

[b]Indicates .01 significance; two-tailed tests.

[c]The variable "number of sex partners" is actually the log to the base ten of that variable.

[d]Indicates .05 significance; two-tailed tests.

Source: Compiled by the authors.

do so because of the stigma attached to exclusive homosexuality. To such persons, self-identification as a bisexual often carries less stigma (Blumstein and Schwartz 1976). Some gays who attempt to represent themselves before other gay men as bisexual rather than homosexual often are ridiculed for false pretentions (which implicitly discredit exclusive homosexuality). However, Table 3.6 shows only a nonsignificant positive association of 0.11 between negative attitudes and sexual identity. This seems to imply that negative attitudes are distributed within the population of male homosexuals independently of their degree of heterosexuality. This implies that heterosexual tendencies or behavior among male homosexuals may not relieve them of stigmatizing attitudes toward other gays. We also note that a heterosexual identification has no significant relationship with self-esteem. Thus any significant degree of homosexuality in a male may confer a "master status," upon which all evidence or claims to the contrary have little effect (Beck 1963, pp. 32-33).

Self-identity as significantly heterosexual has no significant relationships with any of our measures of sexual behavior (see Table 3.6).* However, self-identification does seem to be related to whether a male homosexual becomes integrated into the gay community, since it is significantly correlated with having mostly heterosexual friends, not liking gay couples, not avoiding straights in leisure hours, and to no desire for emotional intimacy with another man. Thus it seems that persons with significant components of heterosexuality in their self-identity engage in sexual encounters with men equally often as do exclusive homosexuals but that their encounters are of the preferentially nonintimate nature. Their participation in the gay community is substantially for purposes of impersonal sex, while they remain unattracted to either socializing with other gay men or relating to other males in an emotionally intimate manner.

The pattern of correlates of heterosexual self-identification gives empirical meaning to the occasionally used distinction between "gay" and "homosexual." Homosexual behavior is not the same as a gay self-identity. Not all male homosexuals have a gay self-identity, although popular thought and political labelers tend to equate the two. It is even possible, though unlikely, for a heterosexual to have a gay identity through sympathy with gay culture. Within this distinction, a "gay" person is one who considers himself or herself as exclusively homosexual and who identifies with the gay community—or at least some particular gay subcommunity. To the "gay" person, gay men are a normative reference group, and their approval is sought. In comparison, the "homosexual" is a person who engages in homosexual behavior but may or may not—and more likely does not—feel any special sympathies or identification with a gay community. To the

---

*We also note that heterosexual identification is not statistically related to marital status ($F = 1.67$; $df = 2,229$; $p = ns$).

"homosexual," the gay community is largely a source of sexual encounters but is lacking in emotional or symbolic significance. Accordingly the presence of "homosexual" persons within "gay" communities seems likely to affect the social integration of those communities. To the extent there are significant numbers of "homosexual" men among the gay population, they are unavailable for participation in gay social—as opposed to sexual—events or for participation in gay cultural or political organizations. Thus it would seem that such homosexuals would be less likely to vote in public referenda for gay rights issues than "gays."

Sagarin (1975, pp. 144-54) has argued that there are no persons who are necessarily gay. There are only persons who engage in homosexual behavior, some of whom adopt identities as "gay." He has further argued that the consequences of adopting such an identity are to foreclose alternative possibilities, chief among them being the possibility of becoming heterosexual or bisexual. We also assume that Sagarin would agree that adopting an identity of heterosexual largely forecloses the bisexual and homosexual alternatives. While not taking up the question of the extent to which sexual orientation is changeable, our data suggest that not foreclosing options also has consequences of arguable desirability. When a person declines to foreclose options by identifying himself as less than exclusively gay, he declines to adopt gays as a reference group. He associates with gays only on a selective—and largely sexual—basis. Through maintaining flexibility of self-identity, he declines the option of participating in, and contributing to, the solidarity of *any* group, whatever its sexual persuasion. He is in, but not of, any group. Given the above-reported negative relationship between emotional intimacy and heterosexual self-identification, it seems that he also may decline the option of paired intimacy, since such pairings foreclose options and largely imply a relatively permanent commitment to a particular sexual community. To the extent that many gays were to forgo their identities as gay persons, the result would be a collection of homosexuals lacking in a reference group, the rewards of ingroup solidarity, any ability to neutralize stigma, political organization and rights, or the ability to resist the labeling attempts of such groups as the psychiatric profession.

In the present chapter, we have found that negative attitudes, dominance, heterosexual self-identification, and, to a lesser extent, self-esteem are related to the ways in which gay men relate to, and feel about, each other. We now turn to a series of multiple regression analyses in order to sort out the relative contributions of these variables. Table 3.7 shows the results of these analyses, with intimacy, number of sex partners, having heterosexual friends, bar cruising, and frequenting the steam baths as the dependent variables. We have omitted avoiding straights and liking gay couples from these analyses, since these two items are largely alternatives to the heterosexual friends item as indicators of social integration into the gay social world. The marital status variable is dealt with separately, through analysis of variance procedures in Table 3.8.

TABLE 3.7

Multiple Regression of Negative Attitudes, Self-Esteem, Dominance, and Heterosexual Identity on Sexual and Attitudinal Measures

Dependent Variable	Variable Entered	By Step		Final			
		R	R^2	Beta	F	N	p
	Emotional Intimacy						
Step 1	Negative attitudes	.30	.09	-.24	13.31	–	.01
Step 2	Dominance	.40	.16	-.25	17.19	–	.01
Step 3	Heterosexual identity	.47	.22	-.23	14.03	–	.01
Step 4	Self-Esteem	.47	.22	.07	0.99	214	ns
	Straight Friends						
Step 1	Heterosexual identity	.32	.10	.26	14.82	–	.01
Step 2	Emotional intimacy	.39	.15	-.23	10.40	–	.01
Step 3	Self-Esteem	.39	.15	.08	1.22	–	ns
Step 4	Negative attitudes	.40	.16	.08	1.18	–	ns
Step 5	Dominance	.40	.16	-.03	0.18	214	ns
	Cruising						
Step 1	Emotional intimacy	.21	.04	-.18	5.52	–	.05
Step 2	Dominance	.25	.06	.13	3.66	–	ns
Step 3	Heterosexual identity	.27	.07	-.11	2.70	–	ns
Step 4	Negative attitudes	.29	.08	.10	1.98	–	ns
Step 5	Self-Esteem	.29	.08	.01	0.03	214	ns
	Frequents Baths						
Step 1	Dominance	.13	.02	.13	3.33	–	ns
Step 2	Heterosexual identity	.14	.02	-.06	0.67	–	ns
Step 3	Negative attitudes	.15	.02	.04	0.22	–	ns
Step 4	Self-Esteem	.15	.02	.01	0.06	–	ns
Step 5	Emotional intimacy	.15	.02	-.01	0.02	214	ns
	Number of Sex Partners						
Step 1	Frequents baths	.41	.17	.38	39.08	–	.01
Step 2	Cruising	.50	.25	.27	18.93	–	.01
Step 3	Self-Esteem	.51	.26	.12	3.36	–	ns
Step 4	Emotional intimacy	.52	.27	-.10	1.88	–	ns
Step 5	Negative attitudes	.52	.27	-.06	0.84	–	ns
Step 6	Dominance	.52	.27	.04	0.32	–	ns
Step 7	Heterosexual identity	.52	.27	-.01	0.03	207	ns

Source: Compiled by the authors.

It is clear that the direct contributions of negative attitudes, dominance, and a heterosexual identity to variation in desired emotional intimacy are all equal. Self-esteem has no direct relationship with emotional intimacy. Negative attitudes, a heterosexual identity, and, perhaps, expectations of dominance seem to be cultural concepts derived from the broader heterosexual culture and transferred to the context of gay interpersonal relationships. The transfer of such attitudes into the gay world creates difficulties in interpersonal relationships, since they all inhibit the development of more intimate pairings.

Turning to the heterosexual friends measure, it seems that only heterosexual identity and emotional intimacy significantly contribute, though in opposing directions, to variation in that measure. Both variables contribute equally to the heterosexual friends measure. Through having a significant heterosexual component as part of their self-identity, it appears that some male homosexuals see little need to have gay friends, as opposed to bed partners. An interesting effect of the emotional intimacy variable appears to be that an interest in an intimate relationship with another male is generalized to seeing friendship relationships with other gay men as meaningful. Thus a desire for intimate sexual

TABLE 3.8

Mean Number of Sex Partners, by Marital Status and Bar Cruising[a]

	Marital Status					
Bar Cruising[b]	Single	N	Married	N	Divorced	N
Low	0.88	28	0.56	54	1.15	24
High	1.07	33	0.85	33	1.34	40

Sources of Variation	SS	df	Mean Square	F	p
Main effects	16.25	3	5.42	16.64	.01
Marital status	10.68	2	5.34	16.41	.01
Cruising	2.64	1	2.64	8.11	.01
Interaction	0.14	2	0.07	0.21	ns
Residual	67.04	206	0.32	–	–
Total	83.43	211	0.40	–	–

[a]The variable "number of sex partners" is actually the log to the base ten of that variable.

[b]The bar-cruising variable has been dichotomized at the median of its distribution.

Source: Compiled by the authors.

FIGURE 3.2

Diagrammatic Summary of Empirical Findings

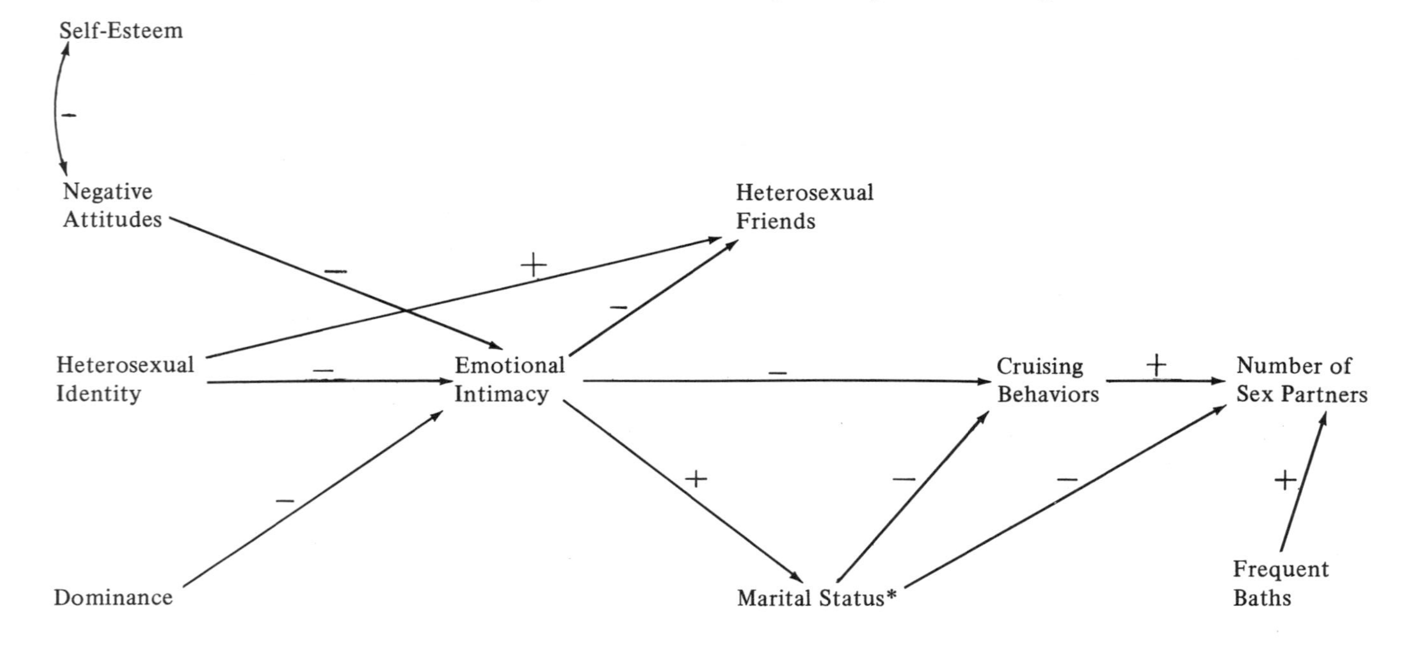

*Being "married" is here considered the positive state of the marital status variable.
Note: (+) indicates positive association; (–) indicates negative association.
Source: Compiled by the authors.

relationships suffuses meaning into gay friendships also. Negative attitudes and dominance have no significant direct links with sexual orientation of friends, since they are only linked indirectly through their relationship with emotional intimacy.

Frequenting the baths has no significant relationship with any of our attitudinal variables. Among the set of variables we have considered, the baths item seems to be rather autonomous and only has occasional weak correlations with them due to its sizable correlation with number of sex partners. The only significant variable in Table 3.7 that is directly linked to cruising behavior is emotional intimacy. Dominance, heterosexual identity, and negative attitudes thus appear to influence cruising behavior through their collective, substantial correlation with emotional intimacy. Emotional intimacy thus appears to operate like a "funnel" through which other attitudinal variables have their effects on the gay male's behavior. Our final behavioral variable, "number of sex partners," is only directly linked to frequenting the baths and cruising behavior. All other variables seem to have no direct relationship with number of sex partners.

Before turning to a more integrated summary of the findings of Table 3.7, we briefly describe Table 3.8. As was reported earlier in Table 3.2, marital status is significantly related to both number of sex partners and cruising behavior. The married have less of both. Table 3.7 shows that both cruising behavior and marital status are significantly and independently related to number of sex partners. Being married inhibits the number of sexual partners.

Concluding Interpretations

Figure 3.2 depicts the pattern of empirical relationships we have found in the data presented. In this diagram, we have left unanalyzed several of the possible relationships, because we simply cannot know which variable may cause which, for example, self-esteem and negative attitudes. We have placed cruising behavior and visiting the baths as causally prior to number of sex partners, since in order to have sex partners, one must, for the most part, search for some. The central role of emotional intimacy in this pattern of relationships is striking. Without this variable, none of the attitudinal measures would be linked to the behavioral measures, except for the link between having heterosexual friends and having a heterosexual identity. The centrality of the intimacy variable in our findings suggests that the ability to view relationships between males in terms of affective intimacy may be the keystone of gay interpersonal relationships. Such affect binds together gay men in both sexual and friendship relationships, while exerting a weaker inhibiting influence on impersonal sexual encounters.

Figure 3.2 also suggests that commitment to heterosexual culture undermines the cohesion of gay communities. In particular, commitment to norms of masculine dominance and of the superiority of heterosexuality over homosexuality erodes a gay male's ability to relate to other gay men in other than sexual ways. Those who remain so committed seem to view the gay world as very largely a sexual community, which is lacking in other purposes. Hence they contribute to, and embody, an impoverishment of gay culture in that for them, gay culture is only a sexual culture and all other life goals are to be attained through participation in heterosexual society.

Our data strongly suggest that attitudes transferred from the heterosexual culture to the gay world are often ill-suited to workable interpersonal relationships in that world. Like other stigmatized groups, gays must overcome their earlier socialization within conventional culture. They must overcome exaggerated expectations of masculine dominance. This may be a particularly difficult change for gay men, or men generally, since relinquishing dominance expectations can readily be confused with relinquishing masculinity. They must also learn to reject popular and authoritative psychiatric interpretations of homosexuals as mentally ill. They also must learn to forgo the temptation to consider themselves bisexual or partly heterosexual. Viewing on's self as bisexual may be a way to avoid the full force of the heterosexual world's condemnation of exclusive homosexuality. It also may be a temporary device for those who are unsure of their "real" sexual orientation and may entertain the possibility of a future orientation that would be different from their present one. However, it also is associated with a lack of intimacy in sexual relationships and a forgoing of gay friendships.

Our data also suggest that many of the sexual behaviors of gay men are substantially, though not completely, independent of their attitudes and friendship relationships. This implies that those formulations of gay relationships in terms of intimacy versus sexual promiscuity (Hoffman 1968, pp. 174-77) are misleading representations of the gay male community. Moreover such views appear to have been formulated in the light of the heterosexual structuring of sexual relationships, which dichotomizes sexual pairings into opposing and incompatible ones of "fidelity" and "infidelity." Such representations can, in themselves, serve to weaken the cohesiveness of the gay community in that they depict the desires of gay men for intimate relationships as unattainable. Through fostering a belief in an unrealistic dichotomy of intimacy versus promiscuity, gay society is represented as one that rarely can fulfill the goals of its members. Alternatively such nonfulfillment of the members' goals has been interpreted as due to overly romanticized and idealized expectations of gay men—hence, as due to psychopathology. Such a representation of the structure of male homosexual behavior can serve as a self-fulfilling prophecy, inducing gay men to forgo the possibilities of intimate sexual or friendship relations for a life-style of hundreds of sexual encounters.

To extend our arguments against a *necessary* polarization of intimacy and promiscuity in behavior, we note that the fact that a given person has sexual encounters with many other men does not necessarily imply he is disinterested in intimacy. An interest in intimacy virtually requires that a person search for others with whom he may be intimate. Accordingly a number of sexual encounters may be an expression of a search for intimacy rather than an expression of disinterest in it. Since the vast majority of our respondents said that they either wanted or had a "long-term lover," we may reasonably assume that for some significant percentage, some of their sexual encounters were expressions of that desire.

It seems that a lack of commitment to the gay community is more likely among gay men of higher occupational status, who because of their commitment to their occupations and consequent immersion in heterosexual society are more covert in their sexual lives (Leznoff and Westley 1956; Weinberg and Williams 1974, pp. 224-25).* Such individuals accord their sexual lives a lower priority in their scale of values, and as Weinberg and Williams (1974, p. 231) report, they identify "more with [their] social class than with homosexuals." However, it is just this reluctance to become socially, as opposed to sexually, involved with other gays that serves to weaken cohesion within the gay community. Without significant involvement in that community, it is unlikely that a gay person can divest himself of the stereotypical attitudes he encountered in his youth and hears daily from his heterosexual associates. Such attitudes render his sojourns in gay settings as visits to a slightly alien society, unencumbered by obligations or commitments. After such visits, he returns to his cultural home in the heterosexual world and there finds acceptance of a defensively created self. Through such vacillation and repeated passing, both sexual and social relationships with other gay men lack intimacy, commitment, and obligation, and the attempts of gay communities to acquire cohesion and political consciousness are thereby weakened.

---

*Note the significant correlation in Table 3.1 between years of education and having heterosexual friends.

4

ADOLESCENT EXPERIENCES AND COMING OUT: OVERCOMING HETEROSEXUALITY

In the preceding chapter, it was shown how the internalization by gay males of the negative stereotypes of homosexuals can affect the individual's potential to become successfully integrated into the homosexual community. In the present chapter, we explore the relationships among teen-age attitudes toward homosexuality, the timing of entry into the gay world, and adult attitudes. We anticipate that adolescent experiences affect adult attitudes and, subsequently, the individual's integration into the gay world.

Several researchers on the careers of gay males have argued that the years immediately prior to an individual's entry into the gay world are a period of internal turmoil and self-doubt (Dank 1971; Gagnon and Simon 1973, pp. 143–45). Since the mean age of coming out, as reported by Dank (1971), is 19.3, the period of internal turmoil is usually the teen-age years. Dank's estimate of 19.3 years is close to the mean of 20.2 (median = 19.2) reported by respondents in our Detroit sample. It appears that during the teen-age years, most future gays have homosexual desires and may occasionally have homosexual sex. But with a significant number of exceptions, they are lacking contact with a community of similarly interested persons. Consequently their interpretations of their own desires and behavior tend to be idiosyncratic and often negative.

The following letter to Ann Landers from a troubled teen-aged gay male seems to be fairly representative of the experience of gays during teen-age years.*

---

*Letter to Ann Landers, *The Idaho Statesman*, February 26, 1977.

> I am a 16 year-old boy. My parents enjoy a very solid economic position in the small town where we live.
>
> Since I was 14, I realized I was a homosexual. Even though I have tried to overcome it, I've been unable to succeed. I finally came to the conclusion that girls are not for me.
>
> I have fallen in love with a kid my age whose parents and mine are close friends. But I can't wait any longer. My life without this kid isn't worth living. It has come to a point where my whole life belongs to him even though he doesn't know it.
>
> Can you give me some advice? Please don't tell me to try girls again. I can't and I won't.

Another poignant example of inner turmoil among young gays was a 20-year-old male living in a small town in Idaho. Believing no one else had homosexual desires and not knowing how to express his, he called the personal crisis "hot line" in the nearby city of Boise. The woman handling his call referred him to the local gay bar in that city. It is evident that an interpretation of one's homosexual desires as unique among humanity could readily lead to self-conceptions that are negative, exotic, and certainly idiosyncratic. Because of the teen-aged gay's common lack of associates who are similarly inclined and because of his lack of a "vocabulary of motives" for his desires and behavior, many during this period acquire or invent views of homosexuality that are, variously, quite unrealistic, overly romanticized, and in conflict with other aspects of the self. Because of the lack of perceived homosexual opportunities, that part of the self remains largely unexpressed in behavior and unintegrated into one's set of roles or identities.

During this period, the information about homosexuals and homosexuality that is communicated to the future gay comes mostly from heterosexuals and is almost always pejorative. In the media and in everyday conversations with heterosexuals, homosexuals are uniformly depicted as mentally ill. At worst, they are described as contemptible, at best, pitiable. These views are most commonly expressed through jokes, put-downs, and on the walls of public restrooms. As Dank (1971) has reported, a significant minority of young gays have learned about homosexuality from books written by psychiatrists. In consequence, the teen-aged gay searching for an identity with which to clothe his desires is offered one that is extremely negative. Some may give in to that identity and conceive of themselves as mentally ill. Of course, such an adopted identity can only cause problems for themselves later if they enter the gay world and attempt or not attempt to become socially integrated into that world.

The adoption of a negative self-image during the precoming-out years and the experience of doubts about one's homosexuality are likely to delay one's eventual entry into the gay world. Such negative views can only serve to exacerbate the internal struggle, since for a person with such views to join the gay community is to join the fellowship of perceived perverts. A number of troubled young gays may attempt a transformation to heterosexuality. The Detroit data show that those repondents who agreed to the item "Before I came out the idea that I might be gay troubled me a lot" were somewhat more likely to have seen a psychiatrist or psychologist, particularly prior to coming out.

Situational or structural factors, in addition to the individual's own attitudes, exert influences on the timing of, and experiences during, coming out. Gay males appear to come out at about 19 years of age. This suggests that the coming-out event is a part of the general acquisition of autonomy experienced by most teen-agers subsequent to graduation from high school. At that time, one is conceded, sometimes reluctantly, the freedom to keep one's hours, establish one's household, and in particular, to find and choose one's associates. Only after leaving high school does the young gay (usually) escape from the supervision of parents and heterosexual teen-aged peers, whose interests he finds uninteresting or even repellent. Through acquiring behavioral autonomy, he also acquires the freedom to define himself as he chooses. Through finding new (and gay) friends, he is enabled in their company to define a new self, and hopefully, to repudiate any negative self-imputations he may have acquired during his years in the teen-age closet.

Of course, some gays may not come out even after they have acquired the freedom of adulthood. In such cases, individual attitudinal factors rather than situational ones are probably more important influences on chosen life-styles. Those who come out later probably have more negative attitudes toward themselves and toward homosexuals generally. Their closetedness is more self-imposed, as compared with that of teen-agers, which is largely due to their immersion in a sea of heterosexual associates and their inability to escape that situation. While we have suggested that those individuals who come out later will have more negative attitudes toward self and other gays than those who came out earlier, an alternative hypothesis must be considered about the relationship of such attitudes and age of coming out.

Is it possible that the relationship of such attitudes and choosing a gay life-style is nonmonotonic, with those coming out quite late and quite early having the most negative attitudes? The rationale for such a hypothesis is that those who come out later have internalized more negative attitudes toward self and other gays; the rationale for negative attitudes by those who come out very early is that the consequences of such "premature" coming out could be disastrous for the juvenile gay. Such juveniles, if their sexual behavior or preferences have become known to parents, peers, police, or teachers are often referred to a variety of official "treatments" and are labeled by institutions, such as schools, through their "counseling" processes. Thus those who come out very early (before 18 years of age) may be more likely to have seen a psychologist or psychiatrist. Or they may have come to the attention of the juvenile court. One of our respondents reported he had come to the attention of the court after having been detected performing fellatio on servicemen in the local bus depot at the age of 13. Even if only peers rather than adults are aware of the young gay's inclinations, he may be subjected to intense ridicule in the very conformist and peer-oriented culture of teen-age society. Any and all of the above experiences could exacerbate the self-doubts the young gay may feel about his inclinations. An attempt is made below to assess which of these two alternative hypotheses about the relationship between teen-age attitudes and age of coming out is more viable.

So far, we have used the expression *coming out* without explicitly defining it. The meaning of this expression is somewhat varied and often depends on who is using the term. One meaning of this term involves the defining of the self as gay. Dank (1971) uses this meaning in his work on coming out. A second and behavioral definition refers to the event of beginning to associate with other gays. Clearly these two events need not be simultaneous, and hence, it is important to separate the two usages. Simon and Gagnon (1967) define coming out as both a behavioral and self-definitional event. Hencken and O'Dowd have offered "self-acceptance" as their definition: "A person comes out of ignorance and self-loathing and self-denial into self-acceptance; one begins to own and accept the identified feelings and desires and to act on them. Both the acceptance and action are crucial. Without the former there is anguished compulsivity; without the latter there is neurotic inhibition" (1977, p. 19). While recognizing that self-acceptance is an important aspect of coming out, we believe that defining coming out in terms of self-acceptance inhibits clear analysis. Rather we prefer to view self-acceptance or its absence as a variable that may or may not follow the behavioral event of coming out or the attitudinal event of defining the self as gay. In short, we approach self-acceptance as a dependent variable.

In the following analysis, both behavioral and self-definitional measures of coming out are used in order to test the hypothesis that those who are most troubled about their sexual orientation tend to delay actual self-identification beyond the time of actually entering the gay world behaviorally. Thus their reservations tend to prolong, and make more difficult, their adjustment to their new life-style. Our self-definitional measure simply asked the respondent at what age he "first defined himself as gay." The behavioral measure asked the respondent at what age he came out (without defining coming out). While we believe that most gay males use the expression *coming out* in a behavioral sense, some probably responded with self-conception in mind. This would inflate the correlation between these two measures of coming out due to self-definition and entering the gay world being correlated. However, in our data, the correlation between the two measures was far from perfect (0.65). This implies they are not simply alternative measures of self-definition, and consequently our behavioral measure has some independence from the self-definitional one. We have also created from these two measures a variable termed *delayed self-definition*, which is the time difference in years between self-definition as gay and behavioral coming out. A positive score on this variable means the respondent delayed his self-definition as gay beyond the time he entered the gay world. This measure should correlate positively with having experienced doubts as a teen-ager about one's homosexuality.

DATA

Table 4.1 gives the univariate distribution of responses to the item, "Before I came out the idea that I might be gay troubled me a lot." The data indicate a bare majority of the Detroit sample were troubled about their homosexuality before they came out. These numbers suggest that the widely accepted notion that gays who have not yet come out have many psychological and identity problems might be exaggerated. Evidently a large minority can make the transition from the world of teen-agers to the gay world without overwhelming difficulties.

The relationships of teen-age guilt, self-esteem, negative attitudes toward other gays, and emotional intimacy with age of coming out and age of self-definition as gay, as well as age of self-definition as gay minus age of coming out are shown in Tables 4.2 and 4.3. Rather than using correlational statistics, a series of one-way analyses of variance was used to test for nonmonotonic relationships. Table 4.2 shows that precoming-out guilt is associated with coming out late. Those who feel guilty about their homosexuality apparently do delay coming out. Since the questions constituting the guilt scale were phrased to refer to feelings prior to coming out, we feel reasonably assured that guilt results in late coming out rather than the reverse.

TABLE 4.1

Degree of Concern about Coming Out (percent)

Before I Came Out the Idea that I Might Be Gay Troubled Me a Lot	Percent
Strongly agree	22
Agree	29
Neutral	8
Disagree	25
Strongly disagree	17
N = 236	

Note: Percents total to 101 due to rounding error.
Source: Compiled by the authors.

The two variables shown to be important in influencing social integration into the gay community–self-esteem and negative attitudes toward other gays (see above)–reveal no significant relationship with age of coming out. Hence our alternative hypothesis that there might be relationships between age of coming out and these attitudinal variables finds no support. Late coming out appears to be related principally to the rather specific attitude of guilt about one's homosexuality and not to the much broader attitudinal phenomenon of self-esteem. However, our measure of self-esteem refers to current rather than past self-esteem, and the latter would be more relevant in this context than the former. We only conclude that present self-esteem does not seem to be materially related to age of coming out.

As shown in Table 4.2, age of self-definition as gay is significantly related to all the presented variables except negative attitudes. The phenomenological event of self-definition seems to have stronger relationships with attitudes than does the behavioral event of coming out. Late self-definition seems to have a debilitating influence on a gay male's attitudes, since it is related to low self-esteem, reduced interest in emotional intimacy, and teen-age guilt. The reader may legitimately ask, "Why should late self-definition be so related? 'Late' is late relative to what?" Table 4.3 attempts an answer by defining *lateness* relative to the behavioral event of coming out. The rationale for such a definition of lateness is that those individuals who underwent periods of time during which their self-definitions were inconsistent with their behavior should have, or have had, negative attitudes. Table 4.3 shows that such inconsistency has no significant relationship with any of our attitudinal measures. Thus, while teen-age guilt is associated with both delayed coming out and delayed self-definition, it is not associated with self-definition being delayed beyond coming out. Inconsistency betwen attitudes and behavior seems to have created no problems for our sample.

In attempting to explain the lack of statistically significant relationships in Table 4.3, we note that what are attitude-behavior inconsistencies to researchers may not be so defined by respondents. During such periods of inconsistency, young gays may have interpreted their behavior to themselves in a number of guilt- or stigma-reducing ways. They may have felt they were simply "going through a phase." Given the widespread belief in North American culture that even heterosexual teen-age males engage in occasional homosexual behavior, this belief may have served as a neutralization for a portion of the Detroit sample and obscured from them the "fact" that they were, or were shortly to become, homosexual. Alternatively they may have felt they were "not really gay" or were bisexual. This could have served to ease their transition into the gay world without leaving residues of negative attitudes. Of course, these suggestions are simply speculations on how individuals might attempt to benignly interpret their behavior in terms other than a full acknowledgment of self as homosexual. From the data in Tables 4.2 and 4.3 however, we conclude that teen-age guilt

TABLE 4.2

Mean Attitudes, by Age of Coming Out and of Self-Definition as Gay

Attitudes	Less than 17	17 to 23	24 and Over	F	df	p	eta
			Age of Coming Out				
Teen-age guilt	9.69	10.38	11.04	5.91	2,228	.01	.22
N	83	98	48	–	–	–	–
Self-Esteem	12.10	12.26	11.84	0.55	2,232	ns	.07
N	87	97	49	–	–	–	–
Negative attitudes	12.73	13.12	13.14	0.28	2,220	ns	.05
N	77	95	49	–	–	–	–
Intimacy	12.84	13.62	11.49	5.13	2,224	.01	.21
N	84	94	47	–	–	–	–

Age of Self-Definition as Gay

Teen-age guilt	9.36	10.35	11.27	9.54	2,219	.01	.28
N	53	122	45	—	—	—	—
Self-Esteem	12.42	12.25	11.30	3.71	2,225	.03	.18
N	57	123	46	—	—	—	—
Negative attitudes	12.78	12.70	13.87	1.64	2,213	ns	.12
N	51	118	45	—	—	—	—
Intimacy	13.44	13.18	11.30	4.87	2,217	.01	.21
N	54	120	44	—	—	—	—

Source: Compiled by the authors.

TABLE 4.3

Mean Attitudes of Self-Definition as Gay Minus Age of Coming Out

	Age of Self-Definition Minus Age of Coming Out						
Attitudes	Less than 0	0 to 1	More than 1	F	df	p	eta
Teen-age guilt	10.40	10.19	10.35	0.17	2,217	ns	.04
N	50	84	86	–	–	–	–
Self-Esteem	11.79	12.45	11.94	1.67	2,221	ns	.12
N	52	85	87	–	–	–	–
Negative attitudes	13.42	12.82	12.89	0.44	2,210	ns	.02
N	50	82	81	–	–	–	–
Intimacy	12.76	13.30	12.63	0.69	2,214	ns	.08
N	50	81	86	–	–	–	–

Source: Compiled by the authors.

seems to delay both coming out and self-definition and that such delayed events are associated with attitudes that could readily impede successful later integration into the gay world.

TEEN-AGE SOCIALIZATION, SEXUALITY, AND AGE OF COMING OUT

It remains a continuing puzzle to students of homosexuality that young gays ever come out in the face of overwhelming pressures to remain in the closet or to become heterosexual. Ellis (1968) uses this phenomenon as the basis of his argument that all gays are psychotic. He argues that they are psychotic because they cannot learn to become heterosexual, despite the immense pressures to become so. We interpret this phenomenon as meaning that their commitment to homosexuality is a deeply internalized aspect of their psyches but not a psychotic one. It is not psychotic because gays typically are sufficiently reality-oriented to wait until they have acquired the freedoms and safety of adulthood before they give substantial expression to their sexual interests. If they were psychotic, as Ellis argues, they would not be rational enough to postpone the fulfillment of their homosexuality until the safety of adulthood. Rather they would have been expressing their sexual interest in overt, detectable, and punishable behavior throughout their juvenile years. Accordingly we interpret the coming-out phenomenon, for the most part, as a rationally timed manifestation of a deeply internalized and enduring aspect of the self.

The question of the extent to which sexual orientation is flexible, and particularly during adolescence, has been subject to dispute. While the data on the degree of flexibility of human sexual orientations are rather complicated, they seem to affirm a substantial degree of deep internalization and inflexibility. Sagarin (1975, p. 150) has asserted that the Kinsey data on male homosexual behavior included large numbers of men who once had engaged in homosexual behavior but no longer did. Such changes in sexual orientation suggested to Sagarin a fair degree of flexibility in sexual identity or orientation. However, until we know whether the men who had once engaged in homosexual behavior were really homosexuals (five or six on the Kinsey scale) or whether they were bisexuals or heterosexuals, who for a short period of time "dabbled" in homosexual behavior, we cannot know how significant Sagarin's assertion is. If such men were not really homosexuals prior to their "reorientation," a situation of substantially less flexibility of sexual orientation is indicated. Under this latter interpretation, flexibility of sexual orientation is limited to small changes—short-distance movements along the Kinsey scale—while complete "conversions" from one exclusive sexual orientation to another is quite rare.

The question of flexibility of human orientation is further complicated by the likelihood that it differs by sex. While Blumstein and Schwartz (1976) argue that there is substantial flexibility in human sexual orientation and that the orientation heavily depends on one's particular situation, all of their data are on lesbians. While data on homosexual behavior in prisons and other unisex institutions have been used as evidence for the flexibility of sexual orientation, the data of such "situational homosexuality" attests to males being largely inflexible and females being more flexible. In analyzing the literature on homosexuality in male and female prisons, Gagnon and Simon show that the incidence of such behavior seems to be about twice as high in female as in male prisons (1973, pp. 245-59). They further show that while the majority of male prisoners who engage in homosexual behavior in prison have also engaged in at least some such behavior on the outside, the majority of comparable female prisoners have not had any significant homosexual experience before coming to prison. These data suggest that while there may be substantial flexibility of orientation among women, the degree of flexibility among men seems rather limited. A further piece of evidence underscoring men's limited flexibility is that Kinsey's bisexual men had remained in that state for an average of only three weeks.* Thus bisexuality among men may be a rather unstable condition, which like the transuranium elements, shortly decays into some more stable state.

In light of the above considerations on flexibility of sexual orientation, a plausible hypothesis accounting for the substantial amount of heterosexual experience typically reported by young gays is that they engage in heterosexual behavior due to the externally imposed demand on them that they appear heterosexual in orientation (Saghir and Robins 1973, pp. 184-204). As Saghir and Robins found, most such heterosexual behavior by gay males, or homosexual behavior by heterosexual males, is limited to the teen-age years and those of early adulthood. After these years, gay men bècome almost exclusively homosexual in behavior. Their motivations for engaging in heterosexual behavior appear to be largely ones of desiring to appear heterosexual, desiring to become heterosexual, curiosity, plus a limited amount of genuine sexual interest. However, to the extent their sexual orientation is largely inflexible, such attempts to become heterosexual could only be expected to complicate their future lives as gays, both psychologically and socially. Accordingly we hypothesize that precoming-out interests in the opposite sex may be positively related to our measures of age of coming out, delayed self-definition as gay, negative attitudes toward other gays, and teen-age guilt and negatively related to self-esteem and emotional intimacy.

Zero-order Pearsonian correlations among our coming-out measures, adult attitudes, and two measures of teen-age sexual interest in boys and girls

---

*This datum is from unpublished Kinsey data and was communicated by C. A. Tripp at the 1976 meeting of the American Sociological Association, New York, New York.

are presented in Table 4.4. The latter two measures each consist of two items (see Chapter 2 on methods). Because the correlation between the two items measuring teen-age interest in boys is only moderate (0.32), we have also included in Table 4.4 all four constituent items to these two scales. Turning to the multiple-item measure of interest in girls (item 8), we see it is positively correlated with a later self-definition as gay and with delayed self-definition. The item of teen-age heterosexual interest (item 5) is positively related to a later age of self-definition as gay, higher teen-age guilt, a delayed self-definition as gay, and negatively related to emotional intimacy. The more behavioral measure of teen-age dating is only related to a later self-definition. These correlations suggest that efforts by young gay males to conform to the heterosexual model in terms of sexual behavior create psychological problems for themselves both during their teen-age years and later. Through prolonging the amount of time they spend in the closet, the problem of resolving their self-definition is carried over into the early years of their explicitly gay careers. Supporting this point, Weinberg and Williams found it was the very youngest adult gay males—those under 26—who reported the most psychological problems (1974, p. 222). We interpret these findings as consistent with our data and suggest they represent a carry-over of earlier difficulties associated with the resolution of an identity conflict.

Turning to the measures of teen-age homosexual interest, engaging in teen-age homosexual sex is strongly related to coming out at an earlier age, moderately related to an earlier self-definition as gay, negatively related to teen-age guilt, negatively related to negative attitudes toward other gays, and moderately (positively) related to a delayed self-definition as gay. It appears that teen-age gay sex, because it is substantially definitionally related to the behavioral item of coming out, reduces the age of coming out more than the age of self-definition and, hence, affects some delay in self-definition.

In Table 4.4, the measures of teen-age heterosexual interest have no significant relationships with the measures of teen-age homosexual interest. While such nonrelationships could be interpreted as meaning that teen-age gay males have flexible sexual identities and, given propitious circumstances, they could have become heterosexual, other interpretations are possible. To the extent their reported interest in heterosexual relationships is one that arises from environmental pressures to imitate the heterosexual model rather than from an "internalized" sexual identity, one might expect little or no correlation between these two sets of measures. Thus if the causes of heterosexual interest among teen-age gays are different from the causes of their homosexual interest, little covariation could be expected. If as Green (1973) and Whitam (1977) have attempted to demonstrate, both deviant and nondeviant psychosexual identities are essentially established during the first few years of life, then later manifested expressions of "alien" sexual identities can reasonably be interpreted as arising out of later situational demands.

TABLE 4.4

Age of Coming Out, Attitudes, and Teen-age Sexual Interests
(Pearsonian r's)

	Variables												
Variables	(1)	(2)	(3)	(4)	(5)	(6)	(7)	(8)	(9)	(10)	(11)	(12)	(13)
(1) Age of coming out	X	-.60[a]	-.24[a]	.03	.06	.65[a]	-52[a]	.05	.23[a]	-.11	.07	-.07	X
N		235	234	234	235	227	234	234	229	225	221	233	X
(2) Teen-age gay sex		X	.32[a]	-.04	-.06	-.36[a]	X	-.05	-.27[a]	.10	-14[b]	.08	.30[a]
N			241	241	242	228	X	241	232	227	225	239	226
(3) Teen-age gay crushes			X	-.09	-.12	-.31[a]	X	-.11	.07	.00	.05	-.03	.01
N				240	241	227	X	240	232	226	225	238	225
(4) Teen-age dating				X	.66[a]	.13[b]	-.08	X	.08	-.08	-.07	.08	.11
N					241	227	240	X	231	226	224	238	225
(5) Teen-age hetero-sexual interest					X	.22[a]	-.11	X	.14[b]	-.15[b]	.01	-.03	.18[a]
N						228	241	X	232	227	225	239	226
(6) Age of self-definition						X	-.42[a]	.19[a]	.28[a]	-.19[a]	.01	-.06	X
N							227	227	220	218	214	226	X

(7) Interest in boys	X	−.10	−.12	.06	−.05	.03	.20[a]
N		240	232	226	225	238	225
(8) Interest in girls		X	.12	−.12	−.03	.03	.16[a]
N			231	226	224	238	225
(9) Teen-age guilt			X	−.17[b]	.15[b]	−.27[a]	.03
N				220	219	229	220
(10) Emotional intimacy				X	−.31[a]	.20[a]	−.04
N					214	226	217
(11) Negative attitudes					X	−.38[a]	−.04
N						223	213
(12) Self-Esteem						X	.01
N							224
(13) Self-Definition minus age of coming out							X
N							

[a]Significant at .01 level; two-tailed tests.
[b]Significant at .05 level; two-tailed tests.
Source: Compiled by the authors.

CONCLUDING DISCUSSION

The question of flexibility of human sexual orientation is an issue heavily invested with political and policy implications. If there is great flexibility of sexual orientation, support is given to the more conservative views on homosexuality. The more orthodox psychoanalytically oriented psychiatrists have taken positions that homosexuality is either a sickness or at least a highly undesirable condition and that it can and should be cured. Indeed an assumption of flexibility of sexual orientation underlies the claim by Save Our Children that homosexuals convert young persons to homosexuality who would otherwise have been heterosexual. This assumption also underlies the view of some gay males that "any man can be made."

On the other hand, most gay spokespersons and some psychologists and psychiatrists argue that "gays are born, not made." Such spokespersons have an evident investment in the question of flexibility of sexual orientation. If sexual orientation is not flexible, attempts to change gays into heterosexuals are ineffective and can only give rise to human suffering. The psychiatrist C. A. Tripp has argued that homosexuality is not an illness and that it cannot be changed. Indeed Tripp asserts that he has been unsuccessful in his extended attempts to locate a single case in which psychotherapy of any form has substantially changed an individual's sexual orientation from homosexual to heterosexual.

We have taken the position in this chapter that sexual orientation is largely established during the first few years of life and that subsequent efforts to alter it, either by the individual or by psychotherapeutic agents, are likely to be ineffective. Proceeding from this assumption, it appears that the juvenile gay male remains largely in a social and psychological closet until adolescence. Until adolescence, it seems that although his psychosexual identity has been established, the more purely sexual parts of that identity have yet to be learned or activated. Such activation appears to arise during adolescence, when peers and parents impose on him expectations that he is ready to become a sexual being. Like other adolescents, he is provided with a number of "sociosexual scripts" through which to express his sexuality (Gagnon and Simon 1973, pp. 73-75).

For the majority of adolescent gays, a problem arises because the sociosexual scripts provided for him are inconsistent with his gender identity or sexual orientation. The resultant conflict appears to be played out during the adolescent years through numerous attempts to conform to the heterosexual scripts. Through dating and occasional intercourse, he attempts to live up to peer and parental pressures. Yet it seems that for many gay males, the scripts are not internalized and remain external to the self. Toward the end of adolescence, he is largely freed from intense and omnipresent expectations that he be heterosexual. Once given most of the freedoms of an adult, he then rejects heterosexual expectations, comes out, and devises a life-style more in keeping with his delayed sexual identity.

We have shown how the period of adolescence, during which the activation of the gay's sexual identity is delayed, often gives rise to a residue of psychological problems, which create difficulties for him during his adult gay career. Teen-age guilt about his homosexuality seems to give rise to a delayed coming out and a later age of identification of self as gay. Late entry into the gay world is also associated with a lessened interest in emotional intimacy with other gay males and with lessened self-esteem. Our data also suggest that to the extent he has made serious attempts to live up to the teen-age heterosexual scripts, he defers the acquisition of a gay identity and has a lessened adult interest in emotional intimacy.

In conclusion, for many gay males, the period of adolescence is a conflictive and confusing psychosocial period. This period draws to a close as the gay male graduates from high school, leaves the parental home, and becomes his own man. For many, however, the conflicts and confusions experienced in the teen-age closet take several years, perhaps a lifetime, to overcome.

5

MARRIAGES BETWEEN GAY MALES

Although a huge number of studies have been devoted to exploring heterosexual relationships, very little attention has been given to enduring homosexual relationships. With the exception of Warren (1974), most of the attention given to homosexual liaisons has been devoted to the more ephemeral encounters negotiated in bars (Hoffman 1968), steam baths (Weinberg and Williams 1975), and public restrooms (Humphreys 1970). The purpose of this chapter is to explore a number of alternative hypotheses about the marital relationships of gay males. In contrast to the heterosexual marriage, the enduring homosexual liaison can perhaps best be described in terms of the characteristics it lacks. Aside from its highly disvalued status, the gay relationship is very largely lacking in institutional supports and cultural guidelines. There are neither legal nor religious sanctions helping to maintain the integrity of the gay relationship. With rare exceptions, there are no children about which the parties to the relationship can organize their marital careers. The lack of children in the gay marriage probably also serves to weaken the ties of the gay couple to the community in that the gay couple acquires no obligations to schools, parental associations, or children's associations.

The gay relationship does not receive the financial subsidies that the heterosexual marriage enjoys, in the forms of reduced taxes and discounts given to married couples by many private associations and businesses. While a number of attempts have been made by gays in various states to acquire such benefits through the legalization of gay marriages, none have been successful to date. Such attempts have been typically defeated on moral grounds, without any significant attention having been given to the financial benefits that would accrue to gay relationships through legalization. It would seem the lack of institutional and financial supports to gay marriages, intentionally withheld by the dominant heterosexual culture, is a potential contributor to the often-mentioned instability and ephemerality of gay relationships (Hoffman 1968, pp. 154-77; Saghir and Robins 1973, pp. 5-58). Since it has been found in a variety of cultures that economic and institutional supports contribute to the stability and longevity of heterosexual liaisons (Rodman 1971; Blood 1972, pp. 48-49), it would seem somewhat arbitrary to argue that such supports have little relevance to the case of gay marriages.

In addition to lacking structural supports, the gay relationship may also be described as lacking cultural guidelines. There are few role models or socialization situations through which the gay individual or couple may learn behavior appropriate to the status of married gay male. While it is possible for gay couples to attempt to borrow cultural guidelines from the heterosexual marriage, such as mutual ownership of goods and social presentation to others as a permanently linked couple, the hostility of the dominant heterosexual world exacts a number of costs from such an "obvious" and visible life-style. For example, there are instances where gay couples have been forced to move due to pressure from neighbors or landlords or due to local ordinances against a residence being inhabited by persons unrelated by blood or marriage. Alternatively when the gay couple adopts a less visible life-style and chooses not to present themselves to others as a unit, it is not possible for them to be rewarded or guided as to behavior appropriate to their married status. The dominant society cannot reward behavior that is hidden from them and will not reward behavior made manifest.

While adult gays in coupling relationships are denied cultural guidelines for the modeling of their relationship, it also seems that they do not experience any situations while growing up in which they may learn appropriate gay role behavior. For example, no mother tells her son that she wants him to find a nice man when he grows up. Furthermore during adolescence, the large majority of future gays have no contact with other gays or gay couples. Whatever impressions the future gay forms of gays or gay couples are largely derived from prejudiced heterosexual sources.

In order to change the situation of young gays having no, or only negative, gay role models, recent attempts have been made in the San Francisco high schools to present an alternative perspective on gays. Within the San Francisco curriculum, gays are depicted as having, or being capable of having, successful and positive long-term marital relationships. They are also presented as socially productive and mentally healthy. However, the success of these efforts to change stereotypes of gays is yet to be proven. A number of macho male high school students respond with derision to any attempts to present gays in a better light. Some appear to have heard such slogans as "Kill a queer for Christ" and to be aware of Anita Bryant's views that gay teachers "corrupt" children by presenting gays in a positive manner. In general, with the arguable exception of the San Francisco case, young gays are lacking visible examples of positive gay relationships.

As a result of the opposition to any presentations of positive gay relationships, most young gays will have few or no ideas as to what an enduring relationship among gay persons is or should be until they socially enter the gay community. Further their impressions of gay relationships during their teen-age years will either be mostly lacking in romantic and emotional content, as opposed to sexual content, or will be grossly overidealized. Until they acquire actual experience (as opposed to fantasized encounters) with other gays, the knowledge of preadult gays about adult relationships are often a mixture of truth, misinformation, stereotypes, and misapplied cause-and-effect relationships. A common example of a misapplied cause-and-effect relationship is the belief that because gay men desire other men they therefore want to be women. In short, their knowledge is a somewhat idiosyncratic approximation of the heterosexual stereotype of gay males as weak, effeminate, perverted, promiscuous, and immoral.

Gagnon's (1967) description of the socialization process in which children learn about sex is structurally comparable to the above-described situation in which preadult gays learn about gay relationships. According to his model, children learn about sex not from those who know most about it—parents—but from those who know least—other children. Because of the cultural norms against discussing sex with or before children, such learning largely occurs in vacuo. This formulation of the socialization process should apply with even greater force to the "nonsocialization" for a gay marriage that occurs among young gay persons. Although it might be thought that heterosexual parents could serve as role models for young gays in the same way that they serve for young heterosexuals, this does not seem to occur. The published research on the topic and our findings on preferred active and passive sexual activities show that the vast majority of gay relationships do not exhibit a role specialization, where one partner is masculine, dominant, and the principal breadwinner, while the other is feminine, subordinate, and the homemaker (Saghir and Robins 1973, pp. 50-58). It would seem that heterosexual marriage cannot serve as a model for the young gay because it cannot answer for him the question, "Which role applies to me—that of husband or wife?" Because of the irrelevance or indeterminacy of the husband and wife roles as models for gay partner roles, the young gay is left free, or adrift, to fashion his own mode of relating to another gay male. Although sometimes the young gay may persist in casting himself and his partner into approximations of the heterosexual husband and wife roles, it seems that in the majority of cases, gays, after some experimentation, opt to play neither role.

Given the structural, cultural, and socialization vacuum within which gay liaisons must evolve, it would seem their marital roles must be substantially self-invented, trial-and-error enterprises. Although there is much trial and error in most heterosexual marriages, it seems clear that this element plays a much larger role in homosexual relationships. Some of the characteristics of heterosexual marriages may be adopted, such as cohabitation. However, it seems that even cohabitation is not always considered a necessary ingredient of an enduring gay relationship. Other characteristics can be borrowed from the experiences of other gay couples, while still others will be worked out entirely on a couple (idiosyncratic) basis. Thus one may expect that homosexual marriages will possess a much greater heterogeneity of characteristics than heterosexual ones. Further to the extent that gay marriages are collectively heterogeneous, there may develop problems of cultural conflict due to a lack of a dominant model for marital relationships within the gay community. In general, when the dominant culture positively avoids making available opportunities for learning about and for rewarding deviant roles or life-styles, problems of perpetuating a deviant culture arise.

The findings and observations to date on the marital relationships of gay males have depicted them as unstable, of short duration, and characterized by frequent conflict and infidelity. Saghir and Robins report that "*only* [italics added] 61 percent of their gay subjects had had liaisons of at least a year's duration with the average length being about three years" (1973, pp. 56-58). They also report that "infidelity was characteristic of the majority of male homosexuals who reported prolonged relationships" (1973, p. 57). By way of contrast, Kinsey and his colleagues (1948, p. 585) and Hunt (1974, pp. 257-58) report the percentage of heterosexually married males who had ever been unfaithful to their wives was a little less than half. Since the latter figures were lifetime incidences, while those of Saghir and Robins referred to fidelity during the three-year average duration of homosexual affairs, the true differences in fidelity are likely to be much greater.

Hoffman (1968, pp. 154-77) interprets the instability and sexual infidelity of such relationships as stemming from mixtures of individual psychopathology and cultural labeling. We have reported some relationship between labeling and experience with exclusive relationships. Warren (1974, pp. 72-76), however, has offered an alternative, more cultural interpretation. She has suggested that the behaviors in gay relationships, such as infidelity, may be nonnormative only within the perspective of the heterosexual community. She posits that infidelity may be more accepted, even expected, as part of the life-style of gay couples. Her suggestion is that fidelity is considered impractical in a "mature" homosexual relationship and is characteristic only of the earliest, or "honeymoon," stage. If the relationship is to endure, the partners will sooner or later come to an understanding, either that each may be sexually unfaithful separately or that both will occasionally have sex with a third person or persons. From this perspective, it is seen as functional to the stability of the relationship to eliminate infidelity as a possible basis of discord. As an alternative, it would also be functional to redefine infidelity, such that it would be disapproved of only when accompanied by affective commitment by one member of the couple toward the outside party.

The ideas discussed above led us to formulate two alternative hypotheses as to the role of sexual infidelity in homosexual relationships. The first hypothesis is the "traditional" one, namely, that infidelity leads to discord and the termination of the relationship. In this case, one would expect fidelity to be a characteristic of the more enduring relationships and that divorced gay males would have been more unfaithful during their marriages than the currently married. To the extent this hypothesis is true, it would seem gay males may have attempted to pattern their relationships after the heterosexual model and to have used the heterosexual definition of fidelity.

The second hypothesis is that infidelity is characteristic of the more enduring relationships. In this case, it is not the *fact* of sexual infidelity that is significant but the affective commitment of the parties to the relationship. Agreement on the permissibility of infidelity would eliminate such behavior as a basis of discord and thereby tend to perpetuate the relationship. To the extent that this hypothesis is true, it would seem gay males have devised a nontraditional pattern for their marriages. Because the present chapter focuses in detail on the gay marital relationship, we use here our first and more complex operational definition of marital status (see Chapter 2 on methods, homosexual marital status [one]). In this definition, being married is defined as having a lover with whom the respondent is currently cohabiting.

DATA

Table 5.1 gives the relationship between age and marital status. As might be expected, the percentage who are single declines with age. However, the percentage who are married shows little corresponding increase. Those who are in their thirties are more often married than either the younger or older gays. Still for no age group is there ever a majority who are currently married. If we combine the married and engaged into a category we label as *currently affiliated*, there is again no age group in which a majority are currently affiliated. The currently affiliated as a percentage of the total only vary from 35 to 46 percent. The marital category that increases with age is the "formerly affiliated"—the divorced plus the formerly engaged.

Despite the roughness of sampling of gay populations, the data summarized above are clearly in striking contrast to corresponding figures for heterosexual populations. Among heterosexual males, the percentage who are married during their thirties and forties varies between 80 and 90 percent (U.S. Bureau of the Census 1975, p. 38). The fact that the percentage of gay males who are married never rises above 50 percent for any age group may itself constitute a structural condition threatening the fidelity and stability of the relationship of the married. When gay males socialize with each other, it is likely that a substantial percentage of their associates will be nonmarried. Such nonmarried associates

TABLE 5.1

Marital Status, by Age*
(percent)

Marital Status	Age			
	18–29	30–39	40+	N
Single	55 (39)	35 (27)	10 (15)	69
Engaged	38 (8)	29 (7)	33 (15)	21
Married	36 (27)	49 (39)	15 (24)	72
Divorced	28 (10)	39 (16)	33 (26)	36
Formerly engaged	47 (16)	29 (11)	24 (17)	34
N	98 –	89 –	46 –	–

$X^2 = 18.51$; df = 8; and $p < .02$.

*Percentages in parentheses add to 100 vertically; those not in parentheses add to 100 horizontally.

Source: Compiled by the authors.

provide opportunities for infidelity or for new liaisons. This situation differs from the heterosexually married, whose friends and acquaintances are also married. In short, the married homosexual is partly immersed in a sea of unmarried peers, who may be open to suggestions of sexual encounters.

It is possible that married gay males, like married heterosexuals, select as their associates other married gay males, thus reducing the chances of sexual opportunities. However, such selectivity would only inhibit infidelity if the married themselves are not disposed to infidelity; the latter case is not supported by our data (see Table 5.2). Indeed the data indicate that married is the least likely of the marital statuses to favor fidelity. It would thus seem that the high percentage of gay males who are unmarried at any one time provides the principal opportunities for infidelity by the married, while the married's disinclination for fidelity provides the motivation for such behavior. We of course recognize that an increase in the percentage married within a group may well increase the rate of infidelity, simply by increasing the percentage of persons who, by definition, are candidates for infidelity—the married. However, we are here suggesting that an increase in the availability of opportunities for infidelty—access to the nonmarried—can also serve to increase infidelity and possible subsequent divorce.

Turning to the row percentages of Table 5.1, the currently unaffiliated, who constitute the principal sexual opportunities for the affiliated, tend to be somewhat younger than the latter. Since the subsequent chapter on age reports

TABLE 5.2

Fidelity Items, by Marital Status

Item	Marital Status				
	Single	Engaged	Married	Divorced	Formerly Engaged
Percentage favors fidelity	44	50	31	72	35
N	68	22	71	36	34
$X^2 = 17.90$; df = 4; $p < .01$					
Percentage never attends steam baths	55	32	47	34	32
N	69	22	73	35	34
$X^2 = 8.17$; df = 4; p = ns					
Percentage with less than ten sex partners last year	45	64	66	13	41
N	64	22	67	31	29
$X^2 = 26.51$; df = 4; $p < .01$					

Source: Compiled by the authors.

a common, though not universal, tendency for gay males to prefer younger or same-age persons, the relative youthfulness of the unaffiliated would tend to increase the appeal of extramarital sexual encounters. Similarly the propensities of the very young (18 to 24 years) to prefer somewhat older partners could well serve to increase their willingness to take up with somewhat older, though married, gay males. It thus seems a variety of structural and attitudinal factors among gay males all operate in the same direction to facilitate extramarital encounters.

Although many gay males get married, they do not stay married. The median duration of relationships is 2.9 years (a figure identical to that reported by Saghir and Robins 1973, p. 57). By way of comparison, although roughly a third of heterosexual marriages terminate in divorce (Fullerton 1977, pp. 440–42), their remarriage rates are sufficiently high such that at no time during the middle years of life is a substantial percentage in a separated or divorced state.

Table 5.2 presents data on attitudes toward infidelity and on various sexual behaviors by marital status. The first item of this table, attitude toward fidelity, reveals that the married are least in favor of it, while the divorced are most in favor. While the finding that the married are the least enamored of fidelity may help explain why gay marriages are characterized by much extramarital sexual behavior (Saghir and Robins 1973, p. 57), that finding is itself somewhat puzzling. Normally one might expect that being married would restrain tendencies toward enjoying many sexual partners. However, it seems that being married produces a sizable reduction in the annual number of sexual partners (see Table 5.2) but may have an opposite effect on attitudes toward infidelity. These data suggest that within the gay culture, infidelity may have been defined in a different way than the one used in heterosexual culture. These data seem to support Warren's (1974) hypothesis that in the "mature" gay relationship, an understanding may be reached that the parties enjoy extramarital sexual encounters as long as those encounters remain purely sexual and do not become a threat to the more personal and social relationshiop of the gay marriage.

The second and third items of Table 5.2 constitute a fairly direct test of Warren's hypothesis. The item "never attends steam baths" indicates that the married are rather average among the various marital groups in their attendance at the baths despite the presumed restrictions of being married. From this, we infer that being married is not an obstacle to enjoying the very impersonal forms of sexual relationship that occur at baths. However, marriage seems to be a substantial restriction on the annual number of sexual partners experienced. From these two items, we infer that being married principally serves to limit those extramarital sexual relationships that are more personal in nature. These would be those encounters that are typically negotiated in the more "social" situations of the gay bar or parties. These more personal encounters would typically entail a number of disadvantages for the married homosexual (heterosexually or homosexually married), who is only interested in the sexual aspects of a relationship (Humphreys 1970). In the more personal type of encounter, more time will usually be required to locate an interested party. In this type of encounter, there may be the risk of information about one's extramarital behavior being relayed back to one's lover through mutual acquaintances. There is also a possibility of a more enduring commitment arising out of such contacts, which could become a threat to the marital relationship. Accordingly it seems that the gay marital relationship serves principally to restrain those extramarital activities that would threaten the existence of the marriage as a social, rather than as a sexual, unit.

Although we have attempted to explain why the married are least committed to fidelity, it still has to be explained why the divorced are so high in their commitment to it. At first look, one might have expected that the divorced would have been least committed to fidelity and that that lack of commitment might have contributed to the breakup of their former marriages. However, we suggest that commitment to fidelity by the parties to a gay marriage is a relatively unworkable adaptive pattern within the gay community. Given the great sexual opportunities repeatedly presented by that community, such an arrange-

TABLE 5.3

Infidelity and Couple's Attitudes toward Infidelity, by Marital Status (percent)

Item	Marital Status			
	Engaged	Married	Divorced	Formerly Engaged
Been faithful last year	23	25	X	X
N	22	67	X	X
	$X^2 = 10$; df = 1; p = ns			
	Couple's Attitude toward Infidelity			
Agreed on fidelity	27	32	61	26
Agreed on infidelity	32	33	14	53
Disagreed	41	35	25	21
N	22	72	36	34
	$X^2 = 18.58$; df = 6; $p < .01$			

*Since our data on infidelity only refer to the recent past, we have no information on the infidelity of the divorced and formerly engaged during their affiliations.

Source: Compiled by the authors.

ment will come to grief on the probable fact of infidelity by one or both partners. In contrast to the heterosexual marriage, we suggest that a commitment to fidelity, rather than infidelity, contributes to the disruption of a relationship. For that reason, the divorced are more committed to fidelity than others.

In order to test the notion that infidelity is the most adaptive pattern within the gay community, Table 5.3 presents data on actual infidelity and on the couple's attitudes toward infidelity by marital status. The item, "couple's attitude on infidelity," was created out of the responses to two questions that were asked of those respondents who currently had or had had a lover relationship: "My lover didn't (doesn't) really mind if I have sex with other guys," and "I didn't (don't) mind if my lover has sex with other guys." The responses to these two questions were then combined to produce the three categories of "agreed on fidelity," "agreed on infidelity," and "disagreed." The data of Table 5.3 show that the divorced are twice as likely to have been agreed on fidelity during their former marriages than the married. This strongly suggests that such a belief may be a positive obstacle to the perpetuation of a gay relationship. The first item of Table 5.3, which concerns actual fidelity, shows that a large majority of the married have been unfaithful during the preceding year. The percentage who have been unfaithful closely replicates the findings of Saghir and Robins (1973, p. 57) on this point.

Table 5.4 shows the relationship between actual fidelity and couple's attitude toward infidelity among the married. As one might expect, there is an association between believing in fidelity and practicing it. However, believing in fidelity makes a difference only when *both* parties to the relationship are agreed on it. There is no difference in the extent of actual fidelity when only one member believes in fidelity. Although belief and behavior have an observable relationship in Table 5.4, we also note that even among those married who are both agreed on fidelity, a majority were unfaithful during the last year. It would seem that even mutual agreement on the desirability of fidelity is an insufficient restraint on infidelity in the gay world. Thus we infer that in a relationship where both parties desire fidelity but at least one behaves in a contrary manner, tensions arise, and the relationship is likely to terminate: hence the high proportion of the divorced who are in favor of fidelity.

A possible ciriticism of the above line of reasoning arises out of the fact that our data are cross-sectional rather than longitudinal. It might be argued that the divorced were not so committed to fidelity when they were married but have become more committed since the breakup of their relationships. This interpretation would be consistent with the common human willingness to impose burdens, such as taxes or fidelity, on groups other than one's own. If this were true, then our data would not show that commitment to fidelity gives rise to divorce. In response to this line of reasoning, we note that the questions used for the item of Table 5.3 concerned with couple's attitude toward infidelity referred to beliefs *during the existence of the marital relationship*, whereas the "favors

TABLE 5.4

Fidelity Items, by Couple's Attitude toward Infidelity[a]

Item[b]	Couple's Attitude toward Infidelity		
	Not OK	It's OK	Disagree
Percentage never attends steam baths	48	46	48
N	23	24	25
$X^2 = .03$; df = 2; p = ns			
Percentage with less than ten sex partners last year	82	45	71
N	22	20	24
$X^2 = 6.69$; df = 2; $p < .04$			
Percentage faithful during last year	46	15	17
N	22	20	24
$X^2 = 6.71$; df = 2; $p < .04$			

[a]Table includes only married gay males.

[b]Because of the obviousness of the relationship, item "favors fidelity" has been omitted from the table.

Source: Compiled by the authors.

fidelity" item of Table 5.2 referred to *current* beliefs. The relative similarity of views by the divorced for both of these two measures suggests a continuity (rather than a change) of beliefs before and after divorce. Accordingly we suggest that the more tenable interpretation of these data is that fidelity attitudes give rise to divorce.

While we have argued that among the married, a commitment to fidelity gives rise to divorce, the case of the formerly engaged seems to present certain difficulties for this interpretation. Since Table 5.3 shows that the engaged are quite similar to the married with regard to couple's attitude toward fidelity, we might have expected the formerly engaged to resemble the divorced on this item. However, they are disproportionately high on their agreement on infidelity. This would seem to call into question our suggestion that a commitment to fidelity combined with actual infidelity tends to disrupt a relationship.

Although the sample sizes for the engaged and the formerly engaged are small, we offer the following tentative interpretation. The cohabitation of the married constitutes a more substantial commitment to a relationship than the separate residences of the engaged. In particular, the social, as opposed to sexual, component of the relationships of the married is greater than among the engaged. In support of this assumption, we note that 50 percent of the formerly engaged, as opposed to 30 percent of all other nonsingle respondents combined, agreed to the item, "Sex is the only important aspect of a gay lover relationship." When the engaged agreed on mutual infidelity, this weakens the basis of the relationship, because sex may be had that is external to that relationship. That is, a relationship which is based principally on sex is weakened when the parties cannot claim a monopoly on the sexual favors of the other. This weakening then serves to eliminate relationships that are already somewhat tenuous. Such an attenuation of bonds probably also occurs among the married when they agree on mutual infidelity. However, because their relationships are based on attachments other than the simply sexual, the resultant weakening may not be sufficient to result in separation, even though the vast majority of the married who are agreed on infidelity are also unfaithful (see Table 5.4). Thus we suggest that when there is a large social component to the relationship, as in the case of the married, a commitment to *fidelity* gives rise to divorce, but when the basis of the relationship is largely sexual, as in the case of the engaged, a commitment to *infidelity* gives rise to termination of the relationship.

We have attempted to show how the marital state of gay males only seems to act as a minor constraint on extramarital sexual encounters. To the extent that it does act as a restraint, it seems that couple's attitude toward infidelity is the crucial variable intervening between marital status and extramarital sexual behavior. Analyzing only the married, Table 5.4 shows that although a mutual agreement on fidelity does seem related to the volume of extramarital sexual encounters, it is unrelated to the frequency of impersonal encounters, such as occur at steam baths. It seems that many gay marital understandings contain an "exception" clause, according to which the parties may engage in impersonal encounters without threatening the relationship.

As a further attempt to assess Warren's hypothesis on the "open" nature of the gay marital relationship, we analyzed the previously given variables on extramarital sexual behavior and attitudes among the married by duration of the marital relationship. These data are presented in Table 5.5 and test the notion that fidelity is principally characteristic of new marriages, while infidelity is the agreed-upon practice of more enduring relationships. The length of marriage variable has been dichotomized at more than two years or less than two years, since more microscopic examination of the data indicates that two years is the most important transition point in such relationships. It is clear that actual fidelity declines substantially after two years of marriage. The items "favors fidelity," "never attends steam baths," and "less than ten sex partners last year" all show consistent, though not statistically significant, trends in the hypothesized direction.

While the data of Table 5.5 support Warren's hypothesis about the mature open gay marriage, it cannot be said that there is a *general* tendency for gay marriages to eventually reach a state of agreed-on mutual infidelity.

The last item of Table 5.5, "couple's attitude toward infidelity," indicates there is a change toward agreement between the couple over time. However, there is no significant change in any one direction. After two years of marriage,

TABLE 5.5

Fidelity Items, by Duration of Marriage

Item	Duration of Marriage	
	1–2 Years	3+ Years
Favors fidelity	41	26
N	22	49
$X^2 = .87$; df = 1; p = ns		
Never attends steam baths	64	39
N	22	51
$X^2 = 3.68$; df = 1; p = ns		
Less than ten sex partners last year	77	60
N	22	45
$X^2 = 1.26$; df = 1; p = ns		
Been faithful last year	46	16
N	22	45
$X^2 = 5.49$; df = 1; $p < .02$		
Couple's attitude toward infidelity:		
Not OK	27	34
It's OK	23	38
Disagreed	50	28
N	22	50
$X^2 = 3.41$; df = 2; p = ns		

Source: Compiled by the authors.

roughly equal percentages are either agreed on fidelity, agreed on infidelity, or remain disagreed. Therefore, although there are substantial measures of truth in Warren's hypotheses, there appear to be multiple careers through which gay marriages may proceed. The couple can come to an agreement on fidelity, or infidelity, or remain disagreed. However, from the above-presented data and arguments, it would appear that the path of agreement on infidelity may be the more enduring and workable arrangement.

As a further comment on the results of Table 5.5, we note that the principal time-related changes are in the sexual behavior items, "been faithful last year" and, to a lesser extent, "never attends steam baths." The attitudinal items exhibit lesser or no changes. These data are consistent with our hypothesis that the sexual opportunity structure within the gay community is the principal factor affecting the sexual behavior of gay males. We suggest that that opportunity structure has a more immediate effect on sexual behavior than on attitudes.

First, behavior is modified to take advantage of opportunities and, then, later, attitudes may change to accommodate one's own behavior.

DISCUSSION

The above data have shown that it is somewhat difficult to speak of a single career for the marital relationships of gay males, because that career seems to be highly contingent on the attitudinal predispositions of the parties involved. To the extent that marital careers are contingent upon individual tastes rather than upon social or institutional expectations, it becomes questionable whether one may legitimately use the term *career* to describe the phases of a gay marriage. Thus while one may legitimately speak of various heterosexual marital careers, since they are quite predictable and based on institutional expectations, perhaps the varieties of gay marriage might better be described simply as "adaptations" based on individual tastes and a prevailing sexual opportunity structure. The heterogeneity of such divergent adaptations seems to arise out of a lack of structural and cultural supports for any single type of marriage, either from the dominant society or from other gays. Since opportunities for infidelity are widely available and since there is much heterogeneity of opinion among gays on the desirability of fidelity, strong cultural support for any one marital adaptation is lacking. Accordingly marital career and life-style appear to be largely subinstitutional phenomena. Gay relationships are thus less influenced by legal, economic, parental, and religious institutions than are heterosexual unions and are more expressions of the personalities of the involved parties.

We suggest that *some* of the marital adaptations of gay males may readily be described as classic instances of social disorganization. While realizing the imprecision of this term, we suggest that such disorganization may be said to exist when the expectations and desires of a segment of a community cannot be predictably pursued through a series of anticipatable situations. When people know what they are getting into and can adapt accordingly (although not necessarily successfully), social organization may be said to exist. It will be remembered that even where both parties to a marital relationship were agreed on the desirability of fidelity, a majority were unfaithful, presumably because of the sexual opportunity structure. This seems to imply that individuals were incapable of adapting their own behavior to both the desired of their marital partners and to their own desires. Further the short average duration of attempted marriages suggests that some gay marital relationships may be instances of social disorganization. However, as a major qualification, we should exclude from the category of "disorganized" those marriages where there is agreement on infidelity and those where there is both agreement on fidelity and actual behavioral fidelity. Such marriages seem to have reached an accommodation between the parties in both attitudes and behavior.

If a commitment to fidelity is the cultural culprit creating disorganization among some gay marriages, it seems likely that gays so committed have borrowed their marital model from the heterosexual culture. The cultural trait of fidelity, which shores up the organization of the heterosexual marriage, when transferred to the gay world, seems to give rise to disorganization. Hence a commitment to fidelity, like negative attitudes toward other gays, dominance expectations, and a nongay self-identity, appears to be another item of heterosexual culture that creates disorganization and a lack of cohesiveness when imported into the gay community by its members.

To argue that many gay marriages are instances of social disorganization is not to argue that gay life as a whole may be so characterized. Weinberg and Williams (1975) have accurately shown how the institution of the gay bath is a highly organized set of expectations and activities. They showed how the gay bath and the gay bar operate in a well-organized manner under a "market mentality," designed for the easy and expeditious acquisition of sexual partners. As they observe, whether or not a situation is socially organized or disorganized depends upon the goals and expectations of the participants in that situation. The gay bar and bath are well organized toward the particular goal of acquiring sexual partners. However, a problem of social disorganization arises when the sexual market mentality is extended into the area of the gay marriage. Whatever the goals of such marriages, the sexual market mentality seems ill-suited to the attainment of those goals. Such an intrusion of the market mentality into the marital institution appears to give rise to the "problem of paired intimacy" (Hoffman 1968, p. 176), that is, to an enduring inability to sustain an enduring relationship of emotional intimacy. Presently the adaptation of the open gay marriage seems to be the most workable accommodation by married gays to the mentality of the sexual marketplace.

DOMINANCE IN GAY RELATIONSHIPS

Cavan (1966, p. 192) has suggested that questions of interpersonal dominance are more problematic among homosexual couples than among heterosexual ones. Among the latter, it is culturally prescribed that the male will be largely dominant and will be the initiator of interpersonal interactions. Thus the male may ask an unknown female to dance but not the other way round. In contrast, the question of who is to initiate interactions between males in gay settings is culturally indeterminate. It seems that the cultural norms permit either to be the initiator. However, when one or both parties may be shy or fearful of rejection, the result may be that both leave initiation to the other, such that a relationship is never established.

While Cavan's observation was based on her experiences in gay bars, in which there were many attractive males standing and milling around but not initiating interaction with each other, her idea can readily be extended to the situation of the gay couple. Hoffman (1968, pp. 183-84) has asserted that within gay marriages, it is problematic which member of the pair is to be dominant or if either is to be dominant. Given that gay males have been socialized into many, although not all, of the cultural norms applicable to males, it might be anticipated that both would expect to be dominant. Or analogous to the bar situation, both might expect the other to be dominant. Clearly both of these possibilities could lead to dissatisfaction with, and termination of, a gay relationship. Accordingly we suggest that the divorced and the single would desire a greater degree of dominance than the married. Below we use marital status definition two, because the cell sizes are larger and because the results are the same as when definition one is employed.

In order to test our hypothesis about stability of relationships and dominance, we asked our subjects to respond to the following two items: "If I lived with a lover (or do live with) I would probably make most of the decisions" (there were five response categories, ranging from strongly agree to strongly disagree); and "In our relationship I made (make) the decisions (there were five response categories, ranging from always to rarely). The second item was asked only of those respondents who had or had had a lover with whom they had gone for at least a year. The univariate distributions for these two items are given in Tables 5.6 and 5.7.

It is apparent from the distributions of these two items that egalitarianism of relationships is the modal expectation and practice. However, there still remains substantial variation about the modal responses, and it is in pairings of gay persons with noncomplementary expectations that we might expect discord to arise. While it might be tempting to compare the distributions of these two

TABLE 5.6

Hypothetical Dominance in Relationship (percent)

If I Lived with a Lover (or Do Live with) I Would Probably Make Most of the Decisions	Percent
Strongly Agree	5
Agree	23
Neutral	37
Disagree	26
Strongly Disagree	7
N = 239	

Source: Compiled by the authors.

TABLE 5.7

Actual Dominance in Relationship
(percent)

In Our Relationship I Made (Make) the Decisions	Percent
Always	1
Mostly	23
Half and Half	60
Occasionally	12
Rarely	4
N = 165	

Source: Compiled by the authors.

items and then infer that in practice, relationships become more egalitarian than anticipated, the wording of the two items does not readily admit such an inference. In particular, disagreement with the first item is consistent with several positions on desired dominance.

While we do not possess actual data on the responses of heterosexuals to these two items, we suggest that within each sex, the variability of responses would be substantially less and that males would respond more toward the dominant ends of these scales, while females would give less dominant responses. In comparison, while the large majority of gay males have undoubtedly internalized most of the cultural expectations appropriate to their gender, their lack of an exclusive and total commitment to the customary male sex role probably encourages variation from, and innovation of, parts of that role. Thus deviation from that role's expectation in such an important aspect as sexual orientation may require adjustments in a number of other parts of the role, for example, in dominance expectations. Accordingly we find a substantial amount of variation in these expectations.

In order to relate the above two dominance items to marital status, the items were trichotomized. The response categories "neutral" and "half and half" became the middle categories of Tables 5.8 and 5.9. It is evident from Table 5.8 that the divorced and single do not desire more dominance than the married. Hence we find no support for the hypothesis that because gay males expect to be dominant in their relationships, their marriages are likely to end in divorce. However, because our data are from a survey taken at one point in time (not panel data), it might be thought that the divorced had greater desires for dominance during their marriages, such desires led to divorce, and that subsequently they have learned from experience and have reduced their expectations of dominance to those similar to the married. This interpretation implies that the single, who have not had the occasion to go through such a learning process, might be expected to have rather high dominance expectations. The data show this not to be the case. Accordingly we do not find support for the hypothesis of problematic dominance relationships among gay marriages. Table 5.9, which compares the married and divorced with respect to decision making during their marriages, similarly shows no significant differences. Both groups are closely similar in their egalitarianism. Again we find no support for the hypothesis of problematic dominance.

The reader will remember that in Chapter 3, we found dominance expectations to be negatively related to emotional intimacy and positively related to number of sex partners, frequenting the baths, and to bar cruising. The last three correlations suggest that dominance expectations may be more significant for the gay man's extramarital relationships than for the marital one. Dominance expectations may partly give rise to the practice of frequent extramarital encounters. However, since such encounters do not seem to be problematic to many gay couples, dominance expectations do not seem to create major problems, either directly in the marital relationship or indirectly through infidelity.

The data of Tables 5.8 and 5.9 suggest that the conventional sex-role definitions of males as dominant in their sexual relations do not create excessive problems for gay marriages. It may be that such conventional conceptions of appropriate behavior are considered irrelevant to the successful gay relationship. Gay couples seem to work out dominance relationships in the absence of cultural guidelines. Whether the relationship tends to eventual equality or inequality may well depend upon the personalities of the parties. We suggest that the cultural model on which many gays may structure their relationship is that of

TABLE 5.8

Dominance Expectations, by Marital Status

	Marital Status		
I Make Most Decisions	Divorced	Married	Single
Disagree	26	39	33
Neutral	46	30	38
Agree	30	31	29
N	74	93	66

$X^2 = 4.57$; df = 4; p = ns.

Note: Percentages may add to more than 100 due to rounding error.

Source: Compiled by the authors.

friendship rather than that of marriage. The friendship role of the conventional culture assumes a substantial degree of egalitarianism but leaves the question of dominance up to the tastes of the parties involved. It is also one that grants the involved parties substantial degrees of autonomy, rather than requiring the closely coordinated activities of the roles of spouses. In particular, the friendship role is not an exclusive one, since persons may legitimately have more than one friend.

A formulation of gay relationships as modeled after the nonexclusive friendship role may help to explain the very common tendency for gay males to have sexual relations with persons other than their principal lover. However, gay males rarely have several principal lovers simultaneously. They typically have a principal lover, while enjoying occasional brief sexual encounters with other parties. Accordingly, we should modify our formulation of gay marriages as friendship relationships to a formulation of "best friend" relationships. While the relationship of best friend is an exclusive one, it permits one to have other friends who are of lesser emotional significance. A friendship interpretation of gay marriages is consistent with the terminology of reference commonly employed among gay males. Gays commonly, though not exclusively, use the expressions *my friend* or *your friend* to refer to a lover, while saying *a friend* to refer to other friends. These expressions seem to be preferred to those of *husband* and *wife*, which commonly have pejorative implications or overtones, particularly for the "wife."

Although the marital relationships of gays tend to be modeled on the egalitarian friendship model rather than the less egalitarian husband-wife model, dominance relationships do occur. Although some of these dominance patterns may be based on characteristics of individual personality, others are based on differential access to resources, for example, money, education, jobs,

TABLE 5.9

Dominance Practices, by Marital Status

	Marital Status	
I Made Decisions	Divorced	Married
Little	23	24
Half and half	63	57
Mostly	14	18
N	70	94

$X^2 = 0.59$; df = 2; p = ns.

Note: Percentages may add to more than 100 due to rounding error. The question of who made the decisions was not asked of the single.

Source: Compiled by the authors.

TABLE 5.10

Dominance Practices, by Relative Incomes

I Made Decisions	Relative Incomes		
	I Made More	I Made Same	He Made More
Little	7	17	28
Half and half	59	64	56
Mostly	34	19	16
N	71	36	50

$X^2 = 12.62$; df = 4; $p < .02$.
Note: Percentages may differ from 100 due to rounding error.
Source: Compiled by the authors.

and so forth. As has been found in heterosexual marriages, differential access to outside resources gives rise to differences in decision-making power within the relationship (Udry 1974, pp. 303-6). Table 5.10 supports the notion that inequality of incomes in gay relationships is associated with inequality in decision making. Those who made more money reported that they also made relatively more decisions. While such income inequality gives rise to inequality of decision making in gay relationships, it seems to us unlikely that the inequalities found in gay relationships come near to approximating the inequalities of heterosexual marriages. Our rationale for this suggestion is that although there are income inequalities, in almost all instances, both parties are employed. It is rare for one party to adopt a domestic role in which he is completely economically dependent on the other. Hence the heterosexual and inegalitarian practice of an employed husband supporting an "unemployed" housewife is largely absent among gays.

CONCLUSIONS

We have indicated that the marital relationships of gay males represent a largely subinstitutional, couple-idiosyncratic adaptation to a situation in which both structural and cultural conditions impair the stability and longevity of such relationships. Rather than utilizing the conventional heterosexual marriage as a model for relationships, it seems that their relationships are patterned after the nonexclusive conventional best friends model. Such an adaptation permits the parties substantial autonomy outside of the relationship. Given this autonomy, plus the great sexual opportunities in the gay world and the lack of cultural constraints against infidelity, the majority of gay relationships are characterized by infidelity. It seems that over time, a large number of gay couples come to an understanding either that infidelity is permissible or that impersonal sex outside of the relationship is permissible. These understandings are in substantial contrast to the conceptions of appropriate behavior among heterosexual couples. Among the latter, sexual infidelity is almost always disapproved of, and there is no agreement that "quickies" are allowed.

It has been suggested that because males are socialized to be dominant in their sexual relationships, this could give rise to disputes over dominance; our data did not support such a formulation. Since gay males seem to model their marriages after the egalitarian model of best friends, matters of dominance are substantially irrelevant to their relationships. It would seem that most gay couples reject the heterosexual marriage as an appropriate model. Of course, as was found in our data, differential access to outside resources gives rise to differences in decision-making power within the relationship, just as it does in heterosexual marriages. This suggests that gay relationships, rather than being dominated by individual personality differences and determined by individual psychopathology, simply reflect in many ways the basic social processes common to both gay and heterosexual groups.

We did not commit ourselves with reference to the much disputed topic of psychopathology among gay males. While psychopathology has been utilized to explain the common tendency for gay males, both in their married and nonmarried states, to have many sex partners, we attempted to use the "obvious" variables of culture and structure to explain their attitudes and behavior. As we have now learned from the experience of many years of psychoanalytic theorizing about deviants, many of the more obvious and important determinants of deviant behaviors can be obscured by a veritable jungle of sophisticated psychologizing.

6

SEX-ROLE AND DOMINANCE INTERPRETATION OF GAY MEN

Most popular thought about gay men and much psychiatric writing on the topic have utilized sex-role concepts to interpret the behavior of persons who prefer others of the same sex for sexual and romantic relationships. The virtually universally accepted dichotomized sex roles of North American culture, which are viewed as the norm, or what is "natural," have been used to explain the behavior of gays. Indeed literally thousands of common activities are accorded symbolic associations with one sex role or the other, for example, mountain climbing versus horticulture, car repair versus dishwashing. Given the "natural" explanatory utility of sex-role concepts, most popular and professional thought has interpreted homosexuality among men as expressing an essential feminine identification. From such reasoning stems the stereotypical view of gay men as effeminate in deportment, largely interested in culturally feminine recreations and occupations, and preferring a passive and submissive role in sexual relationships and activities.

Most psychiatric writing on the topic has proceeded along similar lines of analysis. Yet psychiatrists realized that not all homosexuals could be assimilated into the single category of an essentially female gender identity. Some gay men clearly did not fit the stereotype. Also, if most gay men were interested in playing a feminine role in sexual activities, a set of masculine players was also needed (Bieber et al. 1962; Fenichel 1945; Socarides 1968; Ovesey 1965). Thus psychiatric thought has typically seen gay men as being of two types: a dominant "active" type and a more visibly effeminate "passive" type.

It is interesting to compare the one-category representation of gay men found in popular belief with the two-category version found in much psychiatric writing. We suggest that popular belief utilizes only the feminine category, because to admit the existence of a set of masculine homosexuals would be to acknowledge the existence of a set of basically normal males who differ from heterosexuals only in their sexual object choice. While it might appear that psychiatric theory has a greater degree of accuracy in viewing gay men as existing largely in the two forms (active and passive), such accuracy is only a surface accuracy. If the existence of masculine male homosexuals is acknowledged by psychiatric theory, a problem is raised for that theory in that such men seem to possess an apparent normality other than in their sexual preference. This state of affairs then requires two separate theories of homosexuality—one for active homosexuals and another for passive homosexuals—or an overarching theory that can attribute both forms of male homosexuality to a single cause.

The single cause of homosexuality that most psychiatric theory has employed is that of an essential identification with the other gender. Although the theoretical twists taken by various writers differ, most have maintained that homosexuals, both active and passive, have acquired an identification with the opposite sex. While such an explanation of the case of passive-feminine gay males is fairly straightforward, explanations of masculine homosexuals are more involved. In Fenichel's (1945) formulation, masculine homosexuals prefer a male because they are afraid of the damage to their genitals that would come from inserting their penis into a vagina with "imaginary teeth." As Tripp (1975, p. 79) has ironically commented on this view: "A man can become homosexual because he unconsciously imagines teeth in the vagina, and so, unaccountably, he chooses to place his penis in a cavity where there are real teeth." Others (Bieber et al. 1962, p. 251) explain the masculine homosexual as one who prefers sex with men as a substitute for sex with women. Basically his interest is based on a fear of women rather than a positive attraction for men. His fear, in turn, is based on his beliefs in his own inadequacy as a man. An alternative view of the masculine male homosexual is that through identification with the mother, he has a primary feminine sexual identity and can "behave lovingly toward other men as he wishes his mother behaved toward him" (Socarides 1968, p. 75). When making love, he identifies both with his mother and his sexual partner and, thereby, receives his mother's love. Through such fine reasoning, the primary feminine sex-role identification of both active and passive gay men effects a theoretical unification of polar concepts. Such views assimilate both types of gay men to the cultural conception of the female sex-role, as does the popular view.

Realizing the empirical inadequacy of a straightforward dichotomization of gay men into active masculine and passive feminine types, Bieber and his colleagues (1962, pp. 238–51) created a pair of concepts, "inserter" and "insertee." Their rationale for abandoning the concepts of an active masculine gay and a passive feminine one was that not all of the behavioral and psychological traits attributed to each type were found to be present. Many masculine gay men liked the passive activities of receiving anal intercourse and performing fellatio on their sexual partners. Similarly many apparently more effeminate males liked performing anal intercourse on their partners and enjoyed having their partners perform fellatio on them. Westwood (1960, pp. 127–34) reported that a majority of gay men could not be readily classified into active and passive types in terms of sexual techniques; rather they frequently interchanged roles. Saghir and Robins (1973, pp. 59-61) reported similar findings.

The "inserter-insertee" formulation, while recognizing many exceptions, depicts a state of affairs that can be summarized as follows:

1. Preferences for oral insertee and anal insertee roles are positively associated.
2. Preferences for oral inserter and anal inserter roles are positively associated.
3. Preferences for oral insertee and oral inserter roles are negatively associated.
4. Preferences for anal inserter and anal insertee roles are negatively associated.
5. Preferences for oral insertee and anal inserter roles are negatively associated.
6. Preferences for oral inserter and anal insertee roles are negatively associated.

It is clear that such a formulation of the sexual behavior of gay men in terms of a continuum is still derived from traditional sex-role views; otherwise it would be without foundation (unless, perhaps, one wanted to utilize dominance and submission as explanatory concepts).

Haist and Jewitt (1974) more recently claimed to have found strong support for the pair of concepts devised by Bieber and his colleagues. Their data show strong relationships between preferring either an insertee or inserter role in anal sexual activities and preferring the corresponding role in oral activities. However, we suspect that their results were largely an artifact of the way their questions were put. They apparently dichotomized their subjects according to their answers to the question of whether they preferred an insertee or inserter role in anal sex, while not permitting choices of "both" or "neither." In our data (reported below), we have repaired this methodological deficiency.

While both heterosexuals and psychiatrists appear to take most of the above formulations of gay men quite seriously, we must ask the question of how seriously do male homosexuals themselves take the culturally inherited sex roles? May gay men be reasonably dichotomized into active and passive categories? Is an "inserter-insertee" formulation more accurate? As indicated earlier, there are a variety of possible sex-role interpretations of gay men. Since our data cannot adequately test or speak to some of these alternatives, we restrict our analysis to those on which our data have some bearing. We explore the validity of the inserter-insertee continuum.

In order to explore the validity of this formulation, we propose to examine the relationships between preferences for both active and passive anal and oral types of sex among our Detroit respondents. In the course of this analysis, we have not used forced choice questions but have allowed the respondents to opt for all, some, or none of the four "classical" types of sexual activity among gay men. (We did not include questions on some of the rarer and more exotic sexual activities of some gay men, for example, sadomasochistic practices and scatological activities.) This form of questioning permits the data to exhibit the inserter–insertee dimension, or some other dimension, or various interactions. The particular question asked in our survey was: "How do you feel about each of the following activities: performing fellatio, receiving fellatio, performing anal intercourse, receiving anal intercourse, mutual masturbation, full-body stimulation to orgasm?" The response categories provided were the following: "don't like it"; "it's OK"; and "prefer it."

DATA ON SEXUAL PRACTICES

Table 6.1 gives the frequencies of different types of gay men, the types being defined in terms of preferences for each of the four classical sexual activities. Within this table, there are 16 types, defined by whether the individual likes or dislikes each of the sexual activities. Since the frequencies of this table are a product of both the marginal frequencies of the defining items and the correlations among those items, we have provided two different sets of frequencies based upon the two possible cutting points for liking and disliking. The left column of frequencies is based on a dichotomy of "preferring" responses versus "it's OK" and "don't like it" combined; the right column of frequencies uses a dichotomy of "don't like it" versus the other responses. Traditional psychoanalytic and popular conceptions have focused on the "pure" insertee and inserter types, which are to be found in rows eight and ten, respectively. Such thought has typically ignored the other 14 possible combinations. It is apparent that whatever cutting points are employed, the traditionally hypothesized insertee and inserter types do not constitute a majority of gay men. Indeed neither of these types is even a modal frequency, the most popular combination being an interest in all four activities.

While the data of Table 6.1 do not support traditional conceptions of gay males as inserters and insertees, we may not immediately infer that there is no truth in such conceptions. Since these frequencies depend, in part, on the marginal frequencies of the defining items and since these marginal frequencies, in turn, depend on the uncertainties of the sampling of male homosexuals, it is possible that traditional conceptions may be supported by the interitem correlations but not the marginal distributions. Table 6.2 presents the zero-order associations between the four sexual role-preference items.

The subtable exhibiting the relationship between liking an active anal role and the oral inserter role offers some support for the existence of an inserter

TABLE 6.1

Types of Gay Males, Based upon Preferred Sexual Roles

Preferred Role						
Oral Insertee	Oral Inserter	Anal Inserter	Anal Insertee	Row Number	N[a]	N[b]
+	+	+	+	1	23	115
+	+	+	–	2	12	47
+	+	–	+	3	5	12
+	–	+	+	4	1	4
–	+	+	+	5	1	9
+	+	–	–	6	23	17
–	+	–	+	7	6	0
+	–	–	+	8[c]	10	3
+	–	+	–	9	9	2
–	+	+	–	10[d]	21	5
–	–	+	+	11	9	1
+	–	–	–	12	7	1
–	+	–	–	13	12	1
–	–	+	–	14	28	1
–	–	–	+	15	11	2
–	–	–	–	16	44	2

[a]The cutting point for these frequencies was "prefer it" versus the other two response categories. The response categories were the following: "don't like it"; "it's OK"; and "prefer it."

[b]The cutting point for these frequencies was "don't like it" versus the other two response categories.

[c]The traditionally hypothesized insertee type.

[d]The traditionally hypothesized inserter type.

Note: The symbols indicate that the individual likes (+) or dislikes (–) the activity.

Source: Compiled by the authors.

dimension. Those who like the one activity like the other. However, it should be observed that the oral inserter item has rather low variability. Rather few persons positively dislike having fellatio performed on them. Hence that item cannot readily explain a substantial amount of the variation in the anal inserter item. When we examine the relationship between the two insertee items, the pattern is very mixed. There is a tendency for each of these items to polarize with respect to each other. It seems that the insertee concept, if it has any validity, is more complex than that of inserter.

Traditional theorizing on the insertee-inserter concepts would lead us to expect that preferences for the oral inserter and oral insertee roles should be

TABLE 6.2

Zero-Order Relationships among Sexual-Role Preference Items
(percent)

Response	Don't Like	It's OK	Prefer
		Oral Insertee Role	
Oral inserter role:			
Don't like	29 (6)	7 (8)	2 (2)
It's OK	38 (8)	63 (70)	26 (25)
Prefer	33 (7)	30 (33)	72 (68)
N	21 –	111 –	95 –
	X^2 = 52.43; df = 4; p < .01; gamma = .60; V = .60		
Passive anal role:			
Don't like	41 (9)	35 (39)	32 (29)
It's OK	27 (6)	47 (52)	25 (23)
Prefer	32 (7)	18 (20)	44 (40)
N	22 –	111 –	92 –
	X^2 = 18.68; df = 4; p < .01; gamma = –.21; V = .20		
		Oral Inserter Role	
Passive anal role:			
Don't like	38 (6)	25 (26)	44 (47)
It's OK	25 (4)	51 (53)	22 (23)
Prefer	38 (6)	24 (25)	34 (36)
N	16 –	104 –	106 –
	X^2 = 20.98; df = 4; p < .01; gamma = –.09; V = .22		

	Oral Insertee Role		
Active anal role:			
Don't like	24 (5)	13 (14)	21 (19)
It's OK	43 (9)	40 (45)	29 (27)
Prefer	33 (7)	47 (52)	50 (46)
N	21 –	111 –	92 –
	$X^2 = 5.60$; df = 4; p = ns; gamma = .06; V = .11		
	Oral Inserter Role		
Active anal role:			
Don't like	50 (8)	14 (15)	14 (15)
It's OK	31 (5)	42 (44)	30 (32)
Prefer	19 (3)	43 (45)	56 (59)
N	16 –	104 –	106 –
	$X^2 = 18.21$; df = 4; $p < .01$; gamma = .29; V = .20		
	Active Anal Role		
Passive anal role:			
Don't like	55 (21)	26 (21)	36 (38)
It's OK	16 (6)	48 (39)	33 (36)
Prefer	29 (11)	26 (21)	32 (35)
N	38 –	81 –	109 –
	$X^2 = 14.71$; df = 4; $p < .01$; gamma = .08; V = .18		

Note: Frequencies are in parentheses. Significance tests use a .05 level. Both gamma and Cramer's V are presented due to the nonmonotonicity of some relationships.

Source: Compiled by the authors.

negatively correlated and, similarly, that preferences for the active and passive anal roles should be negatively related. However, Table 6.2 shows that the oral insertee and oral inserter roles are strongly and positively associated. Also, the passive and active anal roles appear to polarize with respect to each other in that the principal frequencies of this subtable are located in the cells of both diagonals. We interpret this as meaning that few persons have lukewarm attitudes toward anal sex. If they either prefer or dislike one anal role, they either prefer or dislike the other role (they do not take a more neutral stance). These data very much suggest that the concepts of inserter and insertee are not polar opposites. Nor do they seem to be simply independent dimensions, since several of the subtables of Table 6.2 exhibit either a relationship in the theoretically "wrong" direction or a polarizing effect.

Entertaining the hypothesis that in these data, oral and anal dimensions of preference may be operative in addition to active and passive dimensions, we dichotomized the four items of Table 6.2, so as to examine the first-order partial relationships. The positive association between the two oral roles remains unchanged when one controls for liking either an active or passive anal role. The first-order partial gamma coefficients are all significant and of a value of 0.70 ± .02. (Data are not shown.) These data suggest that there is a dimension of oral preference among gay men that is independent of active-passive orientations.

The partial relationships between the two anal preference items, however, proved much more complex than those between the two oral items. The relationship between one anal activity and the other was found to be contingent on the person's attitude toward either of the oral activities. For those gay men who disliked either oral activity, the two anal activities were negatively related, that is, they tended to specialize in either one or the other. For those who liked either oral mode, the two anal activities were positively related. The latter pair of partial relationships were both moderately strong and significant, while the former pair of partial relationships were simply statistical trends, with probability values of 0.12 ± .02. These partial relationships are not presented here, although the determined reader may ferret them out of the frequencies of Table 6.1. (By way of interpreting these rather involved relationships, we suggest that disliking either oral mode tends to create active or passive anal specialists, while liking either oral mode creates generalists (that is, nonspecialists) in the anal mode.

We turn to an examination of the partial relationships between the two insertee items while controlling for the two inserter roles. The zero-order relationships between these two roles proved somewhat problematic in Table 6.2, exhibiting a polarized relationship. The partial relationships between the two insertee roles proved contingent on the attitude toward the role of anal inserter. For those who liked the anal inserter role, the two insertee activities were positively and significantly related. For those who disliked the anal inserter role, the two activities were negatively related, although this relationship was only a statistical trend. This finding again suggests that sexual activity preferences tend to come in a "bundle," with likings for one facilitating likings for others. If we look at the relationships between the oral insertee and anal inserter roles while controlling for that of anal insertee, we find a pattern of relationships statistically identical to those that have just been described. Among those who dislike the anal insertee role, these two activities are negatively but not significantly associated. It seems that disliking certain activities gives rise to specialization in preferences. Again the interested reader may ferret these partial relationships out of the frequencies of Table 6.1.

INTERPRETATIONS

The first conclusion we draw from the above data is that the traditionally theorized division of male homosexuals into those who are both orally and anally active and those who are both orally and anally passive seems to fit only a small minority of the cases. The most common set of preferences among gay men is for all roles—both oral and anal and active and passive. Yet since there is an association between liking the role of anal inserter and that of oral inserter, there does seem to be a modicum of validity to the inserter concept. It is the concept of insertee that has fared least well in the present data, and it is that concept which has informed popular and psychoanalytic thought, since it is derived from the notion of inappropriate cross-sex identification. The lack of much empirical support for the active-passive dichotomy renders rather quaint the West German law governing homosexual acts. Under that law, although homosexual acts are legal among consenting adults, adulthood is defined as being over 18 if the party is "active" and over 21 if the party is passive (Geis 1974, p. 47).

The second conclusion drawn from the data is that the concepts of orality and anality may be at least as useful in analyzing the sexual preferences of gay men as those of active and passive or those of insertee and inserter. The association between liking the two oral roles was found to be strong and positive and was not conditional upon the other preferences. However, we should observe that the correlation between the two oral items might also be an indicator of "mutuality" in a relationship, as opposed to one of dominance versus submissiveness. This possibility is explored below in our discussion of dominance in sexual relationships. It also seems that the concept of orality has a greater coherence in terms of the data than does that of anality. The relationships involving the anal items were found to be highly contingent upon other preferences.

We infer from the many instances of conditional relationships reported above that all of the four classical sexual activities of gay men seem to facilitate a taste for each other. An interest in one seems to give rise to a positive interest in several of the others. In short, they all seem to come in a bundle and rejection of any one tends to lead to rejection of some but not all of the others. Perhaps we can infer from this that participation in gay sexual and social activities

TABLE 6.3

Attitudes toward Number of Sexual Activities, by Bar Attendance[a]

Attitude	Mean	N	Standard Deviation	T	p[b]
Number of dislikes:					
Bar attenders	0.57	101	0.80	1.70	$p < .05$
Nonattenders	0.77	120	0.87		
Number of acceptances:					
Bar attenders	1.86	101	1.33	-1.94	$p < .03$
Nonattenders	1.53	120	1.18		
Number of preferences:					
Bar attenders	1.56	101	1.22	0.85	p = ns
Nonattenders	1.70	120	1.16		

[a]Means.
[b]One-tailed t-tests.
Source: Compiled by the authors.

encourages sexual flexibility rather than the sexual role specialization that popular or psychoanalytic thought alleges. Sexual specialization would be found among more "closeted" gays or those described by Humphreys (1970), who frequent public restrooms in order to perform or receive fellatio. In contrast, flexibility would be encouraged by participation in gay society, and particularly bar society, through the experience of having a variety of sexual partners. As a partial test of these hypotheses concerning sexual flexibility, we compared those who frequented bars more with those who frequented them less on the number of sexual activities that they found acceptable. (See Table 6.3.) An activity was defined as acceptable if the subject responded "it's OK" to the item. Using a one-tailed t-test, the bar frequenters were found to be significantly more flexible in sexual activities than the nonfrequenters. They also revealed a reduced number of dislikings of various activities. Accordingly we infer that participation in gay society encourages sexual flexibility and thereby reduces any pre-existing individual tendencies to role specialization consistent with the traditional sex-role models. However, we also note that bar frequenting was not associated with any difference in the number of activities positively preferred. Participation in the gay world thus encourages flexibility but may not affect basic preferences. In order to further test our social integration-flexibility hypothesis, we analyzed the number of preferred, acceptable, and disliked sexual activities by the extent to which the respondent's friends were gay or heterosexual. Using three categories of types of friends, we found no statistically significant differences. Although all of the differences in means were in the hypothesized directions, only the acceptability measure ("It's OK") approached significance ($F = 1.53$; $df = 2,218$; $p = ns$).

DOMINANCE AND SEXUAL PREFERENCES

Some of the more recent interpretations of homosexual roles by psychiatrists and psychologists have abandoned the concept of feminine identification as a major explanatory mechanism. Rather they have interpreted homosexual relationships or desires among men as expressing motivations for dominance or dependency. Such dominance/dependency interpretations may be divided into those that base needs for dominance or dependency on inhibition of youthful assertiveness, particularly assertiveness in the area of heterosexual interests, and those that base such needs on an eroticized admiration of power and masculinity. Ovesey (1965) is the chief spokesman for the former view, while Tripp (1975, pp. 80-94) is the principal expositor of the latter. In Ovesey's fear-based interpretation of homosexuality, the assertiveness of the child is severely inhibited, such that his interest in heterosexual relations is reduced. The gay male therefore interprets most relationships in terms of dominance and submission and attempts to attain reassurance by engaging in sexual acts with other men. Through such acts, he either experiences domination of his sexual partners through assuming an inserter role or experiences dependent reassurance from them through receiving their affection and, in particular, their symbolically powerful penises. The theoretical advance accomplished by Ovesey is that he largely dispenses with the empirically inadequate mechanism of cross-sex identification. Ovesey's point is that the dominance-submission dimension is the axis about which male homosexuality revolves and that only through an understandable confusion do either gay men or psychiatrists interpret homosexuality as inappropriate cross-sex identification. Ovesey's ideas lead us to expect that a gay man's interest in being dominant or submissive should be associated with what activities he prefers in bed. Such an association should be particularly evident for the anal activities, since it is a matter of some indeterminacy just which oral activity could reasonably be considered more dominant.

Tripp's interpretation of male homosexuality tends to place emphasis on the dominance aspect of the dominance-dependency dimension (to the exclusion of dependency as an explanatory factor). He asserts that masculinity and the culturally associated trait of dominance are positively eroticized by gay men and that such motivations are not based on fear. Masculinity is fairly generally desired in a sexual partner. So motivated, gay men feel little need to be either

TABLE 6.4

Sexual-Role Preference Items, by Dominance-Submissiveness
(percent)

Dominance-Submissiveness	Don't Like	It's OK	Prefer	N	Don't Like	It's OK	Prefer	N
	Oral Insertee Role				Oral Inserter Role			
Submissive	4	53	43	72	7	42	51	73
Equal	13	45	42	85	6	54	40	85
Dominant	12	51	38	69	9	40	51	70
	$X^2 = 4.30$; df = 4; p = ns; gamma = –.10; V = .10				$X^2 = 3.75$; df = 4; p = ns; gamma = 0.00; V = .09			
	Anal Insertee Role				Anal Inserter Role			
Submissive	33	33	33	72	18	33	49	73
Equal	28	45	28	87	19	38	44	85
Dominant	48	27	26	71	13	37	51	71
	$X^2 = 9.27$; df = 4; p = ns; gamma = –.15; V = .14				$X^2 = 1.73$; df = 4; p = ns; gamma = .04; V = .06			

Source: Compiled by the authors.

dominant or dependent, because they are not obtaining reassurances or compensating for their own felt deficiencies. Rather they simply want to make love to persons possessing admired traits. Tripp adds that the appreciation of masculine traits can result in a depreciation of their opposites. Thus nonmasculinity in men would be considered undesirable. As such, Tripp's formulation of gay men's sexual interests is essentially one dimensional, as compared with Ovesey's polarized opposites of power and submission.

Using the Detroit data, we cannot fully assess the merits of Ovesey's or Tripp's theories, but we can provide a partial exploration of the role of dominance in influencing sexual preferences. As Tripp argues, masculinity is generally desired in a sexual partner, while femininity is often viewed with distaste. In response to the item, "I like the person I have sex with to be: feminine, about average, masculine," 3 percent responded "feminine," 50 percent responded "about average," and 47 percent responded "masculine" (N = 236). It is clear that while femininity may serve various symbolic functions for the gay community and for some gay men, in practice, it is almost universally felt to be undesirable. Indeed the number of our respondents who said that they liked their sexual partner to be both feminine and older than themselves was zero. If femininity is felt to be appealing, it seems to be appealing only in the younger gay.

In the analysis of dominance (below), we used responses to the following item as an indicator of dominance-submissiveness: "If I lived with a lover (or do live with) I would probably make most of the decisions." We trichotomized the responses to this item into a "strongly agree" and "agree" category, a "neutral" category, and a "disagree" or "strongly disagree" category. Through use of the trichotomy, we obtained a group of respondents who were principally interested in more egalitarian relationships, as well as those who were interested in dominance or submissiveness. While it would be preferable to have a measure of dominance-submissiveness that included a variety of items, such are not available in our data. Yet we have confidence in the validity of this single-item measure because of the variety of variables we have found to be correlated with it.

Table 6.4 presents the relationships between our dominance-submissiveness measure and each of the four sexual activity items. It appears that dominance-submissiveness has no direct relationships with preferred sexual activities among gay men. Interpersonal dominance has no relationship with what goes on in bed. Only the anal insertee role may have a slight, nonsignificant relationship with dominance. In this instance, those are are dominant may prefer to avoid the insertee role but do not differ (from submissives) in their positive preference for it.

Although dominance-submissiveness has no direct zero-order relationships with the sexual-role preference items, it does appear to affect the relationships among those items. Table 6.5 presents the first-order partial relationships among the sexual activity preference items, while controlling for dominance-submissiveness. In these subtables, the "dominant" and "submissive" categories have been combined into an "inegalitarian" category for purposes of maintaining

TABLE 6.5

Associations among Sexual-Role Preference Items, Controlling for Dominance–Submissiveness (percent)

Sexual-Role Preference	Inegalitarians: Don't Like	Inegalitarians: It's OK	Inegalitarians: Prefer	Egalitarians: Don't Like	Egalitarians: It's OK	Egalitarians: Prefer
	Oral Insertee Role					
Oral inserter role:						
Don't like	36	8	2	20	5	3
It's OK	18	55	28	60	79	25
Prefer	46	37	70	20	16	72
N	11	73	57	10	38	36
	$X^2 = 28.25$; df = 4; $p < .01$; gamma = 0.51; V = 0.32			$X^2 = 29.81$; df = 4; $p < .01$; gamma = 0.72; V = 0.42		
	Anal Inserter Role					
Oral insertee role:						
Don't like	18	4	7	6	22	6
It's OK	41	56	54	31	56	43
Prefer	41	40	39	62	22	51
N	22	48	69	16	32	35
	$X^2 = 4.54$; df = 4; p = ns; gamma = 0.03; V = 0.13			$X^2 = 11.15$; df = 4; $p < .03$; gamma = 0.09; V = 0.26		
	Anal Insertee Role					
Oral insertee role:						
Don't Like	7	5	12	23	10	8
It's OK	56	69	32	36	59	29
Prefer	36	26	56	41	31	62
N	55	42	41	22	39	24
	$X^2 = 12.09$; df = 4; $p < .02$; gamma = 0.15;			$X^2 = 9.20$; df = 4; p = ns; gamma = 0.28;		

			Anal Inserter Role			
Oral inserter role:						
Don't Like	27	6	3	12	6	3
It's OK	36	48	39	44	66	50
Prefer	36	46	59	44	28	47
N	22	48	70	16	32	36
	$X^2 = 15.67$; df = 4; $p < .01$; gamma = 0.33; V = 0.24			$X^2 = 4.63$; df = 4; p = ns; gamma = 0.19; V = 0.17		
			Anal Insertee Role			
Oral inserter role:						
Don't Like	5	7	12	13	3	4
It's OK	32	62	34	35	71	46
Prefer	62	31	54	52	26	50
N	56	42	41	23	38	24
	$X^2 = 12.21$; df = 4; $p < .02$; gamma = -.18; V = 0.21			$X^2 = 9.95$; df = 4; $p < .05$; gamma = 0.04; V = 0.24		
Anal inserter role:						
Don't Like	21	5	20	39	10	12
It's OK	21	49	38	35	47	25
Prefer	59	46	42	26	42	62
N	58	43	40	23	38	24
	$X^2 = 12.11$; df = 4; $p < .02$; gamma = -0.14; V = 0.21			$X^2 = 12.57$; df = 4; $p < .02$; gamma = 0.43; V = 0.27		

Source: Compiled by the authors.

sample sizes. Such combining does no violence to the data, since a more microscopic examination of the relationships reveals that in all instances, the associational patterns are similar in corresponding dominant and submissive groups.

We see in Table 6.5 that there are strong, positive, and significant associations between the two oral roles among both the egalitarians and inegalitarians. That the association between these two items is stronger among the egalitarians suggests that their egalitarianism is expressed in a mutuality of sexual preferences. Yet we also note some specialist-generalist tendency among the inegalitarians. In the panel exhibiting the relationships between the oral insertee and anal inserter roles, we find somewhat complex interactions. Among the inegalitarians, there is no relationship. Among the egalitarians, we find a polarization into generalists, who prefer both activities, and specialists, who prefer only one activity. Thus it seems that the concepts of specialist-generalist, rather than those of inserter-insertee, seem more important in explaining the sexual choices of the egalitarians than those of the inegalitarians. In that part of Table 6.5 exhibiting the relationships among the two insertee items, we again see specializations into generalists and specialists, although the relationship is significant only among the inegalitarians. The data also suggest a small net tendency for there to be a positive association between the two insertee items among the inegalitarians. Thus for inegalitarian gays, there seems to be some minor validity to the insertee concept.

The part of Table 6.5 exhibiting the relationships between the two inserter roles makes evident the importance of dominance-submissiveness in analyzing the sexual preferences of gay men. Among the inegalitarians, we find a positive association between these two items, thus suggesting that inegalitarians hold to the symbolic meaningfulness of sexual roles as indicators of dominance and submissiveness. However, among the egalitarians, the concepts of generalist-specialist once more are operative, since the data exhibit a polarization into those who prefer both activities versus those who prefer only one. The part of Table 6.5 exhibiting the relationships between the roles of oral inserter and anal insertee are amenable to an identical interpretation. Among egalitarians, the data exhibit the specialist-generalist pattern. Among the inegalitarians, the data also exhibit a specialist-generalist polarization, with some net tendency for there to be a negative relationship between the two items. This negative relationship is interpreted as an expression of inserter-insertee proclivities among the inegalitarian respondents. We consider the most interesting part of Table 6.5 to be the part that exhibits the relationships between the two anal items. Among the inegalitarians, there is a negative association, which suggests the validity of the inserter-insertee formulation. Among the egalitarians, however, there is a heretofore undetected strong positive association. This pattern suggests a substantial degree of reciprocity of similar sexual favors among egalitarians. Thus equality in a relationship seems to be associated with equality in bed.

In the data of Table 6.5, the marginal frequencies of the "don't like" category for the two oral items were often small. The effect of this was to violate one of the statistical assumptions of the chi-square significance test. In this table, we preferred to maintain the distinction between the "don't like" and "it's OK" categories rather than to collapse the two into a single category. However, we ran a set of alternative tables, with a collapsing (for all tables) involving the two oral items. Of the ten tables involved, seven revealed the same significance (or nonsignificance) as the corresponding subtable of Table 6.5. We briefly deal with the three cases where corresponding subtables differ.

1. Among the egalitarians, the relationship between the two insertee items of Table 6.5 is nonsignificant ($p = 0.056$). In the corresponding alternative subtable, it is significant ($p = 0.046$). This difference requires no modification of our interpretations, since we offered that both egalitarians and inegalitarians exhibited the generalist-specialist pattern, with a secondary tendency toward an insertee-inserter pattern.

2. Among the inegalitarians, Table 6.5 shows a significant positive association between the two inserter roles. The alternative subtable shows a nonsignificant association ($p = 0.14$). This suggests a slight interpretational modification. Although the egalitarians typically exhibit a specialist-generalist pattern, the inegalitarians seem to only occasionally exhibit a rather weak insertee-inserter pattern; at other times, inegalitarians reveal no pattern.

3. Among the egalitarians, Table 6.5 exhibits a barely significant ($p = 0.041$) association between the anal insertee and oral inserter roles. The alternative subtable is barely nonsignificant ($p = 0.068$). We slightly amend our earlier interpretation by offering that while the anal insertee-oral inserter relationship among the inegalitarians suggests polarization, plus some net tendency toward inserter-insertee patterns, the relationship among the egalitarians reveals only specialist-generalist polarization or no pattern.

CONCLUDING INTERPRETATIONS

The data on the effects of dominance-submissiveness upon sexual activity preferences exhibited rather complex patterns. Dominance proclivities do not appear to directly affect the particular sexual preferences of gay men, since Table 6.4 revealed no significant associations between dominance and any of the four classical sexual activities. Rather dominance seems to interact with each of these activities in influencing the relationship of a given activity with each of the others. Thus whether a gay man is dominant or submissive influences the directions of association among the sexual preferences rather than the individual preferences.

The data fairly consistently revealed different patterns of association among sexual activity preferences for egalitarians and inegalitarians. Among the inegalitarians, there surfaced tendencies toward insertee and inserter roles

TABLE 6.6

Dominance–Submissiveness, by Occupational Level
(percent)

Occupational Level	Submissive	Equal	Dominant	N
Low	40	31	29	94
High	25	41	34	124
	$X^2 = 6.01$; df = 2; $p < .05$; gamma = –.0.21; V = 0.17			

Source: Compiled by the authors.

consistent with the theories of Bieber and Ovesey. To the extent that such inegalitarians tend to organize relationships in terms of dominance and submissiveness, we might expect the appearance of the insertee and inserter roles. The inegalitarians also showed a lesser tendency to organize their sexual preferences in a polarized generalist-specialist pattern. Among the egalitarians, there also surfaced two patterns of association of sexual preferences. In one pattern, respondents tended to be bifurcated into those who liked both activities versus those who liked only one. These we termed generalists and specialists, respectively. The second pattern among the egalitarians was one of mutuality. Those who liked one role also liked its reciprocal insertee or inserter role. We interpreted this reciprocity as an expression of individual egalitarian proclivities in interpersonal relationships.

The data strongly suggest that a sex-role interpretation of gay men's sexual preferences is inadequate by itself. A dominance interpretation seems to fare somewhat better. Indeed our data suggest, but do not prove, that whether a gay man's proclivities are for dominance or submissiveness conditions whether or not he utilizes sex-role interpretations to organize his sexual affairs. Inegalitarians seem to utilize such interpretations in bed. Egalitarians seem to pattern their activities more on a model of equality and reciprocity. Such egalitarian modes of relating seem somewhat inconsistent with the power interpretations of Ovesey and more consistent with those of Tripp.

As a final observation, we note that a preference for egalitarian relationships was found to be more common among respondents of higher occupational levels. Table 6.6 shows that gay men of lower occupational levels often are less interested in egalitarian relationships, while tending to prefer relationships structured around dominance and submissiveness. This finding is consistent with much sociological literature, which reports working-class marriages and interpersonal relationships to be less egalitarian than those of the middle class (Miller 1968; Kommarovsky 1964, p. 199; Fullerton 1977, pp. 503-07). The relationships shown in Table 6.6 also make evident that gay relationships are influenced by factors of cultural and social background much as are heterosexual ones. Individuals from backgrounds that structure relationships in terms of dominance and submissiveness will probably so structure their own relationships, whatever their particular sexual orientation.

7

AGE AND SEXUAL CULTURE AMONG GAY MEN

In this chapter, we explore the often reported observation that the culture of gay men is heavily youth-oriented (Hoffman 1968, p. 52; Weinberg 1970; Simon and Gagnon 1967; Warren 1974, pp. 84-85). It is often argued that such an emphasis on youthfulness among gays very largely denies the older members of the community the rewards of sex, sociability, self-esteem, and the neutralization of stigma, which are the principal benefits the community can bestow on its members. In consequence, many gay males and students of homsexuality view aging as a relentless march into social undesirability among an already undesired minority. A common one-liner among gays is, "No one loves you when you're old and gay." Below we elaborate on and extensively qualify (though not negate) the thesis of the youth-orientedness of gay culture.

That the culture of gay men is very youth-oriented has been commented on, observed, and assumed by students of male homosexuality; however, it does not seem to have been directly, or at least numerically, tested. For example, Weinberg (1970), in his study of age-related attitudes and behavior among gay men, assumed the existence of negative attitudes toward older gays rather than directly asking (his subjects) about attitudes toward older gays and toward aging. Lacking direct comparative evidence between the youth-orientedness of homosexuals versus heterosexuals, it is difficult to determine whether gay culture is, in fact, more youth centered or whether it is simply a special case of the more general youth-orientedness of American culture. The view that growing old is a negative experience has been shown to be widely held in the American population (Harris and Associates 1975, p. 2). These authors have reported that 69 percent of the general population believes the best decade of one's life to be during the thirties or younger, while 83 percent say it is in the forties or younger. Further they report that the younger view the lives of the older as less rewarding than the latter view their own lives. Thus while the older do have their own special problems, the younger seem to exaggerate the degree of those problems. Hence it may be that the negative view of aging among gay men (Saghir and Robins 1973, pp. 174-76) is simply a particularized instance of the broader cultural belief.

In comparing the relative degrees of youth-orientedness of gay and heterosexual cultures, one must be cognizant of the research problems that arise due to the fact that most heterosexual males over 30 are married, while most gay males, at any one time, are not married, either heterosexually or homosexually. This problem of finding an appropriate comparison group for gay males was recognized and substantially solved by Saghir and Robins (1973) by choosing as controls single heterosexuals. Since it would seem that the single person of any sexual orientation is likely to place a greater emphasis on youthfulness and physical characteristics than the married, then it would seem that the greater youth-orientedness of the gay culture could be linked more to the fact that most gays are single rather than to their sexual orientation. Accordingly an appropriate comparison of the culture of, say, a gay bar would be with that of a singles bar rather than with the behavior and attitudes of more staid married persons.

We suggest that the greater youth-orientedness of the culture of gay men arises out of that community being populated largely by persons who are single. Such a culture often induces its participants to go to great lengths to present to each other the "cosmetic self" (Hooker 1967) in the available sexual marketplaces. In heterosexual culture, the social affairs of fraternities and sororities are instances in which a highly cosmetic self is expected among participants. It should also be recognized that as with heterosexuals, sexual marketplaces are not limited to such settings as bars, but also may include such settings as work, school, voluntary associations, and so forth (Harry 1970). Across a wide variety of settings, single persons are often sensitive to the availability of potential sexual or marital partners. Such a sensitivity to the availability of partners, with its common emphasis on youth and physical attractiveness, may infuse the social lives of gay men and become a life-style pursued over a period of years. When such a life-style is pursued for an extended period by gay men, subsequent to coming out, the individual gay's sociosexual career approximates a prolonged bachelorhood, interrupted by occasional detours into liaisons lasting from several months to a few years. Thus we may describe the gay sociosexual career as similar in many ways to the heterosexual state of bachelorhood.

We must acknowledge that while the singleness of the gay population facilitates the development of a "singles" culture, that culture also facilitates the singleness of its members, while probably inhibiting the development of a larger gay "married" population (and associated gay married culture). Although we cannot within our own data attempt to solve the question of whether the singleness found in a singles culture is the dominant causative factor in the behavior of gay males, we can observe that the lack of institutional supports for gay liaisons undoubtedly inhibits the elaboration of a more widespread married culture among gay men.

Within gay culture, the dominance of a singles culture seems to have decidedly affected the normative content of the gay marriage. As we saw in the chapter on gay marriages, those marriages that seemed most successful, as measured in terms of duration, permitted impersonal infidelity. Thus the gay marriage appears to have adapted itself to the dominance of single gays. The gay marriage is a blending of elements of both marriage and singleness. In consequence, the differences between the gay marital state and the gay single state are fewer than the differences between the heterosexual marital and single states.

Although gay culture, taken as a whole, tends to approximate a singles culture due to the social and demographic heterogeneity of the gay population, it would seem unlikely that a taste for the young and for youthfulness is characteristic of all segments of that population. In particular, to the extent that gay culture is youth-oriented, it would seem that gay men who do not participate greatly in that culture might be less inclined toward the young. This would suggest that those who do not frequent gay bars—the bastions of youth-orientedness—would be more interested in same-age or older persons. Alternatively we suggest that the sexual culture of gay settings, other than the bar or bath, may emphasize bases of attractiveness other than youth, for example, personality, cultural similarity, or financial standing.

There are several institutions within the gay world that belie the notion that gay culture is overwhelmingly youth-oriented. (What we are discussing here is, of course, a matter of degree.) Harry (1974) has shown that even gay bars vary substantially in the characteristics of their respective clienteles. Particularly in larger cities, gay bars are stratified by race, social class, recreational style, and age. The existence of gay bars for the older gay, or even for the older and middle-class gay, suggests that for a nontrivial segment of the gay community, criteria of cultural and status compatibility will often outweigh the attractions of youth. Many older or middle-class gays may feel repelled by the boisterousness, crowdedness, and occasional effeminacy found at some of the bars of the young.

As in the case of gay bars, it seems that there is substantial demographic stratification of the memberships of homophile organizations. The members of the organizations studied by Weinberg and Williams (1974) were older and more middle class than the patrons of the gay bars in which they solicited respondents. In our own research, it became apparent that homophile organization memberships are substantially segregated on the basis of age and social class. Although we must admit the possibility that bar or organizational settings for the older gay may exist principally because their respective clienteles/memberships have been socially excluded from the settings of the young, to so argue for an exclusionary process rather than for one of similarity and attraction would be to argue that the common social process of attraction based on similarity (which operates in most segments of the heterosexual population) is largely inoperative in the gay world. This strikes us as implausible.

We suggest that the reason the notion of the youth-orientedness of gay culture has received such widespread acceptance is that most of the research supporting this notion has been based on those selected gay settings that are most youth-oriented. Other gay settings and social relationships have been less researched. Among the various gay institutions, certainly the gay bar has received the most attention (Achilles 1967; Hooker 1967; Hoffman 1968; Leznoff and Westley 1956; Weinberg 1970). Similarly Weinberg and Williams (1975) acknowledge that the gay bath is another setting in which considerable, or perhaps exclusive, emphasis is placed on physical attractiveness and youth. Further Humphreys (1970, pp. 108-09) has observed how age plays an important role among his participants in impersonal sex in restrooms in determining the sexual availability of other males and the sexual acts performed with them.

It should be noted that all three of these settings, the bar, the bath, and the "tearoom," are locales of moderate to extremely impersonal interaction, in which the participants get to know each other only through the most superficial, visible, and occasionally contrived indicators of character. In such settings, where as Gagnon and Simon (1973, pp. 149-54) have suggested, the cultural bases of interaction are extremely limited or even "impoverished," a high value is placed on visible physical characteristics. Indeed given the largely sexual nature of the relationships negotiated in such settings, the impersonality of such encounters virtually requires that physical characteristics be emphasized. Within such impersonal settings, it is unlikely that sexual behavior will be converted into social conduct (Gagnon and Simon 1973, p. 153), that sexual desire may be broadened into social affection, or that the criteria of attractiveness employed will be other than those of youth and physique. To the extent that the hypothesis of the youth-orientedness of gay culture is substantially based on such selected settings, it would seem that that idea is in need of qualification.

In the data presented below, we used as our principal measure of youth-orientedness responses to the question: "I like the person I have sex with to be . . . younger than myself, about the same age as me, older than me." This measure is a direct and somewhat stringent test of youth-orientedness in that it refers to sexual behavior—and it is in the area of sexual behavior that various authors have said gays are most youth-oriented. Warren (1974, p. 75) has observed and Cotton (1972) has reported that gay males generally employ the same cultural and demographic criteria in selecting their friends and lovers as do heterosexuals, that is, age, personality, social status, race, and so forth. However, these authors have also asserted that in selecting partners for sexual encounters as opposed to selecting friends, gay men tend to emphasize youth and physical attractiveness. Thus our measure of youth-orientedness speaks to that aspect of gay culture which is inclined toward the young.

DATA

The marginal distribution on the sexual age-preference question was as follows: 26 percent preferred persons younger than themselves, 44 percent preferred the same age, 23 percent preferred older persons, and 6 percent reported no age preference (N = 233). From this distribution, it would be difficult to infer a *general* preference for younger persons. Nearly equal percentages preferred a sexual partner who was older or one who was younger. However, two reasons suggest that we should not place great confidence in such a univariate distribution: (1) the very problematic nature of sampling deviant populations, and (2) if a large percentage of those choosing same-age sexual partners were themselves young, the percentage of our respondents who in fact were opting for the young would be substantially higher than the 26 percent reported above. In order to more securely examine youth-orientedness, Table 7.1 presents the relationship between the respondent's age and the preferred age of sexual partner. Table 7.1 reveals a very strong negative relationship between age and preferred age. A majority of the very young (ages 18 to 24) like someone older, although above age 25, this propensity sharply declines. While a majority of those 25 to 34 years of age prefer someone of the same age, the same-age choice remains a constant 40 percent throughout older age groups. Also, at about age 35, there occurs a sharp increase in choosing someone younger, and the percentage so choosing appears to stabilize at a constant 50 percent for the three older age groups.

TABLE 7.1

Preferred Age of Sexual Partner, by Age
(percent)

Preferred Age	18–24	25–29	30–34	35–39	40–44	45 and Over
Younger	4	15	28	52	50	50
Same age	40	66	51	39	40	41
Older	56	20	22	9	10	9
N	48	41	51	33	10	34
	gamma = -0.54; $X^2 = 58.81$; df = 10; $p < .001$*					

*Significance tests use a .05 level.
Source: Compiled by the authors.

TABLE 7.2

Preferred Age of Sexual Partner, by Bar Attendance (percent)

Bar Attendance	Preferred Age			
	Younger	Same Age	Older	N
Infrequent attenders	27	43	30	117
Frequent attenders	30	54	17	101
	gamma = –0.17; X^2 = 5.30; df = 2; p = ns*			

*Significance tests use a .05 level.
Source: Compiled by the authors.

It might be tempting to infer from Table 7.1 that because the very young like the older and the older like the younger, the older are not excluded from the sexual marketplaces of the younger. However, the wording of our question does not permit such an immediate inference. The expressions "younger than myself" and "older than myself" can refer to wide age ranges. To observers of the gay scene, it seems unlikely that when a 22-year-old says he prefers someone older, he has in mind a 40- or 50-year-old. Similarly it seems unlikely, though less so, that when a 50-year-old says he likes someone younger, he has in mind a 20-year-old. Consequently we can only estimate that when the 20-year-old says "older," he has in mind an upper acceptable age limit of approximately 40. Similarly when the 40-year-old says he likes someone younger, he may have a lower acceptable age limit of about 25 in mind. What we may securely infer from Table 7.1 is that there is not a *general* preference for the younger, as shown by the modal choices of those 20 to 34 years old and the somewhat surprising majority of 18- to 24-year-olds, who prefer someone older. The fact that a majority of the 18- to 24-year-olds prefer someone older may account for the not infrequently observed phenomenon of May–December relationships in the gay community.

The data of Table 7.1 are consistent with our hypothesis that to the extent that gay men become immersed in gay culture, and particularly in gay bar culture, they become more youth-oriented. It seems that a majority of younger gays may enter the gay world with an ideal of an older man as a preferred partner; within a few years, however, they learn from other gays that an interest in substantially older men is considered peculiar. A case in point is a 23-year-old respondent who because he only found men of at least 40 attractive was the object of considerable comment by his age-peers. Table 7.2 presents a more direct test of the notion that gay bar culture is youth-oriented. This table

TABLE 7.3

Preferred Age of Sexual Partner, by Age, by Bar Attendance (percent)

Preferred Age	18-24	25-29	30-34	35-39	40 and Over[a]
	Infrequent Attenders				
Younger	3	10	22	67	55
Same age	28	70	56	22	40
Older	69	20	22	11	5
N	32	20	27	18	23
	gamma = -.68; X^2 = 56.62; df = 8; p < .001[b]				
	Frequent Attenders				
Younger	6	19	33	33	48
Same age	62	62	46	60	43
Older	31	19	21	7	9
N	16	21	24	15	23
	gamma = -.46; X^2 = 9.17; df = 8; p = ns				

[a]Due to small marginal frequencies, the oldest two age groups have been combined.
[b]Significance tests use a .05 level.
Source: Compiled by the authors.

presents the relationship between frequency of bar attendance and preferred age of sexual partner. (The bar attendance variable has been dichotomized into those who attend once a week or less versus those who attend more often.) It is evident from this table that bar attendance does not significantly influence age preferences. However, when we examine the relationship between age and age preference while controlling for frequency of bar attendance (Table 7.3), it becomes apparent why there is no significant relationship in Table 7.2. Most of the relationships shown in Table 7.1 are concentrated in that segment of the sample that infrequently attends bars. Within this segment, there is a very strong negative relationship between age and age preference, while among those who go to bars more often, there is no significant relationship. Although bar attendance has no direct effect on age preference, it interacts strongly with age in influencing age preference. (We should note that due to the small number of persons among the frequent bar attenders who chose someone older, the chi-square value for that panel should only be taken as suggestive.) We infer from Table 7.3 that frequent participation in gay bar culture serves to alter the meanings of age to the young gay such that choices for younger or same-age persons are given greater priority and the penchant of the very young for older men is rapidly eliminated.

Research by Leznoff and Westley (1956) suggests the possibility that the relationships shown in Table 7.3 may be due to a correlation of occupational level with both age and infrequent attendance at public gay settings, such as the gay bar. These authors have observed that high-status homosexuals tend to frequent gay bars less often due to their need to be more circumspect in their sexual behavior. Thus the control variable of Table 7.3—bar attendance—may also control for social status, so that the observed relationships of age and preferred age may be specifications by social status rather than by bar attendance. Using this interpretation, the inverse relationship between age and preferred age would hold only for higher-status respondents, while an emphasis more on youth or same age might exist for lower-status gays.

Table 7.4 presents the relationships between age and preferred age, while controlling for occupational level. "High" occupational status includes upper and lower white-collar respondents. "Low" occupational status includes respondents with manual occupations, service occupations, the unemployed, plus two

TABLE 7.4

Preferred Age of Sexual Partner, by Age, by Occupational Level (percent)

Age Preference	18-24	25-29	30-34	35-39	40 and Over
	High Occupational Status[a]				
Younger	0	21	30	58	44
Same age	88	67	60	33	48
Older	12	12	10	8	7
N	8	24	30	24	27
	gamma = -.34; X^2 = 13.68; df = 8; p = ns[b]				
	Low Occupational Status				
Younger	3	7	28	38	56
Same age	33	57	33	50	31
Older	63	36	39	12	12
N	30	14	18	8	16
	gamma = -.78; X^2 = 26.68; df = 8; $p < .01$				

[a]Students have been omitted from this table.
[b]Significance tests use a .05 level.
Source: Compiled by the authors.

"houseboys." Students have been excluded from this table due to the indeterminacy of their occupational status. It is apparent from Table 7.4 that the inverse relationship of age and preferred age is to be found principally among those of lower occupational status, although there is a similar weaker, nonsignificant trend among those of higher status. (Because of several small marginal frequencies in the high-status section of Table 7.4, the chi-square value should only be taken as suggestive.) An inspection of the row marginal frequencies of Table 7.4 also reveals there is an association between higher occupational status and an aversion to the older. Higher-status persons evidently prefer same-age or younger persons and rather infrequently express an interest in the older (gamma = 0.46; $X^2 = 24.86$; df = 2; $p < .001$).

Because the column marginal frequencies of Table 7.4 reveal the commonly found association between age and higher occupational status (gamma = 0.36; $X^2 = 25.99$; df = 4; $p < .001$), we raise the question of whether the association between occupational status and age preference is due to age rather than to occupational status. When age is controlled, the partial associations between occupational status and age preference remain significant (data not presented).

AGE PREFERENCE AND DOMINANCE

The data have revealed that age, occupational level, and frequency of bar attendance influence sexual age preferences among gay men. It seems that the very young prefer someone older, those 25 to 34 years old opt for same-age persons, while those yet older choose younger or same-age persons. This pattern of choices is found to be strongest among those who participate less in gay bar culture and among those who are of lower occupational status. It would thus seem that there are a variety of sexual preference standards in the gay world and that the dominant choice pattern depends on the particular gay setting in which the individual immerses himself.

While our data revealed that a majority of the very young and two-thirds of the very young of lower occupational status opt for older persons, we have not yet attempted to explain this. The two most obvious explanatory hypotheses are economic benefits and interpersonal dominance. Under the former interpretation, the younger gay may prefer the older man for his money rather than for his other characteristics. As several writers have observed, the gay world, due to its relative sexual egalitarianism with respect to social class, occasionally permits younger attractive persons of limited economic backgrounds access to some of the social, economic, and cultural resources of higher-status gays.

Under the second interpretation, the younger lower-status gay may desire an older man for his presumed dominance and masculinity. Such an interpretation would be consistent with the sex-role literature, which reports a greater normative dichotomization of sex roles among persons of working- and lower-class backgrounds. Both Gagnon and Simon (1973, pp. 147–48) and Weinberg

TABLE 7.5

Preferred Dominance, by Preferred Age of Sexual Partner (percent)

	Preferred Age of Sexual Partner		
Preferred Dominance	Younger	Same Age	Older
He makes decisions	29	28	44
Equality in decisions	30	38	35
I make decisions	41	34	20
N	63	103	54
	gamma = 0.22; X^2 = 7.92; df = 4; p = ns*		

*Significance tests use a .05 level.
Source: Compiled by the authors.

and Williams (1974, p. 222) have reported that young gay males tend to be more effeminate than older gays. Logically such a selected sexual style, and particularly among young gays of working-class backgrounds, might well imply an interest in an older, more dominant sexual partner.

While our data do not permit us to test the notion that younger gays are interested in the older for their money, we are able to explore the alternative hypothesis of desired dominance. Table 7.5 presents the zero-order relationship between preferred dominance and age preference. We see only a nonsignificant trend in this table. In Table 7.6, however, which presents the relationships between preferred dominance and preferred age while controlling for frequency of bar attendance, we see that bar attendance once again serves to specify the associations of preferred age. Only among infrequent bar attenders is there an association between preferred age of sexual partner and preferred dominance. Those who like the older man prefer a more submissive role, while those who like the younger man prefer a more dominant role.

The part played in the above analysis by the bar attendance variable calls for some clarification. In and of itself, bar attendance has no direct zero-order relationship with preferred dominance. At no level of our preferred dominance measure is the difference between the frequent and infrequent bar attenders as much as 4 percent. Yet bar attendance sharply influences the relationships of preferred age and preferred dominance. We infer from these data that participation in gay bar culture deprives age of its traditional symbolic associations with dominance and masculinity. Without such symbolic expectations structuring their conceptions of a preferred sexual partner, participants in gay bar culture who are interested in submissiveness in a relationship will be no more likely to choose the older man than those who are interested in being dominant.

TABLE 7.6

Preferred Dominance, by Preferred Age of Sexual Partner, by Bar Attendance (percent)

	Preferred Age of Sexual Partner		
Preferred Dominance	Younger	Same Age	Older
	Infrequent Bar Attenders		
He makes decisions	23	26	47
Equality in decisions	32	38	39
I make decisions	45	36	14
N	31	50	36
	gamma = 0.36; X^2 = 9.99; df = 4; $p < .05$*		
	Frequent Bar Attenders		
He makes decisions	34	30	41
Equality in decisions	28	38	24
I make decisions	38	32	35
N	32	53	17
	gamma = –.04; X^2 = 1.72; df = 4; p = ns*		

*Significance tests use a .05 level.
Source: Compiled by the authors.

Gay culture, and particularly gay bar culture, erodes the meanings of the traditional cluster of expectations associated with age and sex roles.

Briefly summarizing certain other relationships related to the above analysis, age is related to preferred dominance (X^2 = 12.33; df = 2; $p < .01$). Of the very young (18 to 24 years old), 51 percent prefer a submissive role. Beyond age 25, a fairly constant 25 percent of all the older age groups like a submissive role, about 40 percent of all older age groups like decision-making equality, and about 35 percent of all older age groups prefer a dominant role. Having a higher occupational status is modestly associated with, first, a choice for equality and, second, a preference for dominance (X^2 = 6.01; df = 2; $p < .05$). Occupational status once more specifies the relationships of preferred age of sexual partner with preferred dominance. Among those of higher occupational status, there is no relationship between preferred age and preferred dominance (X^2 = 2.56; df = 4; p = ns). Among those of lower occupational levels, this relationship barely misses significance (X^2 = 8.39; df = 4; p = .08). If years of education is used as an alternative control variable, then only among the less educated is there a significant relationship between preferred dominance and preferred age of sexual partner ($X^2 = 9.89$; df = 4; $p < .05$). Among the more educated, the relationship is not significant ($X^2 = 3.06$; df = 4; p = ns). We interpret the specifying role of the education variable as meaning that among the more traditional segments of the population, that is, the less educated, the traditional meanings of age and sex roles retain relatively more of their strength. Among the more educated, the dominance and masculinity associated with age are less in force.

CONCLUDING DISCUSSION

We have argued that the thesis of the youth-orientedness of gay culture has been overstated. Our data strongly suggest that there is substantial variation between different segments of the gay world in their sexual age preferences. Frequenters of gay bars, middle-class gays, and older gays seem most youth-oriented, while those who go to bars less and working-class young gays seem more interested in relationships with older men. We have attempted to explain the interest by the very young in older men as due to their interest in being the submissive partner in a relationship. Such an interest in being the younger and more submissive partner in a relationship seems to be especially common among the young from working-class backgrounds. A background of working-class socialization, in which sex roles are viewed in the more traditional dichotomous way and in which sex-role relationships tend to be perceived in terms of dominance and submission, explains some of the sexual choices of gay men.

While we have suggested that dominance and submission are key explainers of a mutual sexual interest between younger and older gays, we have not been able to rule out the hypothesis that the young are interested in the older more for their money than for their dominance and masculinity. However, the two explanations are not necessarily incompatible. Given that traditional sex-role dichotomies impute to a dominant male a relative preponderance of economic resources, an economic interpretation could simply be a special case of a dominant sex-role interpretation. On the other hand, we suggest that economic dominance is probably a minor part of most gay relationships. While there may be minor economic flows between parties to a relationship, usually in the form of material gifts, situations in which one party is completely financially dependent on the other seem rather infrequent.

We have suggested that whether one finds an overwhelming youth-orientedness among gays will often depend on which part of the gay world is examined. Outside of gay bars, the emphasis on youth seems to be significantly less. Warren's (1974) research is one of the few that provided observations on age-related sexual preferences of gay men in a nonbar, nonorganizational setting. She has reported that choice of lovers tends to depend on the usual criteria of sociocultural and personality compatibility, while selection of a sexual partner for a brief encounter utilizes more physical criteria, such as looks and youthfulness. While her observations might imply, contrary to our findings, that youthfulness is also a prime criterion of attractiveness in nonbar settings, a reconciliation of our respective research is possible. It appears that most of Warren's respondents were middle- and upper-middle-class gays of considerable economic resources. We note that our data showed that higher-status respondents were significantly more interested in the younger men than were those of lower occupational levels. Accordingly we suggest that occupational level effects a preference for the younger man that is independent of the setting.

We have devoted most of our attention to explaining why the very young should be interested in older men, while largely ignoring the finding that with increasing age, gays first shift to a same-age choice and then to a younger choice. The explanations for this pattern of changes are likely to be the same as those for changes of husband–wife age differences over successive marriages:

> The tendency of men who have been married before to seek a younger wife can be explained simply by noting that the standards of beauty of our culture are centered on the young woman of 20 or so. An older man who has economic resources (is) quite able to compete with younger men for the most desirable sexual partners. The age difference may in fact be an attraction to some women, who may have despaired of the apparent irresponsibility and lack of resources of men their own age, and who find the security of a relationship with a mature and successful man a compelling point in marital bargaining. This is a pattern of many centuries standing (Fullerton 1977, p. 259).

As a further explanation of why older men choose younger partners we add that with advancing years, there is also a decline in the numbers of available same-age partners, whatever their desirability.

Topics that we have not dealt with are the effects of aging on the gay man's morale and the so-called crisis of aging. Since our data and observations do not speak to these topics, we largely limit ourselves to some comments of other writers. West has said:

> many affairs rarely last a lifetime, and in the course of the numerous re-shuffles older men tend to get more and more left out. Many aging homosexuals find eventually that they are left without family, roots, or purpose. Some of them can be seen wearily trailing their old haunts. . . .Others retire to a grimly isolated existence. The dread of growing old is a noticeable feature of male homosexuals (1967, p. 58).

West's observations concerning "reshuffling" and being "left out" are consistent with our data on gay marriages, which found the majority of men over 40 in a "nonmarried" state. Yet as we reported earlier, there is no significant association between age and self-esteem. Weinberg (1970) has also reported that older gay men are no more lonely or depressed than younger gay men. Indeed his data found the very young (under 26) to have the most psychological problems. Our data, as well as Weinberg's, suggest that although gay men have a fear of growing old, they seem to be able to adapt psychologically to a probably less-rewarding life.

In conclusion, nowhere have we attempted to suggest that on the average, the gay world is not more youth-oriented than the heterosexual world. Virtually all of the relevant literature provides evidence for a greater youth-orientedness of the former. Indeed one of the research problems that such a youth-orientedness seems to give rise to is a relative paucity of truly older gays—over 60, say—in most studies of gay men. This paucity was also present in our own sample and suggests that the meaning of "old" will often depend on the cultural context and purpose of research. Our purpose has been to document qualifications and exceptions to the thesis of youth-orientedness.

8

URBANIZATION AND THE DEVELOPMENT OF HOMOSEXUAL COMMUNITIES

The present chapter describes the development and social ecology of gay institutions and communities in North America (the United States and Canada). The relationships among city size, local historical-cultural atmosphere, and the spatial distributions and numbers of such institutions as gay bars, baths, and social service organizations serving gays are discussed. We argue that homosexuals are subject to much the same economic and cultural influences and processes as heterosexuals. When allowed to develop by tolerant or sympathetic political authorities, institutions serving male homosexuals diversify with increasing urbanization in the same ways as institutions serving heterosexuals. Consequently in nonrepressive political climates, the prediction of much of the behavior of gays can be best accomplished by employing the same variables as used in the prediction of heterosexual behavior.

DEVELOPMENT OF INSTITUTIONAL COMPLETENESS

The emergence of a variety of organizations catering to the needs and tastes of a particular minority is problematic for any minority or deviant aggregate of people. When that aggregate is an oppressed group, which often attempts to make its identity and behavior invisible, then the emergence of a variety of organizations to serve its needs in certain urban areas becomes an interesting question within the perspectives of urban sociology. Under what conditions may such organizations arise, even though the population they serve tends to be invisible and often secretive? Under what conditions may such an organization be transformed from "black market" operations to conventional markets?

In approaching these questions, we find the concept of "institutional completeness," introduced by Breton (1964) in his analysis of the ethnic institutions of Montreal ethnic residents, to be useful. Breton introduced this concept to explain the adaptation of ethnic immigrants to urban life. He stated that "ethnic communities can vary enormously in their social organization. At one extreme, there is the community which consists essentially of a network of interpersonal relations; members of a certain ethnic group seek each other's companionship; friendship groups and cliques form" (Breton 1964, p. 194). At this stage in the development of an ethnic community, the level of social organization is quite low; the community consists very largely of sets of interpersonal friendship and kinship networks. There is no institutional specialization within the community. This state of affairs is similar to that described by Leznoff and Westley (1956) for Montreal gays during the early 1950s. The social organization of gays in Montreal at that time consisted of a number of interrelated cliques who socialized in each other's homes and at gay bars—gay bars apparently at that time being the only institution devoted to serving gays.

In discussing the further development and differentiation of ethnic organizations, Breton continues:

> Most ethnic groups probably were at one time—and some still are—of this informal type. Many, however, have developed a more formal structure and contain organizations of various sorts; religious, educational, political, recreational, national, and even professional. Some have organized welfare and mutual-aid societies. Some operate their own radio station or publish their own newspapers and periodicals. The community may also sustain a number of commercial and service organizations. Finally, it may have its own churches and sometimes its own schools. Between the two extremes much variation can be observed in the amount and complexity of community organizations; the degree of institutional completeness in fact shows considerable variation from one ethnic group to another.
>
> Institutional completeness would be at its extreme whenever the ethnic community could perform all the services required by its members. Members would never have to make use of native institutions for the satisfaction of any of their needs, such as education, work, food, and clothing, medical care or social assistance. Of course, in contemporary North American cities very few, if any, ethnic communities showing full institutional completeness can be found (1964, p. 194).

For Breton, ethnic communities go through a life cycle, with a public, or aggregate, of possible users gradually accumulating in an urban area due to migration. Such migration provides a set of opportunities for social entrepreneurs, who establish organizations that persist as long as a public exists to use their services. While ethnic identity is important in the formation and continuance of such organizations, the social entrepreneurs will have a vested interest in these organizations and will attempt in various ways to strengthen the ethnic identity so as to keep their public as large as possible.

The development of gay communities in North American cities can be profitably analyzed as an instance of increasing institutional completeness. As the absolute numbers of gay males in North American cities have increased in size due both to general increases in the local populations and to emigration to the larger cities by gays, opportunities have arisen for social entrepreneurs to provide goods and services to resident gay communities. Moreover, as such providers arise and as institutions develop, gays have been transformed from a statistical aggregate of quasi-isolated individuals into members of a self-conscious and interacting community. If institutional completeness were carried further, there would be a full-fledged political economy for male homosexuals, with a well-developed market providing a wide range of goods and services and a variety of job opportunities for male homosexuals serving other male homosexuals.

Although we do not have demographic data for male homosexuals such as are available for racial groups, age groups, and many other demographic aggregates of the North American population, we do have some data on the ecological distribution and numbers of certain organizations serving gay males by city size. We proceed to an analysis of the numbers, variety, and types of gay bars serving gay males in cities of varying sizes in the United States.

Urbanization and Gay Bars

Harry (1974) has provided an analysis indicating that the number and variety of types of gay bars are related to the size of urban areas in the United States. The gay bar is but one of the institutions serving gay males, and the presence of a gay bar or a number of gay bars is not a strong indicator of the degree of institutional completeness for a given gay community. Still as Hooker (1967) has argued, the gay bar is the most central gay institution, and its presence in a community is the beginning of the development of a set of gay institutions. Further gay bars come in a variety of types, and the presence of a *variety* of such bars may be presumed to be a strong indicator of the presence of a number of nonbar gay institutions.

The basic sources of data for the present analysis were the 1970 U.S. Census of Population and the 1972 *Guild Guide*. The *Guild Guide* lists gay bars by state and city and is considered one of the most reliable of several gay guides on the market. Errors in listings in the *Guide* are very largely due to the frequent opening and closing of gay bars. However, while there may be an erroneous listing for a particular bar in a given city because the bar has been closed, the number of gay bars within that city will have remained fairly constant due to the opening of a new bar. Consequently the general statistical patterns that emerge from the analysis of these data are largely valid.

Four hundred and twenty-six cities were listed in the *Guide* as possessing at least one gay bar, including bars with mixed homosexual and heterosexual clienteles. We coded these cities as to their numbers of gay and mixed bars and as to whether they contained at least one of each of ten types of gay bars. The ten types included: young clienteles; older clienteles; lesbians; black clienteles; same-sex dancing occurring; clienteles containing significant numbers of male hustlers; leather bars, where the customers dress in motorcycle costumes and occasionally indulge in sadomasochistic (S and M) practices; bars where ties and jackets are customary (dressy); and private gay clubs.

TABLE 8.1

Percent of Cities with at Least One Gay Bar, by City Size

City Size (thousands)	Percent	N
-9	3	18,310
10–49	7	1,890
50–99	39	236
100–249	74	98
250–499	100	29
500–999	100	20
1,000+	100	6

Source: Compiled by the authors.

Table 8.1 presents the percentages of U.S. cities (by size of city) with at least one gay bar. It seems necessary for a city to have at least a 50,000 population before it becomes likely to have at least one such bar.* Exceptions to this genralization can be explained by two conditions. First, there are a number of resort areas of small population where gay-oriented businesses are allowed by authorities to remain open due to their great profitability. The flows of gays to these resort areas tend to be both seasonal and temporary, so that the local residents are not obliged to live with gay neighbors the year round. Aspen, Colorado; Saugatuck, Michigan; Provincetown, Massachusetts; Orcas Island, Washington; and Key West, Florida; are instances of such gay resort areas. Second, certain communities near major metropolitan areas serve as weekend retreats for homosexuals, as well as heterosexuals, in the area. Their proximity to the big

---

*Karlen (1971, p. 51) cites Paul Gebhard as making a similar observation about city size and the presence of a gay bar.

TABLE 8.2

Percent of Cities with a Given Type of Gay Bar, by City Size*

	City Size (thousands)							
Bar Type	-9	10–49	50–99	100–249	250–499	500–999	1,000+	Total
All mixed	42	38	31	11	0	0	0	27
Young	34	33	47	67	90	95	100	50
Dancing	24	18	34	58	81	95	100	38
Lesbian	7	3	19	25	58	85	100	20
Impersonators	16	8	12	16	32	75	100	18
Hustlers	0	5	9	16	39	65	86	14
Private club	4	6	9	12	29	50	86	12
Older	6	4	4	10	29	50	100	11
Dressy	6	4	5	10	29	50	86	11
Leather	2	3	1	0	13	45	57	6
Black	0	1	0	3	3	35	86	4
N	55	147	93	73	31	21	7	426

*The 1970 census lists only six cities over 1 million, although seven are indicated above. The difference arises because the *1972 Guild Guide* lists all Los Angeles noncentral city bars as being in the metropolitan area. This area was coded here as a separate city with over 1 million population. The difference between the 31 cities listed above as having a 250,000 to 499,000 population and the 29 listed by the census is due to rounding error.

Source: Compiled by the authors.

city serves to explain the presence of a gay bar in a community of modest size.

In Table 8.2, city size is cross-tabulated with a variety of types of gay bars. Smaller cities (but not resort areas) have predominantly "mixed" bars. Evidently the gay populations within such communities have not reached sufficient numbers to be able to support a bar of their own and must share a local bar with heterosexuals. For urban centers with over a 50,000 population, the Pearsonian correlation between number of gay bars and city size is quite strong, being 0.78 among those cities having at least one such bar.

In general, larger cities usually have a greater diversity of types of gay bars. The Pearsonian correlation between population size and the number of types of gay bars a city contains is 0.53. Although the variety of gay bars a city contains increases substantially with city size, large cities seem to also have a number of the mixed gay and heterosexual bars. (The correlation between city size and the ratio of mixed to all-gay bars is a barely significant -0.10 $N = 426$, two-tailed $p = 0.04$).

Guttman scaling was attempted on the data of Table 8.2, since the data seemed to show a measure of cumulativeness. That is, as city size increased, there was not simply an addition of a greater variety of bars but the increments seemed to occur in a particular order. The bar types formed an acceptable scale if only the following types were included in the scale: young, dancing, hustler, older, dressy, leather, and black.* Since black gays are a minority of a minority, it is understandable that only the very largest urban areas would be able to support a black gay bar.

The relationships between size of urban area and number and types of gay bars is determined by the size of the available bar clientele, the bar-going propensities of each type, and the propensities of each type of clientele to segregate themselves into separate settings. For instance, because lesbians have lesser bar-going propensities than do gay males, lesbian bars seem fewer in relation to the numbers of lesbians than gay male bars in relation to their numbers. Similarly hustlers must necessarily have fairly low self-segregative tendencies; otherwise, a hustler bar would be a market of many sellers but no buyers. The relative infrequency of leather and black bars appears to be due to the small numbers of relevantly interested gays. We note that we could find no metropolitan area of less than 1 million population with an exclusively leather bar.

The tendency of certain types of gay bar clients to segregate themselves from other gays will normally serve to hasten the appearance of that type of gay

---

*The scale had a coefficient of reproducibility of 0.95, a minimum marginal reproducibility of 0.81, and a coefficient of scalability of 0.72.

bar in the course of urbanization. Such self-segregation is exemplified in the dressy gay bar. The clientele of this type of gay bar is typically older (30 to 60 years old). As such, the dressy gay bar is a subtype of the older bar. Also, the clientele of the dressy bar tend to be heavily middle or upper middle class. Given their social status and age, they voluntarily segregate themselves from other gays, so as to avoid the frenzy of the young bar, possible exploitation by persons of substantially lower status, and to find companions with similar cultural interests. To the extent that the set of gay bars a city possesses is varied, individuals of similar age, social status, culture, and recreational interests will be able to meet socially for purposes of sharing interests other than purely sexual ones. The differentiation of gay bars, and of other institutions, which increases with city size, probably provides a more satisfying life for gays in the larger city. The variety of available gay life-styles permits a closer fit between the sexual, social, and cultural tastes of the individual and the opportunities for the expression of those tastes.

Gay Life in Rural Areas and Smaller Towns

The analysis of the relationships of city size to number and variety of gay bars invites the question of whether there is any gay life or community in towns too small to support even a mixed bar. To date, all of the research and observations of gay life have been based on larger cities or on resort areas, such as Fire Island. Based on our observations of gay life in southwest Idaho, we make a number of suggestions as to the modus operandi of gays in smaller towns and rural areas. Gay life in such communities appears to be largely lacking in specialized gay institutions. Such communities are at the opposite pole of social organization from that of institutional completeness. For gay residents of small towns, the gay life consists primarily of friendships and acquaintanceships with, perhaps, a dozen other gays. This stands in great contrast to gay life in the larger city, where a gay may typically be acquainted with hundreds of other gays.

Entry into the local gay networks in a smaller town is only negotiated with some difficulty and substantial circumspection. Given that there are no gay bars or other locales where the person entering the setting may assume that others present are gay, becoming acquainted with others already integrated into the local gay network requires time. The newcomer to such a town may search among his daily contacts for those individuals who could reasonably by hypothesized to be gay. Such indicators as being unmarried and older or being somewhat effeminate can serve as possible hints that another is gay and may be tentatively approached for purposes either social or sexual. Alternatively city parks and rest stops along the local freeways are occasionally frequented by gays from smaller towns and rural areas. Such locales also serve as places where social and sexual contacts may be made. Subsequently the gay newcomer to an area may effect entry into the local networks of acquaintanceship. Of course, the frequenting of such locales is fraught with danger, since after several years of use by gays, the local police undoubtedly become familiar with the activities of gays.

Due to the lack of exclusively gay settings and institutions in smaller towns, most gay socializing occurs either in the anonymity of public settings, such as parks or beaches, or in private settings, such as at private parties. Given that in smaller towns a large percentage of the population can identify a substantial percentage of the other residents, great circumspection in behavior is usually required. Information in such towns travels very fast, and if the individual has a job of some prominence or visibility, it travels even faster and more widely. Some gay individuals in smaller towns often defer any sexual behavior until those times when they make trips to a nearby city, where there are gay bars or baths. Alternatively they may choose to do their cruising in nearby small towns, where there is less likelihood that they will be identified.

One effect of the highly clique-oriented and secretive nature of gay life in smaller towns is that the behavior and identity of gays is not only successfully concealed from heterosexuals but may also be concealed from a number of other gay residents of that community. Thus even though there may be, say, only two dozen gays in a small town, some will not know others or will only "know of" them but not be acquainted with them. While the acquaintanceship networks among such gays may be extensive in that most are familiar with a few others, they are not the sort of networks in which all are familiar with all.

We here turn to a brief analysis of the opening of the first gay bar in Boise, Idaho, as an event that helps reveal the nature of gay life in smaller towns. Boise's first gay bar opened in July 1976. At that time, Boise had a population of 98,000, with approximately another 100,000 population in the surrounding, but not adjacent, smaller towns. Until that opening, it appears that the principal locales for gay social and sexual activites were private parties and one of the city parks. Also, a number of gays occasionally frequented a local bar that was mixed and in which they were a substantial minority.

From the day of its opening, the gay bar was a thriving business. The very rapid growth of the bar's clientele occurred in the virtual absence of any formal advertising. It was not listed in any of the gay guides. While its opening was announced in the *Advocate* and the *Northwest Gay Review*, the former being published in Los Angeles and the latter in Seattle, these publications were not then available to local gays, except by subscription. We estimate that very few Boise gays actually subscribed to these publications.

The rapid growth of the Boise bar's clientele points up several distinguishing characteristics of gay life in smaller towns and cities. First, the lack of generally available advertising indicates the existence of long chains of acquaintanceships among gays in and around Boise and that these chains were able to develop, although not flourish, in the absence of formal gay institutions. Apparently most of the bar's new clientele originally heard of its existence through acquaintances. It is possible, although unlikely, that a few gays may have heard of the existence of the bar from heterosexuals.

Another illustrative effect of the opening of this bar was that a significant percentage of its clientele were residents of smaller communities 15 to 50 miles distant. Such persons quickly developed the practice of visiting the Boise bar on weekends, where they would be reasonably secure that information about their activities would not be transmitted back to their home communities. A good number of the gay residents of the smaller surrounding communities would meet at the Boise bar other gays from their home communities with whom they were not acquainted or of whom they had only heard. Such meetings of gay co-residents from smaller towns support the notion that although such communities have gay networks, they are far from being densely interconnected.

Third, the fact that the new bar advertised in magazines that were published in distant large cities, rather than publishing in the local paper, indicates the partial dependence of small town gay communities on the more institutionally developed gay communities of larger cities. The communication devices of larger cities, both formal and informal, help smaller town gays to overcome their relative lack of means of identifying each other, communicating with each other, and subsequently of becoming more organized.

Several new gay institutions were organized in rapid succession following the opening of the Boise bar. A Metropolitan Community Church (MCC) was established. Since the MCC is a California-based organization, the founding of a unit in Boise once more indicates the partial dependence of small town communities on those of larger cities. A series of shoftball events was begun. An annual picnic was established. A women's discussion group was formed. The rapidity with which these institutions was formed seems in part due to the fact that Boise was long "overdue" for the establishment of a gay bar and other gay institutions. Given its size, the arrival of an explicitly gay set of institutions to Boise was late in coming.

The lateness of arrival of gay institutions to certain cities can be partly explained by special historical and cultural circumstances and partly by out-migration of gays from smaller towns to larger population centers. For example, Boise is widely known for the large-scale purge of gays that occurred in the mid-1950s (Gerassi 1966). Also, the highly religious and conservative culture of the state of Idaho generally could only be considered a drawback in the eyes of many gays. Having a very negative view of Idaho in general, and Boise in particular, many gays in other cities would be reluctant to move there. Such nonmigration partly explains the slowness of gay institutions to develop in that city.

It would seem that a factor common to most smaller towns is a substantial outmigration by gays to larger cities. Schofield's (1965, p. 101) data from Great Britain indicate the relative frequency of moves by male homosexuals to London or other large urban centers. In larger cities, the gay person need be less circumspect in his behavior. His fearfulness is less. Also, the large city offers him a variety of social and sexual rewards, which are substantially lacking in smaller towns. Thus because of both greater rewards and reduced fears, the lights of the metropolis gleam brightly for the rural gay.

One consequence of the outmigration by small town gays is that the development of a set of gay institutions in the smaller city is inhibited. A substantial segment of a gay bar's potential market simply moves away. Those left behind tend to have especially strong reasons for remaining. Such reasons would typically be owning a business or a farm, being heterosexually married, having many relatives in the area, or having a position of prominence. Such factors as owning a business or farm have also been shown to reduce the geographical mobility of the general heterosexual population.

The outmigration of gays to larger cities tends to be age-related and to alter the age distributions of the gay population left behind. As has been repeatedly found among heterosexuals, geographical mobility is greatest among the young, and particularly among those in their twenties. Shortly after graduation from high school or college, large numbers of persons make long-distance moves to urban areas, if no longer to central cities (Sjaastad 1962; Freedman 1957). Among gays, the effects of large-scale outmigration would be to leave behind those who are still in their teens, and who have probably not yet come out, and those who are over 30. Since at least within the gay world, older persons tend to be somewhat less active sexually and socially, their presence in large numbers in a city would inhibit the formation of an active gay life. Also, since older gays tend to have somewhat more substantial occupations and for that reason are often somewhat more closeted (Leznoff and Westley 1956), their closetedness is a further inhibiting factor for the development of gay institutions. Accordingly it seems that large-scale outmigration by younger mobile gays may inhibit gay life in smaller cities, both through a reduction in actual numbers available to support a gay community and through leaving behind the least active segments of a potential gay community.

Toward Greater Institutional Completeness: The Gay Ghetto

After the establishment of gay bars, a next important step along the road to institutional completeness for the gay community is the development of neighborhoods having substantial concentrations of gay residents. Based upon her observations of gay life in Los Angeles during the late 1950s, Hooker noted that

> although homosexuals as a total group do not have a bounded territorial base, they are, nevertheless, not randomly distributed throughout the city, nor are the facilities or institutions which provide needed services and function as focal gathering places. Mapping

> the residences of persons known to us, or known to subjects who have supplied us with their addresses, and noting the residential areas of the city described by them as having heavy concentrations of homosexuals resulted in large cluster formations. In these sections, apartment houses on particular streets may be owned by, and rented exclusively to, homosexuals. Single streets or individual dwellings may have only one or two non-homosexual families. The concentrated character of these areas is not generally known except in the homosexual community, and in many instances by the police. The (gay) population is also distributed widely throughout the city and its suburbs since other factors than association affect the choice of residence (1967, pp. 171–72).

Such residential concentrations of gays as observed by Hooker, while not constituting the full-fledged gay ghetto of more recent years, provide a number of functions for gays. Having many gay neighbors in an apartment building is a useful protective device in that one may be assured that one's neighbors will not complain about one's sexual activities. It also provides one with greater access to information about forthcoming events in the gay community and about past events (in the form of gossip). Further gays will be more willing to exchange with each other the variety of small services that neighbors exchange than they would if their neighbors were heterosexuals. Many gays take care in selecting their residences to ensure that their dwellings are substantially insulated from the sight and hearing of heterosexual neighbors.

Residential and organizational clustering are, of course, common phenomena in urban North America. What is new in the larger urban areas is the open, up-front nature of neighborhoods of male homosexuals and their rapid expansion during the last ten years, particularly in such urban areas as San Francisco, Manhattan, and parts of Los Angeles county. Those areas of larger cities that have tended to become gay earlier seem to have been principally ones containing substantial numbers of apartment buildings and of older houses. Housing in such areas is both cheaper than single-family dwellings and more suited to the smaller sizes—one to two persons—of gay households. Later in the development of a city's gay community, there may develop suburban single-family dwelling gay areas, as the number of upper-income gays increases to a size sufficient to support such a concentration, for example, Marin County, California. While we have emphasized the economic factors underlying the development of gay districts, political ones are also important. A social history of the emergence of gay areas, such as Greenwich Village in Manhattan or Castro and Market in San Francisco, would include an analysis of the tolerance of police and political authorities for male homosexuals at different historical periods.

Once an area begins to develop concentrations of resident gays, cumulative effects lead to the further elaboration of gay organizations and commercial establishments. Such elaboration leads to the emergence of the full-fledged gay ghetto. Levine (1977) has argued that "ghetto" is an appropriate concept to apply to predominantly gay residential and commercial areas in North American cities, the social requisites of a ghetto being social isolation, segregation, and the development of a special subculture. He found such ghettos to exist in small areas of Boston, Chicago, San Francisco, Los Angeles, and New York. Of course, only a minority of the gay men of such cities live in these ghettos.

Unlike black or Latino ghetto residents, the inhabitants of gay ghettos seem to be highly age-selected. Impressionistic evidence suggests that the Castro-Market ghetto is populated by gays with a median age of roughly 30, with very few being in their early twenties and even fewer in their fifties or sixties. This suggests that residence in such ghettos is a phase in the career of many gays. Among those who choose to live in the ghetto, the time they spend there is, we suspect, something less than five years. At the end of this time period, some begin to feel "fagged out." They tire of the unceasing stream of sexual partners, loud music, liquor, and parties and then move to less frenetic settings.

The national gay newspaper, the *Advocate*, recently described the development of a ghetto of male homosexuals in the Castro area:

> Single men with excess income began moving in, buying up the old houses and using their leisure time to renovate the area. By 1967 a few gay bars were doing business. By the early 70's, gay business people began leasing the deserted storefronts. The trend became an explosion in 1974. Housing costs skyrocketed. Young single men could afford it. Middle-class families, meanwhile, couldn't afford to pass up the top dollars offered for their homes. The gay population dug in (February 9, 1977, p. 20).

By 1978, the invasion process was sufficiently complete that the *San Francisco Chronicle* (January 3, 1978) published a lengthy article entitled "The Last Straight Bar in the Neighborhood."

For the city of San Francisco as a whole, there are well-developed social services, including health and welfare organizations catering to male homosexuals, which advertise in gay-owned newspapers. There also exist a variety of organizations serving both social and political functions for the community. There exist gay caucuses of the Democratic and Libertarian parties, and a committee of the local American Civil Liberties Union works for gay rights. Travel bureaus arrange tours for gays, for example, "opera tour of New York," "gay Toronto," and "wilderness river running with real cowboys." Competitive marketing attempts to appeal to gays by advertising in gay newspapers. Thus one San Francisco beer company had a "beer man" contest in local bars to choose a "hunky dude" to advertise the beer to homosexual communities. An image of the "macho gay dude"—the antithesis of the effeminate homosexual—usually in the nude, is a common part of advertising directed to gay communities across North America. While the expansion of organizations providing such services to gay males is centered in the largest North American cities, they also service a much broader market. Gay tourists, who visit from other large cities and from small towns, partially (and intermittently) depend on the variety of things offered by the gay institutions of the big city.

San Francisco and a few other large North American cities give evidence of a great measure of institutional completeness for gay communities. However, full institutional completeness is not readily possible for a gay community, or for most minorities, without their seceding from the surrounding society's political and economic institutions. Particularly in the world of work, gays must participate in basically heterosexual institutions. Only in those instances where gays work in establishments catering largely to other gays can individuals be completely surrounded by gay institutions. However, such extreme completeness may not be desirable for gays, despite its many benefits, since such an extreme implies a segregation from the dominant institutions of North American society.

Gay Capitalism or Capitalist Exploitation?

The development of gay ghettos, the proliferation of political and social service organizations, and the rise of gay culture since 1960 have been described above. The convergence of these trends created an identifiable market of gay men currently being developed for its profit potential by capitalist entrepreneurs. The implications of this market approach for gay culture and consciousness may be severe. Hence we undertake an analysis of how this market seems to have developed.

Before the late 1960s, few products or services were marketed for an explicitly gay clientele. A few bars and baths were available in some metropolitan areas. Also, some theaters and restaurants tolerated gays on the premises. Occasionally some of these establishments would eject their gay clientele in an attempt to acquire a heterosexual clientele. Some of the bars and baths, particularly in New York City, were reputed to be Mafia-owned. Mafia and other underworld entrepreneurs have traditionally provided services and products to various deviant categories for a fee—usually, a very high fee. For example, drinks in some of New York's gay bars were 100 to 200 percent more expensive than in nearby heterosexual bars. One very popular gay bar in Detroit—the Woodward—was repeatedly ticketed for watering the drinks with tea or water. On a few occasions during the 1960s, such pricing provoked demonstrations by outraged gay clienteles.

Since the middle 1950s, nonprofit service organizations have been providing some products and services for gay audiences. Newsletters of such organizations as the Society for Individual Rights (SIR) in San Francisco included articles on gay consciousness, political activities, announcements of dances, plays put on by gays, and an "advice to lovers" column. *One* magazine began to publish photographs of partially nude males for its audience. (It should be remembered that the period being described was prior to the advent of universally available commercial pornography.) Some service organizations published classified ads for males wanting other males; others organized outings, picnics, weekend motorcycle runs, and camping events. Others provided mimeographed leaflets or maps for visitors to their city listing restaurants, bars, and baths.

The emergence of large concentrations of gays in ghettos, of nationally distributed newspapers, such as the *Advocate*, and of publicity concerning gay culture led to more magazines and newspapers being established as profit-making enterprises rather than as nonprofit service organizations. Similarly services such as dances, coffee houses, and personal and legal advice, which formerly had been offered largely by nonprofit organizations, now were offered by commercial establishments.

The phenomenon of the gay businessman began to emerge. Whereas most of the earlier establishments catering to gays seem to have been owned by heterosexuals, during the 1960s, gay entrepreneurs began to both capture and expand the various gay markets. Gay capitalism as an ideology has some similarities to the black capitalism of the 1960s. Gay small businessmen did not necessarily advertise "buy gay," but through advertising in gay publications and holding benefits and other functions, the identification between being gay and buying gay was made to the potential customer. Examples of such functions have been softball or bowling leagues sponsored by the gay bars of Detroit or San Francisco.

Some gay businessmen began to form associations to protect their interests. Examples include the Tavern Guild and the Golden Gate Businessmen's Association in San Francisco. Since members of these associations have the resources to publicize persons and events, aspiring gay politicians have gone to them for money and support during political campaigns in San Francisco. Some heterosexual politicians have also sought their support. These associations have also contributed to various gay causes, such as the Miami gay rights issue publicized by Anita Bryant.

After 1965, the range of services and products offered to gays expanded immensely. Products currently offered include films and magazines of male nudes; gay pornography; T-shirts for Anita Bryant opponents; slick format magazines, such as *Blueboy, Mandate, Queen's Quarterly, In Touch*, and *After Dark*; cosmetics for males; dildoes; S&M implements; massage oils; amyl nitrite stimulants; and clothing. Services include travel agencies for gays, gay resorts, wilderness trips, opera tours of Europe, legal services, and illegal services, such as male "models" and gay hotels.

By the 1970s, the potential of the gay market had come to the attention of legitimate heterosexual businessmen rather than just underworld entrepreneurs. Gay males were discovered to have considerable discretionary income. A readership survey of the *Advocate* (with a circulation of 50,000) found the median income of readers to be about $15,000, with 59 percent owning some stocks, 90 percent owning stereo equipment, and 10 percent owning their own businesses. It should be observed that such a readership survey is grossly biased toward the wealthier part of the gay population. Still it indicates the existence of a considerable gay market with discretionary income.

With a readily identifiable market, the *Wall Street Journal* ran several lengthy articles on the *Advocate* and on the "new sales target" of homosexuals.* In the article on the *Advocate*, the *Journal* noted that since former Wall Street analyst David Goodstein had bought it, it had expanded readership in 1975 and expected to turn a profit in 1976. The article discussed the problems the *Advocate* had in getting advertisers and getting distribution on newsstands, as opposed to pornography shops.

In the article on selling to homosexuals, the *Journal* quoted a Columbia Pictures executive: "Market research shows us that the gay audience is a highly movie-oriented audience. We can no longer afford to ignore this market." Columbia Pictures planned to spend $200,000 in 1975 advertising and promoting to gays. A Falstaff beer executive said they gave $100 to a benefit for deaf gays. "I try to participate as much as I can. We do a lot for the gay community and it has helped our sales. The gay community here (San Francisco) is big and strong and it is an important factor in our business. I guess we do business in about 90 percent of the gay bars in San Francisco." Another beer executive said: "The gay population is a big market and there is no reason for us to ignore it." The *Journal* said that in the field of publishing, "companies are offering at least ten times as many books aimed at homosexuals as five years ago." For example, Bantam Books produced a 150,000-copy first printing of Patricia Warren's *The Front Runner*, a love story about a homosexual track star and his coach. Department store managers were quoted by the *Journal* as saying they were bringing out "campy lines of products" for the gay market.

Over the last three decades, the entrepreneurs catering to the gay market appear to have been of three kinds. First, there were heterosexual and underworld businessmen running gay bars and baths. Later, there developed numerous establishments, principally retail ones, owned by gays. More recently, legitimate heterosexual businessmen have begun selling to gay men. The latter appear to operate more in the fields of manufacturing and distribution than do the gay businessmen. With the recent recognition by businessmen that there is a large gay market, a number of advertising firms have come into existence that cater to the needs of heterosexual firms attempting to expand into the gay markets. Some gays have come to feel beseiged by advertisers and hucksters. Certainly

---

*"A Homosexual Paper, 'The Advocate,' Widens Readership, Influence," November 3, 1975; "Campaigns to Sell to Homosexual Market Are Being Launched by More Big Firms," May 13, 1975.

they can now feel sympathy for the housewife, who for decades has been beset by white tornadoes, Mr. Cleans, and friendly laundry advisors.

It is difficult to assess what may be the future effects of the discovery of the gay market by the business world. One possible effect is that gay culture may become one of trinkets, erotica, exotica, and fads resembling some segments of teen-age culture. Another possibility is that through the acquisition of cultural objects specially designed for the needs of gays, gay consciousness may be heightened. Whatever the future effects, it seems clear that the discovery of the gay market has moved gays a step closer to the mainstream of American consumer culture.

POLITICAL AUTHORITIES, THE CLIMATE OF OPINION, AND GAY INSTITUTIONS

While we have emphasized demographic and economic factors as the principal forces behind the elaboration of gay institutions, that elaboration is also dependent upon local political conditions. Such elaboration would not be possible without the at least tacit support of political authorities at the city or county level. Local governments in North America have a panoply of powers through which they can influence the development of many kinds of activities within their jurisdiction. Typical powers that have been used to prevent the development of gay institutions have been zoning powers; prohibiting persons unrelated by blood or marriage from living together in certain areas; differential use of police power, as in the cases of raids on gay bars; power over liquor licensing (or at least pressures on state alcohol control boards); and uneven enforcement of loitering ordinances. A further power that has been used to suppress the growth of gay institutions has been the selective and arbitrary refusal of permission for gay groups to utilize public meeting places. An instance of this was the refusal by the city of Boise to allow a lesbian discussion group to hold meetings at a city community center.

The Los Angeles area provides a clear example of how variation in attitudes toward gays between differing jurisdictions can greatly influence the growth of gay institutions. The police chief of the city of Los Angeles proper, Ed Davis, has been vehemently outspoken against gays for many years. He has quoted the Bible against homosexual behavior, denied the existence of "victimless crimes" ("There is no such thing"), and has selectively used the vice squad, particularly the Hollywood division, to arrest homosexuals in gay bars for soliciting. In general, the Los Angeles police department, certainly by reputation and probably in fact, has virtually patented the practice of entrapment.

In contrast to the situation of gays in Los Angeles, there have developed several gay ghettos immediately outside of the city boundaries, chiefly in West Hollywood. It is an unincorporated area of Los Angeles county and, hence, is under the jurisdiction of the county sheriff's department. The many gay institutions present in West Hollywood include gyms, baths, public restrooms, restaurants, markets, apartment houses, discos, bars, churches, and other organizations serving a wide variety of gay tastes. The original mother church of the MCC is located a short drive down the freeway. The Los Angeles Gay Community Services Center has a Fountain House, partly funded at one time by county revenue-sharing funds, to help jobless and homeless male homosexuals in the central Los Angeles area. In 1977, a movement was begun to establish a privately funded retirement home in the Los Angeles area for aged male homosexuals.

We have described the emergence of the West Hollywood gay ghetto to illustrate the importance of the attitudes of local political authorities for the emergence of gay institutions. Once legal and quasi-legal restrictions on gay activities have been removed and the aggregate of gays (including tourist gays, who may return as permanent residents) has reached a size that will support a set of gay institutions, social entrepreneurs will begin to service the gay market. A political economy of the gay community develops. Both the profit and nonprofit sectors receive the attentions and organizing efforts of social entrepreneurs. Political organizations come to lobby for sympathetic candidates and may, in some districts elect openly gay candidates to local office.

The development of institutionally complete gay communities is contingent on the removal of legal and quasi-legal restrictions. The removal of such restrictions has been part of a process of continuing struggle in all North American municipalities. In general, the dominant heterosexual authorities have resisted the removing of each and every barrier to the development of gay institutions. Although occasionally, segments of the heterosexual community have been willing to support and enact such laws as consenting adults laws and ordinances forbidding job discrimination, most of the removal of restrictions has been through gradual and less formal discontinuance of discriminatory policies and practices or through simply allowing antique laws to fall into disuse. The latter less formal and less public form of change has permitted the development of gay communities, while avoiding the implication that gays have a legitimate life-style; public legal enactments generally tend to confer such legitimacy.

Changes in both the attitudes of local political authorities and in those of the broader public help to foster the growth of gay institutions. Local groups have often acted and organized to exclude gays and their establishments from their neighborhoods. In the development of the Castro district of San Francisco, gay businessmen formed their own Castro Village Merchants Association, to protect their economic interests after the heterosexual businessmen had acted to exclude gays from the local neighborhood merchants association. Similar exclusionary activities have been attempted in residential areas. For example, Chicago Boulevard is a street of old, mansionlike homes in Detroit; after the original wealthy inhabitants had left, the area was inhabited by a mixture of gays and middle-class black families. The latter attempted to utilize the local neighborhood association to exclude such "undesirables" from the area. These instances of exclusion (or attempted exclusion) exemplify the step-by-step nature of the growth of gay institutions in the face of continuing resistance from both public and private groups.

In conclusion, once gays are granted a measure of tolerance by local political authorities and once they have aggregated together in sufficient numbers, there rapidly develops a gay community, a set of gay institutions, and in larger cities, an approximation to institutional completeness. Concomitant with these developments, there also arises a distinctly gay culture, typically consisting of a set of recreational "styles," plus common, and usually negative, attitudes toward the dominant heterosexual world.

THE ISSUE OF GAY CULTURE

Some writers have questioned whether the gay community can have a well-developed culture. Gagnon and Simon have asserted that

> in contrast to ethnic and occupational subcultures the homosexual community, as well as other deviant subcommunities, has very limited content. This derives from the fact that the community members often have only their sexual commitment in common. Thus, while the community may reduce the problems of access to sexual partners and reduce the guilt by providing a structure of shared values, often the shared value structure is far too narrow to transcend other areas of value disagreement. . . . The important fact is that the homosexual community is in itself an impoverished cultural unit. This impoverishment, however, may only be partially limiting, since it constrains most members to participate in it on a limited basis, reducing their anxiety and conflicts in the sexual sphere and increasing the quality of their performance in other aspects of social life (1973, pp. 153–54).

While there is an element of truth in the thesis of cultural impoverishment of the gay community, these authors have overgeneralized this hypothesis. There may be such impoverishment at certain times, in certain places, and in certain social settings, but as a categorical assertion, the proposition is simply untrue.

We recognize the truth of the cultural impoverishment thesis for certain gay settings, in which the interests of the parties present are limited to the negotiation of (mostly brief) sexual encounters and which exclude an emphasis on any romantic content, as well as all other cultural content. Settings satisfying these criteria are gay baths and public terminals, such as those studied by Humphreys (1970). In such settings, the social organization is almost exclusively focused on purely physical encounters, and the opportunities for cultural elaboration are severely limited (Weinberg and Williams 1975). Also satisfying these criteria would be those gay bars in which cruising is the exclusive purpose of the parties present and in which conversation that is not sexually oriented is considered an inconvenience. In such settings, the only culture is physical culture and the only self the "cosmetic self" (Hooker 1967). If the cultural impoverishment thesis of Gagnon and Simon is based on observations of such settings, then it is valid.

The thesis of cultural impoverishment also appears to have some applicability to those gay communities in which the surrounding political climate has severely limited the extent to which gays may readily interact with each other. Thus in small towns lacking a gay bar, the principal instances of gay behavior may consist of cruising the local parks and terminals. Similarly in small towns that possess a gay bar, some individuals may limit their attendance at gay bars or may not participate in the gay community, in order to avoid identification by heterosexuals. In such places, the conditions that prevent the development of gay institutions would seem to also limit the social, and hence cultural, content of interactions among gays.

We also recognize that the thesis of cultural impoverishment may apply to two categories of gay individuals, as opposed to gay communities. First, since heterosexually married men who engage in homosexual behavior have strong reasons to limit the extent of their participation in the broader gay community, they appear to chiefly go in for one-night stands, cruising public terminals, or to only engage in homosexual acts when away from their families (in distant cities). As Humphreys (1970) has reported, half of his sample of tearoom participants in impersonal sex were married. Such persons could readily be described as "(gay) culturally impoverished." Second, as argued earlier, some gay individuals have not been able to effectively neutralize the stigma of being gay and, in consequence, participate in the gay community on a limited and largely sexual basis. They avoid entering exclusive relationships and develop few or no gay friends. Such persons can also be considered "(gay) culturally impoverished." The above settings and types of individuals exhaust the instances for which we believe the thesis of cultural impoverishment has validity.

As more North American communities have developed a variety of gay institutions in which gays participate, the thesis of cultural impoverishment has become less and less valid. In the course of the development of gay institutions, the purely sexual ones of the restroom, the bar, and the bath appear to be the first established. Writings such as those of Leznoff and Westley (1956) and, probably, those of Simon and Gagnon (1967), which were based on observations of earlier decades, appear to have taken the cultural impoverishment of the gay institutions of that time as a constant within gay culture rather than as an historical variable. The severe constraints on gay activities and organizations of earlier decades substantially prevented the elaboration of a variety of gay organizations and particularly those that were more visible to the general public, for example, gay dances, picnics, political organizations, travel tours, and welfare organizations. The fairly systematic oppression of gays and their institutions of earlier decades maintained institutional narrowness within the gay community and, hence, cultural impoverishment.

An important and crucial early step toward the development of gay institutions and gay cultural enrichment was in gaining access to the use of the federal mails for gay organizations (DeVall 1973). This apparently minor step, which was achieved during the 1950s by some of the older gay organizations, was crucial to the development of a gay culture. It provided a means whereby gay organizations could communicate with their members, an essential requirement for all voluntary associations. It thus provided the basis upon which the level of social organization within gay communities could rise above that of cliques and friendship networks and begin the "take-off" toward institutional completeness.

Gaining access to the means of communication not only provided the basis for the formation of gay organizations but also provided the basis for the formation of a more diversified gay culture. In order for a culture to exist, it must be communicated among its members. Without access to formal means of communication, the culture of a group, like the group, is limited and local in content. For gay communities, this may often mean that members' interests are predominantly focused on local gossip and sexual adventures. Given access, even if simply in form of a *Gay Guide*, individuals of similar tastes and cultural and recreational styles may seek each other out, persons can become aware of issues and events affecting them in other parts of the country, and new inventions or styles may be introduced into the culture.

The rise of gay institutions and media helped to provide gays with a sense of collective identity through increasing awareness of the existence of each other. Prior to this, they could be readily described as a "historyless people." While many gays had been aware of a number of noted historical figures who were homosexual, these individuals were not seen as connected through participation in an ongoing community. Such figures were seen as relatively isolated individuals, who might have had a lover and a few gay friends, for example, Oscar Wilde. It was not possible for them to be seen as representatives of an organized collectivity, since little collective organization existed.

Given the rise of gay organizations and media, it became possible for there to be a recorded history of the gay collectivity rather than a history of gay individuals, consisting principally of biographies. Gay representations of themselves, their communities, and culture have become collective and sociological in nature. Gays began to "know that many personal troubles . . . must be understood in terms of public issues" (Mills 1959, p. 226). Evidence of a growing sociological interpretation of gay phenomena is to be found in articles in the *Advocate* in recent years. The advent of a collective identity among gays has enriched gay culture in that it has made salient to most the meanings of the collective struggle for civil rights. As in the case of Jews, a significant segment of gay culture consists of the history of oppression by other groups. In short, gay culture has had a large segment of political culture rapidly added to it.

Perhaps the greatest efflorescence in gay culture within the last two decades has been in its recreational content. Using culture content as a variable, we contrasted the conditions of Humphreys' (1970) restroom traders of sexual acts by anonymous persons with the variety of styles and tastes of West Hollywood or Castro-Market. These tastes include, but are not exhausted by, the following:

1. "Drag" events, in which male performers dressed in colorful female costumes entertain gay patrons and enter contests.
2. S and M settings, in which individuals affect sadomasochistic interests, sometimes genuinely but more often not, and wear leather and motorcycle garb.
3. Opera and high culture events, participated in mostly by upper-middle-class gays.
4. Decorative and artistic interests, which seem to be extremely widespread among gays, for example, interior decorating, floral arranging, theater (particularly Broadway), and painting.
5. Outdoor recreational interests, particularly in the Western United States, for example, hiking, backpacking, and river-running.
6. Softball and bowling leagues organized by gay commercial establishments in a number of larger cities.
7. "Camp" behavior as a personal style, often accompanied by a highly cultivated and sharp wit.

In conclusion, it would seem that the Gagnon and Simon thesis of cultural impoverishment was a time-bound hypothesis that had a measure of validity for certain gay settings, for some gay individuals, and for earlier decades. However, the growth of gay institutions during the last 15 years, the rise of a sense of collective identity, the creation of a sophisticated political culture, and the efflorescence of a variety of gay recreational styles has significantly expanded the content of that culture.

9

GAYS AND WORK: DISCRIMINATION AND ADAPTATION

All studies of male homosexuals that give data on years of educational attainment uniformly indicate that gay men seem to have substantially more education than the general population. Our data find 69 percent of the Detroit sample had at least some college education. Weinberg and Williams (1974, p. 95) reported 82 percent of their U.S. respondents had some college education. Gagnon and Simon (1973, p. 141), using Kinsey's data on males, found 70 percent to have had a college education to some degree. Other researchers (Warren 1974; Siegelman 1972; Saghir and Robins 1973, p. 12) reported high levels of educational attainment among their homosexual samples.

Although it is possible that all of these studies suffer from the same deficiency, namely, an undersampling of less-educated male homosexuals, the fact that these studies were from a variety of time periods and places and used various methods of obtaining respondents suggests that male homosexuals probably are more educated than the general population. If this is true, it implies that male homosexuals may have several assets, in addition to their high educational levels, to offset the multiple discriminations they face in the world of work and achievement.

Several hypotheses are discussed here concerning the ways male homosexuals relate to the world of work. We also attempt to explain why, on the average, they seem to have such high educational achievement.

CAREER CHOICES OF MALE HOMOSEXUALS

Consistent with the findings of other studies, the occupational distribution of the Detroit sample contains few blue-collar respondents and a large percentage of respondents in lower white-collar jobs. The distribution is as follows: 18

percent employed in upper white-collar jobs, including managers of businesses, the professional strata, and college teaching; 35 percent in lower white-collar jobs; 12 percent in manual jobs, 24 percent in service occupations; 6 percent in school; and 5 percent unemployed.

Why is there such a low percentage of blue-collar respondents in the Detroit sample and in all other samples of male homosexuals in North America? Rather than sampling bias as an explanation for the paucity of blue-collar male homosexuals, it seems plausible that male homosexuals deliberately choose non-blue-collar jobs because they anticipate greater discrimination from blue-collar workers than from workers in other occupational strata. Given the great emphasis placed on masculinity in working-class circles (Miller 1958) and the greater homophobia found among blue-collar workers than among workers in other occupational strata (Nyberg and Alston 1977), the gay male has some real basis to fear discrimination in blue-collar work if his sexual preference becomes known to co-workers. Potentially, he could face verbal ridicule and possible physical assaults from co-workers. To the extent that large numbers of male homosexuals, regardless of the occupation of their fathers, exclude blue-collar occupations from their job horizons, this would have an almost automatic effect of raising their actual occupational levels. If they exclude blue-collar jobs from their occupational choice, male homosexuals would often have to seek more than a high school education in order to qualify for white-collar occupations.

A further hypothesis to explain why male homosexuals avoid blue-collar jobs is that such jobs are inconsistent with their sex-role identities. To the extent that gays have not internalized or have actually repudiated some of the more macho elements traditionally attributed to the masculine role, they may find manual jobs inappropriate to their self-concept. Such traits as toughness, strength, and physical aggressiveness seem to have been rejected by many gays as not particularly desirable characteristics. These traits are also occasionally ridiculed by other gays in symbolic "put-downs" of the cultural values of heterosexual males. Having rejected a number of the values of heterosexual masculinity, and not considering more "feminine" occupations to be inconsistent with their self-concepts, gays seem to often avoid the manual jobs associated with traditional masculity.

While these ideas may explain why male homosexuals seem to be underrepresented in blue-collar jobs, they do not explain why male homosexuals gravitate to the jobs they do hold. The Detroit data and most of the other studies cited suggest that male homosexuals are overrepresented in lower white-collar and service occupations, for example those of bartender, waiter, grade school teacher, store clerk, file clerk, and florist. Karlen (1971, p. 514) has suggested that the clustering of male homosexuals in lower white-collar jobs represents a "striving for gentility." Given that a white collar and clean hands seem to have symbolic value in the prestige structures of industrialized nations, male homosexuals may gravitate toward such occupations to partially offset their socially discreditable condition. Instances of excessive, and probably defensive, pretentiousness by gay "ribbon clerks" provide some impressionistic support for this interpretation of gay occupational choices. The similar condition of "white-collar gentility" described by Frazier (1957, pp. 76–78) for the black bourgeoisie suggests that a minority group may parody the attributes of "respectability" of the dominant group in the society.

An hypothesis closely related to the striving for gentility suggested by Karlen is that such lower white-collar occupational choices represent a desire for "niceness." "The stress on 'niceness' in upward striving families often takes a toll in children's aggressiveness and sexuality" (Karlen 1971, p. 514). To the extent that such "gentility" and "niceness" motivations are important in the occupational choices of male homosexuals, it seems that they may incur a cost in terms of income. Although lower white-collar jobs may have some of the symbolic trappings of respectability, they often are quite low paid; frequently workers in such jobs receive much lower wages than unionized blue-collar workers. While the strength of gentility motivations among male homosexuals in North America cannot be estimated from the data in any of the studies cited above, both impressionistic evidence and the fact that such motivations seem to operate in the general population (Blau and Duncan 1967, pp. 62-63) suggest some support for this line of argument.

An alternative hypothesis is suggested by Gagnon and Simon (1973, pp. 154–57), who state that "certain marginal, low-paying, white collar jobs" facilitate a homosexual life-style, whereas many professional and managerial positions are incompatible with that life-style. Lower white-collar and service jobs typically require limited commitments to the job in terms of time and afterwork activities. Thus having a service or lower white-collar job permits one to devote large amounts of time to the hedonistic culture of the gay world, that is, to "boozing and cruising," maintaining irregular hours, and traveling to other cities to "make the scene."

In contrast to the freedom for recreational pursuits that lower white-collar and service jobs provide, upper white-collar jobs may constrain male homosexuals in both their visibility as homosexuals and their participation in the gay social world. Gagnon and Simon (1973, pp. 154–55) and Leznoff and Westley (1956) have suggested that because their exposure as homosexuals would often be disastrous occupationally, gays in these occupations are more covert in their participation in the gay world. They limit their amount of participation and resist the call of gay hedonism. Male homosexuals in upper white-collar occupations may visit cities other than the one they work in on weekends and holidays in order to participate in gay social worlds, or they may combine travel for business with "cruising and boozing." Briefly the Gagnon and Simon thesis is that there is an incompatibility between participation in the gay world and occupational achievement. Time constraints force a choice between the two sets of activities.

To the extent that there is a negative effect on both participation in the gay social world and high visibility of participation, it would be rational to choose a service or lower white-collar occupation, where sexual orientation is less important to employers or co-workers. However, there is some evidence that participation in gay social worlds may not have as occupationally destructive an effect as Gagnon and Simon have suggested. The fact that such a large percentage of male homosexuals have been able to acquire high educational levels provides a hint that this line of argument has limited utility in explaining the occupational distributions. If participation in gay social worlds were such a substantial drawback to occupational achievement, it would seem that such participation would also interfere with educational achievement.

While Gagnon and Simon could argue that excessive participation in the gay community only comes later in life, after most of one's education has been completed, and, hence, is a liability only to occupational attainment, their own assertions, plus other data, do not support such an interpretation. Gagnon and Simon (1973, p. 146) argue that shortly after coming out, the gay male goes through a period in his career when he invests most of his energies in sex and socializing in the gay world. But the average age of coming out both in the Detroit sample and in Dank's (1971) study is approximately 19 years of age. Thus entering the gay social world seems to precede or to occur at the same time as college attendance and, therefore, could be expected to have a maximal effect on college attendance. Yet this does not seem to be the case.

Data reported by Weinberg and Williams (1974, pp. 224-26) seem to disconfirm the thesis of the destructiveness of participation in gay worlds. Their data reveal no relationship between occupational level and volume of participation in gay social worlds. Thus sheer volume of such participation—within limits—appears not to be a liability for occupational advancement. What does appear to be relevant to occupational advancement or its lack is the *visibility* of the gay person's participation. Both Weinberg and Williams (1974, pp. 224-26) and Leznoff and Westley (1956) reported that higher-status gay men were more covert in their participation with other gays. By being more covert, they were able to avoid discrimination against themselves by heterosexual employers and co-workers. Accordingly while heavy involvement in gay leisure activities may help to explain the occupational choices of some male homosexuals, such involvement in and of itself does not seem to be a great liability for advancement if one is not openly gay before heterosexual colleagues.

A condition limiting the social mobility of gays that has been unnoticed in the literature is that the mobility of one generation of gays cannot directly affect the status of the next generation. Since gay men have a very low reproduction rate and since, presumably, only a small proportion of their biological offspring would be gay, direct inheritance of economic level is impossible. This implies that gays cannot benefit from cumulative intergenerational upward mobility. Possibly this phenomenon can partly explain the relative lack of gays in the upper economic levels. The noninheritability of economic level between generations of gays also implies that gays of a later generation cannot be directly affected by the disadvantages of, or discriminations against, the preceding generation. Thus it seems that the occupational levels of gays are determined solely by the levels and mobility of the preceding generation of heterosexuals, plus their own mobility.

GETTING AHEAD GAY

While it appears that male homosexuals have high levels of educational attainment, they do not seem able to convert their educational attainment into higher-income or higher-status occupations. Rather they seem to cluster in the lower white-collar strata. If, as we have tried to show, the Gagnon and Simon thesis of occupational destructiveness is not a valid explanation of the occupational distribution of gays, job discrimination against gays offers itself as a likely explanation. Below we discuss the various forms in which that discrimination seems to manifest itself.

Discrimination against gays may be either direct, as in those instances where a gay male is fired or not promoted, or it may be indirect. Indirect discrimination is operative where gay males avoid entering certain lines of work in anticipation of discrimination. As argued earlier, gay males seem to avoid many blue-collar jobs because they anticipate discrimination. Other lines of work that are avoided appear to be police work, military service, business management, and professional sports. In such occupations, any known homosexual behavior or overt expression of sexual preference for other males is highly disapproved of or forbidden by law or administrative policies. For example, if after administrative review, some homosexual behavior is discovered, military officers and enlisted men can be discharged with less than honorable discharges, such discharges often entailing subsequent employment problems (Williams and Weinberg 1971). Similarly in selection of candidates for police work, many departments require that the candidate take polygraph tests in order to determine the candidate's sexual orientation. Some police departments even use past homosexual behavior as an indicator of tendencies to molest children. In the business world, some corporations require polygraph tests of their prospective managers in order to weed out those with homosexual orientations. Also, some firms will not hire single males over 30 years of age. In higher education, discrimination against gay teachers appears to be fairly common. Lipset and Ladd (1976) found in a national survey of professors that 40 percent of those professors 55 and older would "ban homosexual teachers," as compared with only 14 percent of those under 35. Since age and rank are highly correlated in academia, the greater discriminatory tendencies of the older professors implies greater discriminatory attitudes among full professors, chairmen, and administrators, that is, among those making personnel decisions. The discriminatory practices in certain occupations are fairly widely known, or anticipated, among male homosexuals. In consequence, many choose work environments where they may feel more secure.

West has suggested that some

> male homosexuals get themselves into occupations where suspected sexual deviation won't count too much against them. Designing, acting, personal service occupations (e.g., waiters, stewards, hairdressers) are thought to attract male homosexuals; and on account of this some normal young men decline to take up these careers (1967, p. 57).

The service jobs of male nursing, hospital orderly, and librarian should also be mentioned. While it is possible to interpret the concentration of gay males in these occupations as due to the "feminine" or "maternal" nature of these jobs, discrimination in other occupations is also a likely influence. Being barred from entering other types of work, either directly or indirectly, male homosexuals may choose those occupations where they feel the most secure. Thus discrimination in certain occupations may account for the concentrations of gays in other lines of work.

The above occupational processes appear to be similar to those that have resulted in high concentrations of blacks in certain sports (Edwards 1973, pp. 200-02). Due to discrimination in other occupations, sports has been one of the few lines of work permitting the possibility of long-distance social mobility for blacks from lower-income backgrounds. If discrimination were lessened in the better-paying occupations, the concentration of blacks in sports and of male homosexuals in the more "feminine" occupations would probably decline.

An additional effect of discrimination against gays is that some have gone in for self-employment (Weinberg and Williams 1974, pp. 227-28). Clearly self-employment offers substantial protection against discrimination. Typical lines of work for self-employed gays are those of hair dressing, barbering, pet care, floristry, and the ownership of a variety of other retail establishments. Such freedom from discrimination has probably fostered the growth of gay capitalism. Gays often tend to hire other gays as employees, either through friendship connections or due to sympathy for gays generally. An obvious consequence of this process is that gays may tend to be clustered, not only in certain lines of work but also within certain firms.

Direct job discrimination against male homosexuals appears to be somewhat infrequent, although far from rare. Weinberg and Williams (1974, p. 108) reported that "only" 16 percent of their respondents said that they had had "problems on any job . . . because people suspected or know that [they] were homosexual." Saghir and Robins also reported that 16 percent of their subjects "felt that homosexuality had an adverse effect on their jobs" (1973, p. 173). While 16 percent may not seem sufficiently high to reach a conclusion that there is substantial job discrimination against gay males, it is probably quite high to the gay man, who occasionally wonders whether he is to be among the 16 percent. In both of the studies cited above, those who said they had experienced job discrimination had experienced it directly through being fired or being asked to resign.

It is probable that direct job discrimination against gay males is substantially higher than reported in the studies above. Many male homosexuals may be discriminated against without their ever having known about it. Yet they are not hired and not promoted because of their sexual preferences. The reasons officially given usually present the appearance of being legitimate, for example, lack of experience, "overqualified," job already filled, "wouldn't fit in." Many administrators prefer to avoid the somewhat embarrassing situation of directly or publicly denying jobs to persons on the basis of sexual orientation. Other reasons for job denial are preferred. Consequently in studying job discrimination against gay persons, gays would often be the wrong ones to ask. Rather studies of employers would be better ways to get at such discriminatory processes.

Job discrimination against gays can occur either at the time of initial employment or afterwards, in decisions to retain or promote. The discriminatory processes operative at these times are somewhat different. At the time of initial hiring, most gays go to some length to avoid giving any indication of their sexual orientation. Typically they will avoid, if possible, mentioning their nonmarried state or their living arrangements. However, since almost all employers require information about marital status, even if only for tax purposes, concealment of this information is difficult. Many employers use marital status as a major indicator of sexual preference, or at least of emotional stability. Some even have policies not to hire single persons or single males at managerial levels.

The problem of concealing a single marital status becomes increasingly difficult with age. While employers are willing to consider being single a legitimate condition for those under approximately 30, beyond that age, it is often taken as a symptom of abnormality. Singleness beyond 30 is considered a more certain indicator of abnormality among males than among females. If a woman is older and unmarried, it is presumed that the reason for it is that she could not get married due either to personal unattractiveness or lack of opportunity. If a male is single and over 30, it is presumed that the reason he did not marry was because he chose not to and that he is an alcoholic, emotionally unstable, or gay. Both of these interpretations flow rather directly from traditional sex-role conceptions, which view men as dominant and aggressive and women as powerless creatures of circumstance.

While it is likely that most male homosexuals, if reasonably young, are able to negotiate successfully the initial hiring process, the problems of retention and advancement become more fraught with hurdles. Although it is possible to control much of the information given out about one's self at the time of initial hiring, more information is gradually revealed to employers and work associates over a period of time. To some of the latter, one's continued nonmarried state may become an object of curiosity or a sign of homosexuality. Similarly one's living arrangements, friends, practice of not dating females, style of dress, and general deportment can become indicators of sexual orientation. In order to become labeled as "homosexual" or "probably homosexual" by work associates, it is not necessary that many of the work associates be sensitive to, or conjecture about, one's sexual preference. One or two items of information that become known to only one or a few co-workers will typically be sufficient for the question to be communicated and raised among the wider set of work associates. Thus 61 percent of Weinberg and Williams's respondents said that at least some of their work associates were familiar with their sexual orientation, although only 27 percent of their employers were so aware (1974, p. 105). In general, for the majority of gays, their sexual orientation is often known or suspected at work, and thus the opportunity for employers to engage in discrimination later is increased.

Sometimes the employer's awareness may come about only after a positive relationship with the gay employee has developed and after the employee has consciously communicated his orientation to his employer. Alternatively the employer will often develop an awareness of the employee's sexual orientation despite the attempts of the employee to conceal it.

Promotion of an employee who is known or suspected of being homosexual is often a particularly problematic event both for the employee and the employer. Many persons, particularly males, find the idea of having a gay boss threatening and repugnant. Popular conceptions of gay males as "weak, effeminate, and sick" are strongly incompatible with the notion of gays having positions of authority. Further a male homosexual's nonmarital status can be used to mount the argument that since he has no dependents, he does not merit the prestige and salary associated with promotion. If there is competition among similarly situated co-workers for a given promotion, it is virtually certain that heterosexual competitors for the promotion will attempt to introduce sexual orientation as a job-relevant criterion.

Of course, the gay employee may have some resources at the time of consideration for promotion. Over the period of his employment at a given firm or agency, he will probably have acquired a number of heterosexual friends at work. Also, there will now be available to employers and work associates evidence of work competence. Information that the gay employee is competent and likeable creates obstacles to the immediate use of sexual orientation as prima facie evidence of nonemployability or nonpromotability. As Farrell and Nelson (1976) have argued, it is easier to apply negative labels in secondary relationships to persons about whom little is known, for example, at the time of initial hiring. Thus ignorance facilitates discrimination. Accordingly due to familiarity with the gay employee and his work record, it is possible, with some luck, that he may be judged on his merits.

A good work record and having friends at work, however, will not guarantee success on the job. In those types of work where the employee's personality or colleagiality are considered important, there is more opportunity for the introduction of prejudicial criteria into personnel decisions. Even when most of one's co-workers like the gay employee, the presence of one or a few persons who dislike him for his sexual orientation can be sufficient evidence of a lack of colleagiality to prevent promotion or retention. Further although the employer or co-workers may say that they do not care if the employee is gay, they may also be concerned about public relations and the opinions of groups external to the employing organization. Some gay men have had their careers cut short because their employers were concerned about the views of the public, of customers, or of the board.

To the extent that there is differential job evaluation of gay employees in the workplace, the male homosexual must be substantially better than his heterosexual colleagues in order to receive "equal treatment." In order to protect himself from discrimination, he attempts to make his work record impeccable and to perform at his maximum capacity. Similar processes appear to be operative among blacks in professional sports. In his study of professional sports, Edwards (1973, pp. 190-205) documented that the average performance records of blacks on a variety of criteria are better than those of whites. His explanation of these differences is that the criteria for blacks are higher than those for whites, with the result that blacks must be better than whites in order to be employed in professional sports. Similar processes are probably operative in many of the workplaces of gays, and gays employed in higher-status jobs probably have better work records than their heterosexual colleagues.

While gays have many disadvantages in the workplace, they also seem to have some special resources facilitating occupational success. Lack of ties to spouses and children and frequently weakened bonds with relatives (Saghir and Robins 1973, pp. 170-71) allow them greater geographical mobility. Thus they are generally freer to move long distances in search of better jobs or to accept transfers imposed by employers. Further their lack of obligations to spouses, children, and relatives enables them to devote large amounts of weekend and evening time to their occupations. They also are freed from the tensions of balancing work demands against the demands of spouses and children. Through utilizing such time resources, they seem often to be able to offset the disadvantages imposed through workplace discrimination.

Whether the gay male devotes his time to occupational achievement or to the pleasures of gay hedonism is probably an individual choice, conditioned substantially by the nature of his work. Higher-status jobs demand more of a psychological (and time) investment than do the more routine blue-collar or service jobs (Hall 1969, pp. 47-53; Dubin 1956, pp. 131-42). While the higher-status jobs call forth more effort from employees, it is likely that gays have more to give to their jobs due to their freedom from familial obligations. Thus many homosexuals in high-status positions may be "married" to their work, while participating only selectively in the gay leisure world.

A final observation should be made about the recent entry of females and gay males into formerly "alien" occupations. With the rise of the women's movement and associated efforts to sexually integrate occupations formerly closed to one sex or the other, females and gay males appear to have moved into certain new occupations. We suggest that a significant number of the "pioneers" in previously all-female or all-male occupations are gay persons. For gay men, the relevant occupations are airline steward, telephone operator, and nursing. For gay women, the relevant occupations are police work, cab driving, and law. A plausible hypothesis for the willingness of homosexuals to enter such occupations earlier than heterosexuals is their lack of commitment, or even opposition to, traditional conceptions of sex-role appropriate occupations.

CONCLUSIONS

In the preceding pages, it was suggested that the principal resources for male homosexuals in an occupational world dominated by heterosexuals are their higher-than-average educational attainment and freedom from domestic commitments. These have enabled some male homosexuals to partially offset the frequent discrimination against them. Gays in higher white-collar occupations often have better records of job performance than heterosexuals.

Because of discrimination, male homosexuals are distributed quite unevenly in the occupational structure. They have tended to avoid blue-collar jobs with traditionally defined macho codes. When they do occupy such jobs, they typically are highly secretive of their sexual orientation. One effect of such secretiveness has been the lack of visible occupational role models for male homosexuals aspiring to these occupations. For example, only after David Kopay, a professional football player, came out was there any visibility for male homosexuals in this traditionally macho occupation. Only after such authors as Merle Miller and Christopher Isherwood, a legislator such as Elaine Noble in Massachusetts, military personnel such as Sergeant Leonard Matlovich, and other persons in high-status occupations became leaders in the gay liberation movement or spoke and wrote of their homosexuality have positive role models been available (as opposed to historical figures, such as Walt Whitman).

Traditionally, male homosexuals have tended to be somewhat clustered in occupations where they felt secure against discrimination and where the nature of the jobs were defined as "feminine." Such concentrations have tended, in a self-fulfilling manner, to confirm the popular stereotypes of male homosexuals as effeminate.

10

GAY LIBERATION: ACTION AND REACTION

Homosexuals in America have been labeled *sick, deviant,* and *criminal* for hundreds of years. How does a social movement develop among such deviants, with the goals of changing the social status of the deviants, the laws relating to their behavior, and the attitude of the general public toward that deviant behavior? And how do countermovements develop to challenge those hard won changes in legal and informal norms and practices? In this chapter, those questions are explored through an analysis of the gay liberation movement, as it developed in the United States and Canada after 1950.*

PRECONDITIONS AND PRECIPITATING FACTORS

Gusfield (1968, p. 445) has defined a social movement as "an explicit and conscious indictment of whole or part of the social order, together with a

---

An earlier version of parts of this chapter appeared in "Gay Liberation: An Overview," *Journal of Voluntary Action Research* 2 (Winter 1973): 24-35.

*Several sources were used in preparing this chapter. Leaders of some gay organizations in San Francisco were interviewed. Published interviews with gay leaders were also examined (for example, Tobin and Wicker's *The Gay Crusaders: In-Depth Interviews with Fifteen Homosexuals* (1972). Articles on homosexuality by social scientists were examined to see if there were any changes in perspectives on homosexuality among the "experts." Survey data from several studies were used to obtain indications of the acceptance of the goals of the gay liberation movement by various segments of the population. Katz's *Gay American History* (1976) is a pioneering anthology on the history of homosexuality in America.

conscious demand for change. It has an *ideological* component—that is, a set of ideas which specify discontents, prescribe solutions and justify change." One of the tasks of a social scientist is to specify the preconditions that facilitate the development of such social movements. Certainly discontent in a population before a movement emerges is a necessary precondition. Frequently, however, this discontent is defined in purely private terms. Indeed it may be useful for agents of social control to encourage this private definition of the source and solutions to life problems. When people begin to redefine their private ills in terms of public policies and social definition of their situation and when they seek to change the attitudes and behavior of the public, rather than seeking salvation in themselves as individuals, the basis of a political movement is laid.

One important precondition of gay liberation was a *political climate* that was tolerant enough to allow explicitly and openly gay organizations to exist without continuous harassment. Political regimes may break up or prohibit gay gatherings in places such as bars, store fronts, and homes. Argentina during the 1970s and the USSR since the 1930s have been such nations. Driving homosexual behavior underground does not stop it, of course. Indeed some forms of homosexual behavior, such as the "tearoom trade" described by Humphreys (1970), which is especially abhorred by many heterosexuals, may be increased by political harassment. Where homosexual behavior is oppressed, most male homosexuals continue to "pass" as heterosexual. When the costs of openly declaring one's homosexuality are great, there is little incentive to form explicitly gay political organizations.

In political regimes that tolerate dissent by those seeking alternative lifestyles, such as was found in America after 1960, gays may feel a sense of rising expectations with regard to the possibility of their social and legal status being changed through use of the political processes. Gay literature is filled with references to the successes of blacks in changing their social and legal status. When persons see that change is possible, that others have been successful, then they are invited to change their own situation through collective action.

Individuals sharing a distressing condition must somehow make connections with each other and explore the possibilities for change. This requires the existence of a social world of shared communication. Shibutani (1955, p. 566) defines a social world as "a culture area, the boundaries of which are set neither by territory nor by formal group membership but by the limits of effective communication." If we conceive of a social world as a series of overlapping communication networks, some formal, some informal, then we can understand how ideas may be shared among participants. The social world, and particularly the new formal organization that may develop within a social world, becomes a forum for exploring alternative definitions of self and society. It provides both security and encouragement for potential participants.

This is not to imply that a social movement will emerge out of every social world of the discontented. The social world of homosexuality existed for at least

100 years in one form or another in major American cities before it began to be transformed into gay liberation. Although it is virtually impossible to write a full history of underground behavior, there are accounts of gay bars, whorehouses, and "cruising grounds" that operated during the nineteenth century in American cities (Drew and Drake 1969, p. 141).

The written word is important in the transformation of a social world into a social movement. The first-known gay magazine in the United States, *One*, began publishing in 1951. One of the first battles of the beginning gay liberation movement (then called the *homophile movement*) was with the U.S. Post Office Department. The Post Office refused to deliver gay literature. After several court cases, such literature was delivered (there is some evidence that the postal agents and the Federal Bureau of Investigation keep track of some gay liberation mailings and leaders).

Publications such as *One* in the 1950s, *Vector* during the 1960s, and a host of publications during the 1970s provided a written history of gay life in America (including published interviews and memoirs of gays) going back to at least the 1920s. This attempt to rediscover and, in some ways, to reinterpret the past in order to discover the roots of present conditions is an important function of such ingroup journals in any social movement. A second function of the written media is to keep readers informed of current political events affecting the group. Gays living in small towns in Iowa, for example, could not keep informed of demonstrations and manifestos by gay spokesmen in New York City except through the gay media. The heterosexual press ignores many social movements, and until about 1970, most of the major newspapers and other media ignored the gay liberation movement. A separate press can both spread the word and serve as a forum for the exchange of ideas.

Besides the preconditions for a social movement, precipitating events may be important, because mobilization of potential activists can occur around the conditions highlighted by these events. For example, the Santa Barbara oil spill served as a rallying point for the environmental movement. Two such events will serve as examples for the gay movement. Both of them involved gay bars. As indicated elsewhere in this book, gay bars have been central to the gay social world. The policies of public agencies, such as the police and liquor boards, are important to the existence of these bars in all towns in North America. The arbitrary and discriminatory actions of these public agencies toward gay bars have occasioned bitter hostility among gays. Using plainclothes policemen to arrest patrons in gay bars for "soliciting" or some other vague crime was common in many urban areas until after 1970.

The first incident of protest occurred in San Francisco (Achilles 1967, p. 236). The Black Cat Bar was an old gay watering spot in North Beach. For years, the state alcoholic beverage control board had attempted to close the bar. After many legal appeals, the California Supreme Court ruled in 1954 that homosexuals, if properly behaved, had the legal right to congregate. When the Black

Cat was finally closed by the board in 1964 for "lewd and indecent acts" among the patrons, the closing attracted a large coverage in the local press. The climate of public tolerance in San Francisco, which was manifested in the case of the Black Cat, may help to explain why the gay liberation movement found a receptive audience among heterosexuals in that city. Achilles (1967, p. 237) gives an account of the closing:

> The public response [to the closing], while it manifested more amusement and curiosity than actual sympathy, seemed an illustration of the sophisticated and liberal attitude upon which San Franciscans base their city's image. . . . This self-conscious liberalism has attracted a large homosexual population and the gay life in the city is unusually visible.

The second incident that serves as an example of a precipitating event began with the usual raid by police. The Christopher Street riots, or the Stonewall riots (named for the bar in Greenwich Village where the incident occurred) were precipitated by a police raid in June 1969. Gays fought back; they shouted slogans and resisted arrest (Teal 1971, p. 17). In this case, instead of there being merely some public interest in a bar raid, formal organizations began to be developed almost immediately afterwards. Gay leaders and gay newspapers seized upon this event as heralding a new era of "gay resistance," and demonstrations and marches were organized in a number of large American cities in succeeding years each June to commemorate the event. These later demonstrations came to be called *Gay Pride Parades*. A few American cities have recently given official recognition to Gay Pride Week, for example, Portland, Detroit, San Francisco, and Seattle.

PERSPECTIVE ON ORGANIZATION

While the gay liberation movement began in informal discussions, it moved on to formal organizations, which first had to fight for the right to use the mails or to exist at all. One of the first organizations of male homosexuals was formed in Chicago about 1924. Apparently the leaders were soon arrested by the police, and nothing else developed until the 1960s in that major city (Katz 1976, pp. 385-96). In 1950-51, the Mattachine Society and One, Inc., were organized in Los Angeles. The leaders of Mattachine considered themselves daring at the time to organize for political action and even more radical to suggest the integration of gays into the larger society and to define gays as a minority group (Teal 1971, p. 43; Katz 1976, pp. 406-20).

Most of the gay social and political organizations have been local, since they usually have had neither a national organizing campaign nor the ability to sustain a national membership. Local organizations are realistic as a strategy in that the constraints of local government agencies, such as police departments, and local public opinion are the crucial factors with which gays must deal. At the local level, however, organizations sometimes rise and fall with great rapidity.

One safe way to establish a continuing basis for an organization is to provide social service functions. One is then not open to criticism if political tactics fail, and there are always people who need and want one's services. Thus SIR in San Francisco for a number of years provided weekly dances and theater (camp musicals) for gays. Political nights for local candidates to speak to the gay community were considered a great innovation when begun in the late 1960s. But in the 1970s, many disco bars, baths, and other community service organizations opened, thereby destroying the semimonopoly SIR once had on gay social services.

While SIR had over 1,000 members in 1971 and candidates in municipal elections openly courted the votes of gays by appearing at SIR candidate nights, by 1976 the organization was bankrupt. The unwillingness of leaders to engage in demonstrations as well as internal dissension and arson (which burned out a large part of the SIR social center) destroyed the organization.

The rise of new organizations in the late 1960s, such as the Gay Activist Alliance (1969-70) and the Gay Switchboard in Berkely, provided an outlet for some younger gays, who criticized SIR and the whole homophile movement. These younger gays were concerned with establishing the legitimacy of an alternative life-style for gays that was not patterned after heterosexual institutions. They were critical of gays "marrying" each other and were particularly critical of SIR's ties with the gay bars, which they called *ghetto bars*. For these gays, the gay liberation movement began with the Stonewall riots. In San Francisco, the sentiments of this segment of gay liberation were expressed in Wittman's article, "Refugees from America: A Gay Manifesto" (1972).

The development of a separate gay church was another "radical" innovation for the time. Troy Perry, a gay fundamentalist minister, argued that gay churches could be important because other reform movements, including the civil rights movement among blacks, had their own churches. Through this church, gays would develop a consciousness of themselves as self-respecting individuals who were accepted by other people. And through the church, political action would be formulated. To these ends, Perry entitled his autobiography *The Lord is My Shepherd and He Knows I'm Gay* (1972). He has led fasts, marches, and demonstrations in cities across North America.

The rise and decline of several gay organizations in New York City and San Francisco indicates that at different periods, different organizations could be considered as being in the vanguard. A multiplicity of organizations has allowed activists to be drawn from many areas. Although differing in ideology and tactics, gay organizations were formed to (1) provide social, legal, and welfare services not provided by the heterosexual community to self-acknowledged gays; (2) explicitly attack the mental illness and criminal models of homosexuality, which have been part of the conventional wisdom of American public agencies; (3) negotiate with public agencies to reduce repression and change the social and legal status of homosexuals; and (4) help gays redefine their self-identities in more positive terms than those traditionally available in North American culture.

Humphreys has argued that fragmentation is a grave weakness of the gay movement. He described the demise of the North American Conference of Homophile Organizations (NACHO) in 1970 at length. To Humphreys, its demise

> illustrates the futility of attempting to impose old organizational forms upon nascent social movements. . . . The wonder is not that so many homophile organizations fail but that so many do so well. Subject to rip-offs, embezzlement, panic, and ideological conflict, these marginal groups are doubly jeopardized by the lack of sanctions and rewards that might combine to shore them up (1972, p. 97).

Humphreys was writing from the perspective of the late 1960s, when the controversies over the Vietnam War, hippies, and student revolts were still raging.

By the late 1970s, the gay movement had become institutionalized and stronger, despite the passing of NACHO. The above-described specialization of gay organizations on the local level functioned to strengthen the movement rather than to fragment it and to bring more recruits to some kind of political action. On the national level, coalitions of organizations and lobbying groups were institutionalized with boards of directors, business meetings, and paid executive directors. The Gay Rights National Lobby and the National Gay Task Force worked in concert and without acrimony to lobby the administrative and legislative branches of the federal government.

One of the movement's emerging cleavages in the late 1970s has been between the gay churches and service organizations and the profit-oriented businesses, such as bars and baths. Gay churches, such as MCC, Integrity (Anglican), and Dignity (Catholic), made remarkable gains in their membership in the 1970s. For example, Dignity doubled in membership between 1975 and 1977, despite the continued disapproval of the Catholic hierarchy and the silencing of the noted theologian Father John McNeil on the topic of homosexuality. While differing in theology among themselves, the several gay churches have collectively emphasized loving relationships between homosexuals, permanent coupling, and social services. They disagree with the individualism, hedonism, and sexual adventurism of the bar and bath culture. It is possible that by the 1980s, the gay bar will cease to be the central institution of gay culture and that churches or other organizations will assume that role. If that occurs and if gay intellectuals begin to explore how many businessmen serving the gay community have used the tools of advertising, control of markets, and techniques of people-management (such as the playing of loud music in bars in order to inhibit conversation and encourage drinking), it is possible that the two cultures will conflict more openly.

In the 1970s, gay persons began forming caucuses within established heterosexual organizations. Besides the gay affiliates of the churches, a number of professional organizations sprouted gay caucuses. Examples are the caucuses of the American Sociological Association, American Library Association, the ACLU, the American Bar Association, and the American Anthropological Association. Some of these caucuses sought changes in the profession or supported the cases of individual women and gay men. Others sought to use the profession to change the attitudes of the larger society. For example, the sociologists' Gay Caucus successfully sought to enlist the American Sociological Association in forming a task force in 1977 to review the literature on homosexuality and to make public research that disputed the myths and stereotypes fosted by antigay spokespersons, such as Anita Bryant.

Writers such as Humphreys (1972) and Sagarin (1969), who predicted the decline of the gay movement, were talking about an early and somewhat exotic phase of the movement, in which radicals and drag queens were significant and highly visible components. Sagarin may have been correct about a small segment of the movement when he said that the contradictions in it were likely to prevent it from becoming other than "isolated and cultist, sinking deeper into untenable ideological distortion as it proclaimed only what its members wanted to hear and what they need (or feel they need) to believe" (1969, pp. 108–10). But the second, broader, and less radical gay movement of the 1970s was characterized more by pragmatic, realistic political strategies, seasoned leadership, and stated goals that were possible to obtain within the structure of a liberal, democratic nation.

Instead of dying out or becoming weak through factionalism, as some had predicted in 1972-73, the gay movement was more vital a decade later than other movements spawned in the late 1960s. There seem to be several reasons for the continued strength and recent resurgence of the movement. Yearwood and Weinberg (1977) have argued that there are strong sociological parallels between black and gay organizations and that gays have learned political lessons from the black movement. Also, the more recent upsurge of attacks on gays—the Anita Bryant phenomenon and the general backlash against liberations movements in North America in the late 1970s—have led some gays to realize the precariousness of their gains made during the last decade and the need for political strength and organizational coherence. Further the general level of sophistication of the gay leadership may have increased over the last decade.

In pursuit of their goals, the organizations of the gay movement sought for allies in other organizations and movements. Probably the most helpful source of support for the movement has been the women's movement. In searching for other allies, they have been able to penetrate only a thin segment of middle-class, liberal Americans. Some support has come from the ACLU. Ministers and laymen in some high-status Protestant churches have worked to have church positions reviewed on homosexuality. Both the United Church of Christ and the Society of Friends have published books in which homosexuality has been redefined from a sin to a "state of loving one's own" (Weltge 1969; Heron 1963). Both the Presbyterian and Unitarian-Universalist churches have taken steps to explicitly welcome homosexuals into their congregations.

Nowhere have the tenuous relationships between social movements and the gay liberation movement been more evident than in the reactions of the so-called counterculture, the black and socialist movements. Even the Sexual Freedom League in San Francisco had some internal battles before homosexual expression was accepted within the group. By 1971, however, the underground press had begun to carry articles on police suppression of homosexuals and the place of homosexuals as victims of a police state (*The Militant*, April 16, 1971). During the 1970–71 school year, the National Student Association established a special national office to help gay liberation groups forming on college campuses (*Advocate*, February 2, 1972). There were some very brief alliances with socialist groups. Howard has argued that "it is clear that the gays were swept up in a radical movement which they had not initiated and that the fate of gay liberation hinges on the fate of that radical movement in general" (1974, p. 135). However, the lack of support for homosexuals—or even opposition—by leftist groups indicates the inaccuracy of Howard's statement. Also, as leftist groups declined during the 1970s, the gay movement grew.

The allies of gay liberation have come from diverse parts of North American culture. Some leftist political groups, Jewish groups, some Protestant churches, the ACLU, and some scholarly and professional associations, such as the American Psychological Association, the American Sociological Association, the American Federation of Teachers, and national librarians' associations have passed resolutions at various times in support of some of the goals of gay liberation, including passage of consensual sex acts, equal employment opportunities, and an end to police harrassment.

SUMMARY OF FACTORS CONDUCIVE TO THE DEVELOPMENT OF GAY LIBERATION

In summary, the following factors were identified as having been especially conducive to the development of gay liberation after 1950 in North America. All of these factors interacted to produce a favorable climate for the development and continuation of gay collective social action and social organization.

1. The political regimes and police of some cities allowed homosexuals to congregate openly and to organize for political action.
2. There was a general growth in North America in a liberal attitude toward alternative life-styles, including their sexual aspects, and an increasing willingness to discuss sexual behavior.
3. Some gay intellectuals questioned traditional practices and attitudes and encouraged the search for a new collective identity in their writings.
4. Voluntary organizations to propagate gay liberation ideas on a regular basis and sustain goal-directed activity were formed.
5. The development of new channels of communication, such as specialized newspapers, which carried the message of gay liberation and current political events affecting gays, greatly broadened the number of potential recruits to the movement.
6. Successful role models were available for gay liberation from other social movements active in America during the 1960s.
7. At least a few charismatic leaders emerged who could arouse potential activists by their personal appeal.
8. Some high-status individuals and established organizations supported some of the goals of gay liberation, helping homosexuals organize and negotiate with the power holders in the United States and Canada.
9. Competition and interaction between segmentary and decentralized movement organizations made the gay movement stronger and less likely to become conservative as quickly as would be likely if only one organization were dominant in the movement.
10. A developing collective identity embodied explicit criticism of the status quo and provided a justification and rationale for homosexual life-styles.

SURVEY DATA ON HOMOPHOBIA

Several surveys completed between 1970 and 1977 provide cross-sectional data on attitudes and opinions about homosexuality in America and Canada. Levitt and Klassen (1974), using a 1970 probability sample of U.S. adults, concluded that prejudice against homosexuals consists of more than just esthetic repugnance. Substantial majorities of respondents in 1970 would deny homosexuals employment in teaching, government service, or medicine, and believe that homosexuals seek to become sexually involved with children, are security risks, and that homosexual acts are "vulgar and offensive." Some 46 percent did not agree that homosexuals should be allowed to organize for social and recreational purposes. Some 60 percent disapproved of actions by state legislatures to decriminalize sexual acts between persons of the same sex.

These findings from the 1970 national survey differ little in substance from surveys on more localized populations done during the 1960s. In a 1965 survey (Simmons 1965), 49 percent of the persons sampled labeled homosexual as *deviant*, more than any other so labeled on a list presented to the respondents including rapist and thief. In a 1966 study of the San Francisco area, a liberal urban area, the researchers (Rooney and Gibbons 1966) found support for changing laws so homosexual conduct between consenting adults would be legal (55 percent), but only 38 percent agreed that "homosexuals should be allowed to organize in order to obtain the civil liberties they are denied" (1966, p. 410). The authors concluded that their data

> seem to add up to a picture of middle-class citizens who would allow women to obtain abortions fairly easily at the same time they would have homosexuals and drug addicts hounded and harassed. The Society for Human Abortion is faced with a more congenial social audience than is true of the Mattachine Society, the Daughters of Bilitis, Synanon Foundation (an organization for ex-drug addicts) and those groups staging "puff-ins" and other agitation in favor of legalized marijuana (Rooney and Gibbons 1966, p. 410).

In a study in Washington State, an attempt was made to discern if judges and laymen shared a commonly accepted moral standard (McConnell and Martin 1969). The authors asked state court judges, members of a Kiwanis Club, college students, and a sample of residents of Spokane to rank 35 crimes, ranging from murder to jaywalking, as to the seriousness of the offense. They compared this to the legal ranking of the crime by severity of penalty. The Spokane residents and college students ranked homosexuality between consenting adults second in severity (murder was ranked first), while Kiwanis members ranked it third (behind murder and armed robbery) and the judges ranked it tenth. At the time of the survey, the legal rank of severity of punishment for acts between consenting adults (oral copulation) was third (behind murder and armed robbery).

What happened after the gay liberation movement received full publicity in the early 1970s? Do later surveys indicate changes in the attitudes of the American people toward homosexuality? Analysis of a 1974 nationwide survey (Nyberg and Alston 1977) indicates little change in attitudes by white adult residents of the United States. In the total sample, 72 percent believed that homosexual relations were "always wrong." Males and females were equal in their rejection.*

On selected sociodemographic characteristics, there was considerable variation in attitudes toward homosexuality. Catholics and Protestants were more

---

*The question on the 1974 survey was: "What about relations between two adults of the same sex—do you think they are always wrong, wrong only sometimes, or not wrong at all?"

disapproving than Jews and "no religion" persons, but these latter groups were small subsamples. The authors suggested that regular church attendance is correlated with negative attitudes toward homosexual relations among Methodists, Presbyterians, Lutherans, and other Protestants, but active church attendance for Baptists and Episcopalians was correlated with less prejudice. Liberalism toward homosexuality in the 1974 study was correlated with liberalism toward premarital and extramarital sex, but still 48 percent of those sampled said premarital sex was "not wrong at all," while also saying that homosexual sex was "always wrong."

Education, age, and size of city of residence were related to attitudes toward homosexuals and homosexual acts. All of the national surveys indicated that the larger the urban area, the more educated the respondent, and the younger the respondent, the more likely he or she was to favor rights for homosexuals. These findings of correlations between demographic characteristics and opinions on homosexuality were consistent with a large number of other surveys, which show greater tolerance for minorities by civic leaders, urbanites, Jews, and more educated segments of the U.S. and Canadian populations (DeVall 1974).

By far the most extensive analysis of the intercorrelations of demographic variables with opinions toward homosexuals was Sherrill's (1977) analysis of a 1973 survey.* In this sample, 70 percent agreed that "homosexuality is always wrong." However, a majority of respondents stated some belief in gay rights: 60 percent would allow a gay to speak in their town; 53.5 percent would not remove a gay book from the library; and 47.3 percent would allow a gay to teach in college. Sherrill went beyond other researchers in his scaling attitudes toward dissenters. Developing a "puritanism index," Sherrill found Americans in 1973 to be puritanical (74 percent, for example, had not seen an X-rated movie in the previous year, and 71 percent believed sexual material led people to commit rape). However, of the most puritanical respondents, 17.9 percent supported all gay rights, and among the least puritanical, 89 percent supported all gay rights. Racist attitudes, puritanical attitudes, and sexism were all positively correlated, according to Sherrill. Homophobia was part of a "broader pattern of intolerance"; there were "no three wholly distinct dimensions" (Sherrill 1977, p. 35). As in all the other surveys to date, Sherrill found education was related to more positive support for gay rights. He observed that "many aspects of oppo-

---

*The National Opinion Research Corporation, as part of its 1973 annual poll of social attitudes, asked 1,504 respondents questions on civil liberties drawn from Stouffer's *Communism, Conformity and Civil Liberties* (1955). The questions listed "homosexuals," "socialists," "atheists," and "admitted communists" and asked if these people could "speak in your town," if "books by these people [should be removed] from the library," and if they should be allowed "to teach in college."

sition to gay rights and civil rights in general take the guise of 'protecting youth' from 'corrupting' influences" (Sherrill 1977, p. 40).

From their analysis of the 1974 survey on attitudes toward homosexuality, Nyberg and Alston suggested that there is no "strong evidence that a moderation in public attitudes has occurred . . . and that liberal attitudes exist in socio-democraphic 'pockets' that are unrelated to either sex or age differences" (1977, p. 106). They suggested that attitudes toward homosexuals will remain relatively constant in the future, because demographic trends indicate less in-migration to urban areas. Smaller towns are increasing in population, while urban core cities are declining. There is a decreasing aspiration toward a college education by high school students. Thus the liberalizing effect of college (much disputed, of course) will not be as prevalent in the future as during the 1960s.

Contrary to these conclusions are the results of 1977 U.S. (July) and Canadian surveys (May), both conducted by the Gallup organization. In the U.S. sample, the question was asked, "Do you think homosexuals should or should not have equal rights in terms of job opportunities?" Some 56 percent said "yes, should have." There was no significant difference between men and women, but the larger the city (500,000 or more), the more was the support of gay job rights. Unmarried rather than married, younger more than older, and Catholics more than Protestants supported equal job opportunities. The college-educated person (64 percent) was much more supportive than a person with only a grade school education (36 percent). However, when asked about specific occupations, respondents were less supportive: only 27 percent thought homosexuals should be elementary school teachers; only 36 percent thought priests or ministers could be homosexuals; 44 percent thought medical doctors should be allowed to be homosexual; and 68 percent said it was all right for sales people to be homosexual. In the Canadian survey, 52 percent said homosexuals should be protected from job discrimination under a proposed Federal Human Rights Acts.

Given the findings of the 1977 Gallup polls, it appears that opinions toward some gay rights among the U.S. and Canadian populations have changed during the past decade, with more favorable attitudes by a majority of respondents than before. Whether the recent resurgence of conservatism in North America, decline in college attendance, and move to fundamentalist religions will signal a renewed homophobia in the population is difficult to determine. Certainly the organized opposition to homosexuals has become more vocal in the late 1970s than at any time since the McCarthy era of the 1950s. In the following section, the organized opposition to gay liberation is discussed.

ANTIGAY CRUSADES AND NEOCONSERVATISM

During the latter half of the 1970s, a resurgence of conservative populism developed in the United States similar to that of the 1920s, when the Ku Klux

Klan (KKK) and other racist, conservative, Christian, and nationalistic organizations attacked blacks, Jews, and Communists. One part of this neoconservatism has been a number of crusades against homosexuals. Since the above-cited survey data show that homosexuals are condemned by majorities of almost all segments of the U.S. population, they constituted a politically vulnerable part of the set of newer movements and cultures composing the liberal and cultural left. The successes of the gay movement in getting consenting adults laws and nondiscrimination ordinances in employment and housing passed served as concrete issues around which conservative elements organized.

Neoconservatism organized itself to fight a wide variety of issues, only one of which was that of gay rights. These issues included the Equal Rights Amendment (ERA), bussing, the Panama Canal Treaty, environmental laws relating to land use, prayer in public schools, abortion, government regulation, and gays. There are some indications that the gay rights and women's movements were "targeted" by conservative action groups because they were considered highly vulnerable. Clearly the presence of lesbians among the supporters of the ERA has received considerable attention from conservative opponents of that amendment.

The thrust of latter-day neoconservatism has been principally moral rather than economic. It has used the family as its major symbolic rallying point. It perceives gay rights, women's rights, bussing, and abortion as threats to the American family. As a value, the family, perhaps even more than the flag, has been highly serviceable, apparently being capable of transforming the "gas-guzzling car" into the "family automobile." The family is one of the principal components of the set of "old middle-class values" so dear in conservative rhetoric.

These perceived threats to the family have served as the points for launching a series of "symbolic crusades." Gusfield (1963), in his book on the Prohibitionist movement, described a symbolic crusade as a moral movement by which one status group attempts to preserve its life-style and defend its status against threats from groups with different life-styles.*

In the longer run, symbolic crusades may be considered relatively harmless phenomena, in that some may simply reinforce status group values without having further effects on the social or legal structure or interfering with social change. For example, using the model of a symbolic crusade to analyse two antipornography campaigns during the late 1960s, Zurcher et al. (1971) con-concluded that such crusades were simply a "safety valve" reaction to social

*Social status is the distribution of prestige among individuals or groups in a social system. Life-style refers to a system of values, customs, and habits distinctive of a status group.

change. Only when the crusade is supported by those in political or economic power does such a crusade assume larger implications for relations between status groups or for social change.

For several reasons, we disagree with Zurcher's view of symbolic crusades as relatively harmless safety-valve phenomena. Symbolic crusades focus on issues that are highly variable in their meaning for different people. For example, pornography is an important part of the lives of extremely few persons other than pornographers. Most persons can take it or leave it. This is vastly less true for gays, who are not in a position to readily dispense with the gay aspect of their identity. Also, symbolic crusades conducted on a local basis, as have been many of those involving gay rights, can become national issues when picked up by the national media. The Dade County battle over gay rights is a case in point. When given such attention, local issues can serve as a means of recruitment into a broader set of issues, such as those constituting neoconservatism. Through using single issues, such as gay rights or abortion, a broader movement may be able to consolidate a wide following from formerly disparate segments of the population.

Some evidence indicates that leaders of the neoconservative movement have attempted to utilize local symbolic crusades to organize broad support for conservative candidates for political office. As summarized by Sasha Gregory-Lewis, some of the leaders of the new right in the late 1970s attempted to unite fundamentalist Protestants, Mormons, Catholics, and blue-collar workers.

> Radical right technicians have found that one of their most successful contemporary tools is the conversion of civil concerns into moral issues cloaked in the myth of the "American family," a weapon that is being used in fights against federal welfare programs, federal support for education, federally financed child care, and a host of other human-oriented issues.*

Gregory-Lewis has documented numerous organizational, financial, and membership linkages between the recent antigay crusades and other persons and organizations constituting the neoconservative movement. Some of these linkages are explicit in Bryant's autobiography, *The Anita Bryant Story: The Survival of Out Nation's Families and the Threat of Militant Homosexuality* (1977). Other persons and groups involved in several of the movements of the radical

---

*Sasha Gregory-Lewis, "Danger on the Right," *Advocate*, November 16, 1977, pp. 16ff.; see also: "Unraveling the Anti-Gay Network," *Advocate*, September 7, 1977, pp. 10 ff.; "Battle with the Right Looms in Golden State," *Advocate*, August 10, 1977, pp. 11ff.; and "Stop ERA: A Choice or an Echo," *Advocate*, November 2, 1977, pp. 12ff.

right are State Senator John Briggs of California (initiator of a petition to bar homosexuals from employment in California schools); Los Angeles Police Chief Ed Davis, active in campaigns against "pornography pollution" and "kiddie porno" (a thinly veiled attack on Los Angeles homosexuals); the American Conservative Union (mentioned by Bryant); Phyllis Schlafly's anti-ERA group; the Eagle Foundation; the Conservative Caucus; the Committee for the Survival of a Free Congress; the Christian Crusade (dedicated to electing Christians to legislatures); and the Gun Owners of California. We are not presenting a conspiratorial interpretation of neoconservatism, although it would be conceptually difficult to distinguish between "conspiracy" and "intergroup political planning." Rather the set of issues constituting the neoconservative movement have a certain natural coherence. As shown by survey data on homophobia, homophobic persons also tend to be racist and sexist.

Also opposing the gay rights movement are such ultraconservative organizations as the KKK and the neo-Nazi organization, the National White People's Party. The latter group, in their magazine, *Thunderbolt* (June 1977), called homosexuality a "threat to the nation and a part of the Jewish conspiracy." In a two-page article praising Anita Bryant—"Jewish Leadership of Queer Rights Movement"—they stated:

> We will never accept this evil and will continue our work in uncovering the forces which are working day and night to subvert our White Christian civilization. Survival of the White Race depends upon the maintenance of the American home, marriage, and reproduction of ourselves within our offspring—THAT IS WHAT LIFE IS ALL ABOUT.

While such extremist groups are an embarrassment to neoconservatism, they seem to be a logical cultural extension of the latter.

Some conservative organizations in their propaganda and organizing tactics have played on the prevailing homophobia in order to recruit supporters for other causes. Leaders of conservative organizations have attempted to exploit antigay feelings among those who felt "things have changed too fast," and gays had "gone too far in flaunting their life-style." Several aspiring politicians, such as California State Senators John Briggs and H. L. Richardson; Police Chief Davis, who recently has been running for California governor; and U.S. Senators Jesse Helms and Orin Hatch, have attempted to capitalize on antigay feelings to gain publicity and further their political careers. Similarly motivated politicians have also used the laetrile issue for career gain. In consequence, the gay movement has had to face opposition from the rather well-organized neoconservative groups, as well as from the occasional opportunistic politician who is willing to use such easy targets as homosexuals, welfare cheaters, or laetrile.

With few exceptions, efforts by gays to effect legal changes in their own status seem to have called forth vocal opposition from neoconservative groups, churches, and opportunistic politicians or to have provoked the creation of explicitly antigay organizations, such as Save Our Children. In Seattle and Portland, the official proclamation of a Gay Pride Day or Week led to the creation of antigay groups. Another instance was Eugene, Oregon, where the city council passed a gay rights ordinance. Conservative churches there organized a successful petition to have the issue placed on the next popular ballot. Against the churches there were aligned the ACLU, the Eugene Women's Commission, the Lane County Democrats, the Governor's Task Force on Sexual Preference, the National Organization of Women, plus numerous professionals from that liberal university town.* The outcome of the future referendum seems promising for the gays, although it should be noted that a similar gay rights referendum was held in Boulder, Colorado, a liberal university community, and was decisively defeated in 1972.†

Of course, the most famous gay rights battle occurred in Miami in the spring of 1977. Since this imbroglio seems to have been a watershed in the development of the gay movement, we treat it at some length below. The precipitating event in this instance was the passage of a gay rights ordinance in January 1977 that banned discrimination in jobs, housing, and public accommodations in Dade County on the basis of "sexual or affectional preference." This passage motivated Anita Bryant and others to create the organization Save Our Children as a mechanism for battling gays in Miami, and, subsequently, nationally. On the antigay side, there were aligned Save Our Children, the Conservative Union, the Catholic Church, the governor of Florida, and Senator Briggs, who went to Miami to campaign for repeal of the gay rights ordinance. Also against the ordinance were numerous conservative churches and some Orthodox rabbis.

On the progay side, there were grouped the newly formed Dade County Coalition for Human Rights; the National Gay Task Force; several nationally prominent media personalities—for example, Ed Asner—who campaigned in Miami for the ordinance; former San Francisco Sheriff Richard Hongisto; the *Advocate*, which collected several thousand dollars in funds from its readers for the battle; and several national professional organizations. The Dade County Coalition spent over $350,000 during the campaign, compared with $150,000 spent by Save Our Children.‡ For historical background, it should be noted that homosexuality had been a political issue before in Florida. In 1964, a committee of the Florida Legislature dedicated to prying homosexuals out of positions of influence and staffed by an ex-vice squad policeman and Baptist leader from

---

*See *Willamette Valley Observer*, "Gay Rights Vote Mobilizes Militant Opposition," October 21, 1977, pp. 9ff.; "Gay Rights Activists Outmaneuver Accusers," October 28, 1977, pp. 10ff.

†Subsequent to the writing of this chapter, gay rights ordinances were repealed by very large majorities in Wichita, St. Paul, and Eugene.

‡The full story of the Miami battle can be found in the *Advocate* from January through August 1977. During these months, the *Advocate* covered the campaign in microscopic detail.

Miami (John Sorenson) issued a report entitled "Homosexuality and Citizenship in Florida," in which homosexuality was described as "the greatest Abomination."

It seems likely that Anita Bryant's national prominence was a major factor in transforming this battle into a national issue. Other cities, such as Detroit, had passed similar ordinances in recent years without the event becoming a national issue. As an occasional singer, author of many books on religion, a beauty queen, a media figure in advertising for Florida orange juice, a star in Orange Bowl parades, and a self-proclaimed Christian witness, she succeeded in attracting the attention of the national media to the events in Miami. According to some reports (*Newsweek*, June 6, 1977, pp. 6-22) she had been looking for a crusade to lead in order to bear witness to the Christian family, and the passage of the gay rights ordinance had provided her with a ready-made issue.

The arguments and imagery on the antigay side were classic and were formulated in terms of morality rather than civil rights. For example, Anita Bryant was quoted as saying: "There are a lot of things that are destroying our children. There's drugs, alcohol, abortions. . . . So it's not a matter of human rights. It's a matter of human rot" (*Newsweek*, October 3, 1977, p. 11). She also was reported as saying that "the recruitment of our children is absolutely necessary for the survival and growth of homosexuality. Since homosexuals cannot reproduce they must recruit heterosexuals in order to freshen their ranks. . . . I would rather see the schools burned down than have my children taught by a homosexual teacher" (*Newsweek*, June 6, 1977, p. 18). These highly emotional appeals were responded to favorably by many Miami residents, a few of whom even adopted bumper stickers saying "Kill a Queer for Christ."

The progay side attempted to formulate the issue as one of civil rights. In part, this was intended to appeal to Miami's large Jewish community. They attempted to define Bryant as part of the lunatic fringe and spent considerable money on ads in local newspapers attempting to refute the charges of Save Our Children leaders concerning gays as child molesters. However, it seems that they were not able to successfully set aside the issues of morality and conflict of lifestyles, since Save Our Children television ads repeatedly contrasted the "wholesome" image of Bryant and her family with scenes of drag queens and gays kissing on the streets of San Francisco in the 1976 Gay Pride Parade.

When the votes were counted, the gay rights ordinance had been repealed by a vote of 69.3 to 30.6 percent. Nearly 50 percent of the eligible voters had turned out—a very high percentage for a special election. From the viewpoint of the gays, all of the "wrong" people had voted. The precincts with high percentages of blacks and Jews had low turnouts—only 10 percent in the case of blacks—and these precincts split 50-50 on repeal. The areas with high percentages of Catholic and Cuban residents had a much higher turnout and voted overwhelmingly for repeal of the gay rights ordinance.

The repeal of the gay rights ordinance in Miami prompted the formation of antigay activities and organizations in a number of states and municipalities. An Indiana legislator began a movement to recriminalize homosexual acts in that state as part of his perennial campaign for governor. Senator Briggs initiated his referendum to ban gays as teachers in California. A Los Angeles group was born that advocated the death penalty for gays. There also occurred a national rash of assaults on gays.

The response of gays nationally has clearly been an unprecedented resurgence of activism. In San Francisco, Save Our Human Rights was formed, which raised $23,000 and 700 members in three weeks. Immediately after the Miami vote, gay demonstrations took place in several major cities, the one in San Francisco including an estimated 100,000 to 300,000 persons. A number of new gay organizations came into existence. As often occurs in the occasionally self-destructive gay movement, these new organizations gave rise to intergroup rivalries and accusations of opportunism. A very few of the new organizations were outright fund-raising (for profit) devices. Also, most of the older gay organizations and media experienced large increases in membership, donations, and readership.

It seems clear that the major effect of the Miami defeat for the gay movement has been the politicization of many formerly inactive or closeted homosexuals. Some have had their identities transformed from homosexual to gay by the Miami defeat. Others, in response to the Miami events and the national blossoming of antigay groups and movements, came to realize that these events could be re-enacted in other municipalities. Many have experienced a newly felt obligation to contribute to gay causes. A few, of course, have closed even tighter their closet doors.

11

POLICY CONSIDERATIONS AND THE FUTURE: A PLACE IN THE SUN?

In this final chapter, we undertake a discussion of a number of possible legal and institutional changes that would benefit gays and, to a lesser extent, heterosexuals. Our intent is to suggest a number of meliorative changes in the area of public policies bearing on gay men. We do not here undertake a full-scale discussion of all of the gay-related public policies, since in some policy areas, relevant data simply do not exist. For example, concerning the issue of gay parents adopting or raising children, such data are only just now coming into existence. In consequence of the lack of data bearing on a number of gay-related issues, we limit our discussions to those on which there are at least some (if hardly conclusive) data.

In the absence of data directly relevant to policy issues, popular prejudice has been delighted to fill in the gaps. Examples of gratuitously provided popular views of homosexuals include: (1) homosexuals must recruit children in order to "freshen their ranks" (Anita Bryant); (2) "Any woman who wants to be a patrol officer has got to be a lesbian"–asserted by a Boise chief of police in 1977; (3) homosexual teachers convert children to homosexuality by being homosexual role models (underlying this assumption are the two dubious assumptions that children *can* be converted by such superficial influences and that gay teachers do not go to great lengths to conceal their sexual orientation from students); (4) gay men will constantly importune heterosexual males if given a chance (this self-flattering notion assumes that gay men find heterosexual men attractive despite evidence that many gay men say that heterosexual men are incredibly poor sex partners). This list of gratuitous assumptions about gay males could be extended to great length.

It appears that opinion on policies bearing on the lives of gays exists on two different levels. There is informed opinion, as represented by the staffs of commissions and task forces. Such opinion has been generally in favor of the decriminalization of morality offenses and represents the views of the most-educated segments of the North American population (Nyberg and Alston 1977). However, such opinion represents the views of a limited minority of the general population and is only found to any great extent in such social enclaves as the liberal professions, major urban centers, and within some of the federal bureaucracies, such as the National Institute of Mental Health (NIMH). The second level of opinion on gay-related public policies is popular opinion, which is the view of vast majorities of the population outside of selected liberal enclaves. Because such opinion is the view of the vast majority of people in North America, many of the attempts to decriminalize morality offenses have been nullified by (fairly general) public indignation.*

The division of public opinion into informed and popular opinion is also a rough division into national and local opinion. While informed opinion tends to be concentrated in a few urban centers of national influence–New York, Boston, Washington, D.C.–popular opinion governs at the local and state levels of government in the rest of the nation. Within the latter political arenas, conservative views on morality–for example, views on pornography, bussing, and homosexuality–have traditionally had a greater influence on public policy. Because questions of morality have almost exclusively been within the jurisdictions of state and local governments, the rights of gay persons have been dealt with in political arenas least favorable to their advancement; hence the very slow and piecemeal progress of legal rights for homosexuals.

Given the conservativeness of state and local political arenas, it may seem somewhat surprising that by 1977, 19 (38 percent) of the 50 states had passed consenting adults laws and approximately 40 municipalities had passed ordinances against job discrimination based on sexual or affectional preference. Rather than asking why there has been so much opposition to the advance of gay rights, we find interesting the question of why gays have been able to make the progress they have. A variety of reasons explain the progress of gays, but most important among them have been sheer political luck and the presence of numbers of persons of enlightened opinions in strategic political locations. In the states of Illinois (1962) and Nebraska (1977), gays were lucky to obtain the passage of consenting adult laws in the course of a general revision of those states' criminal codes. Because the consenting adults provisions did not have to be voted on separately, they did not obtain much prepassage publicity. Further because these provisions were not voted on separately, state legislators were not obliged to publicly vote for their passage on the legislative floors. We note that in one of the several votes of the House of Commons on decriminalizing homo-

---

*Case studies of the failures of the Commission on Obscenity and Pornography and other social science-based commissions are discussed in Komarovsky's *Sociology and Social Policy: The Case of the Presidential Commissions* (1975).

sexual acts in Great Britain, there were 164 votes for decriminalization, 107 against, *and over 350 abstentions or absences* (Geis 1974, p. 44). In similar fashion, a ban on job discrimination based on sexual orientation became part of the Detroit city charter in the course of the adoption of a new charter by that city's people. This provision in the Detroit charter received very little attention in the course of adoption. Accordingly in some political arenas, policies benefiting gays have been enacted through the insertion of progay provisions in broader legislative packages. This tactic, of course, is not a new one, having been used uncountable numbers of times by economic interest groups seeking special tax or tariff advantages.

That progay provisions, in a number of cases, have been passed through their insertion in broader legislative packages does not in and of itself explain such a passage. Sponsors for those provisions are needed who are both sufficiently enlightened and courageous. Fortunately in recent years, there have been public officials on key committees who were of sufficiently informed opinion that they were willing to sponsor and push for legislation benefiting gays. Also, informed opinion is occasionally to be found among the staff persons of legislative committees. Such informed opinion was present among the staff of the Oregon Committee on Minority Affairs and Aging, which drafted a bill proscribing job discrimination against gays in 1977. It evidently was "too much present," because the staff had included a gay affirmative action provision in the bill, which, when discovered, resulted in the bill being tabled until the next legislative session. Informed opinion can also be occasionally found in the governor's mansion. The forceful assistance of California's Governor Jerry Brown made passage of a consenting adults law possible through breaking a tie vote in the California Senate. In general, much of the progress of gay rights over the last decade can be explained by political luck, combined with persons of informed opinion occasionally being in the right place at the right time.

In some other cases, gay rights have been able to advance due to the presence of strong local liberal traditions. This appears to have been true in such places as Oregon, Massachusetts, and Ann Arbor, Michigan. Because such places largely lack organized highly conservative groups, gay rights provisions have passed without substantial opposition. Such was not the case in New York City, however. In 1974, the city of New York entertained an ordinance banning job discrimination against homosexuals. In this case, there was substantial opposition from the Catholic Church and from the police and firemen's associations. The ordinance failed. Accordingly when there are genuine local liberal traditions and conservative morality is largely lacking in organization, gay rights have a reasonable chance of advancement.

The cause of gay rights has fared poorly in states possessing organized conservative groups, particularly when progay provisions had to be voted on singly. The case of Nevada illustrates this point. Nevada and Arkansas are unusual among states in possessing consenting adults laws that explicitly exclude homosexual acts from their protection. When the Nevada law was passed (1977), it faced the organized opposition of the Church of Latter Day Saints. That opposition was partly mollified by the exclusion of homosexuals from the protection of the law. Also, since this law was being considered at the same time that Nevada was entertaining passage of the ERA, the two issues became symbolically entangled (as being threats to the family). Both failed. Similarly in Florida, the ERA and gay rights became entangled to the mutual disaster of both.

As argued above, gay rights have advanced due to the combination of luck, persons of informed opinion being at the right place at the right time, local liberal traditions, and the lack of organized conservatism. Gay rights have failed when put in popular referenda (Dade County, Florida) and in states with organized conservatism. While gay rights may well make further advances, it seems likely that those advances will largely be made in states where advances have already been made. As more and more states have passed consenting adults laws, the remaining states increasingly constitute a highly conservative bloc; inroads here may come slower and slower, if at all. For instance, it is virtually inconceivable that such states as Utah, Arkansas, Oklahoma, or Louisiana will pass consenting adults laws in this century. (We note that Arkansas recently reinstated its sodomy law—it had been struck down by the Supreme Court for vagueness—while the legislatures of both Louisiana and Oklahoma passed resolutions commending Anita Bryant for her contributions to American culture.) In terms of geographical expansion of gay rights laws, the gay movement may have just about run its course.

A further reason why there are probably limits to the geographical expansion of gay rights is that there is little prospect of assistance to that cause coming from the federal government. It is extremely unlikely that Congress would approve the addition of "sexual or affectional orientation" to extant civil rights bills. Indeed when the Department of Health, Education and Welfare recently (1977) decided that homosexual couples showing "evidence of marital stability" could live in public housing, Congress quickly passed a bill overruling the department. Neither is major assistance to the gay rights cause to be expected in the near future from the U.S. Supreme Court. In what was probably the most important case dealing with gay rights to date (*Doe v. Commonwealth's Attorney*, 96 s. ct.1489 [1976]), the Court upheld a Virginia sodomy statute by arguing that the "right to privacy" does not extend to homosexuality but only to the "sanctity of the home and nurture of family life." Accordingly the states are free to legislate against homosexual behavior subject only to other constitutional constraints. While the federal courts of the 1970s have provided some assistance to gay rights in the areas of what is relevant evidence of criminal conduct and of due process, they have not made promising decisions on such major topics as the validity of sodomy laws, gay marriages, or job discrimination.* In summary, the

*For summaries of recent cases relating to homosexual behavior, the reader should

future progress of gay rights will be subject to the above-described political constraints. Progress is possible in selected local areas, in settings where there are strategically placed sympathetic persons, where advances have already been made, and where organized gay groups and their supporters act to take advantage of timely opportunities.

CONSENTING ADULTS LAWS

The effects of the presence or absence of consenting adults laws are much disputed both among heterosexuals and homosexuals. Although there are claims that such laws have a variety of effects on both heterosexuals and homosexuals, there seems to have been no research comparing gay life in jurisdictions with and without a consenting adults law. The 1969 NIMH Task Force on Homosexuality claimed that "the existence of legal penalties relating to homosexual acts means that the mental health problems of homosexuals are exacerbated by the need of concealment and the emotional stresses arising from this need and from the opprobrium of being in violation of the law" (1969, p. 18). However, this statement's validity is based principally on the expert status of the members of the task force rather than on any research evidence. Lacking any research evidence on the effects of such laws, the ideas presented below must be considered more in the nature of proposals for research than as matters of fact.

The suggestion that the criminalization of homosexual sex results in lessened self-esteem among self-identified homosexuals has several testable implications. It implies that homosexuals in states with a consenting adults law should have higher self-esteem and mental health than in those without such legal protection. Although this proposition strikes us as empirically dubious, it should be tested. However, even if it were found to be true that gays in states with consenting adults laws were mentally healthier, such a difference could readily be attributed to the (probably) more conservative attitudes prevailing in states lacking such a law. If self-esteem is more affected by the attitudes of persons with whom one has day-to-day contacts than by distant statutes, the direct effects on self-esteem of such laws could be minimal. Further, it may be that rural-urban differences in the self-esteem of homosexuals within any given state are substantially larger than differences between states. Such suggested rural-urban differences would presumably be due to rural areas having substantially more conservative attitudes in matters of morality.

The notion that the criminalization of homosexual behavior affects self-esteem has the further implication that gays should have lower self-esteem than

---

consult the *Sexual Law Reporter* or the legal review section of the *Journal of Homosexuality*.

comparable heterosexuals. On this point, there is substantial evidence, although its implications are arguable. Saghir and Robins (1973, pp. 109-30) compared gays and heterosexuals on a variety of indicators of psychopathology and found only that the gays seemed to drink somewhat more. Such a difference in drinking patterns could easily be attributed to the importance of the gay bar in the gay world rather than to any differences in psychopathology. Siegelman found that "the homosexuals, compared to the heterosexuals, described themselves as less well adjusted on four scales, better adjusted on three scales, and not different on six scales" (1972, p. 9). He also found that in those instances where homosexuals fared less well on adjustment, they also appeared to rank high with respect to effeminacy. On this point, it seems clear that the visibly effeminate homosexual is likely to have received more negative feedback from heterosexuals, and such responses could readily explain his lower adjustment. Consistent with an interpretation of negative feedback for effeminate homosexuals are the findings of Myrick (1974). He found that while the homosexuals he studied had lower self-esteem, personal competence, power, and self-acceptance than did the heterosexuals, the overt homosexuals scored lower on these scales than did the covert ones. Accordingly it seems that lessened self-esteem is characteristic principally of those homosexuals who, through their overt self-presentation, stimulate negative responses from heterosexuals. For those who practice more covert styles, the differences are slight to nonexistent. On the whole, the relevant research comparing the mental health of homosexuals and heterosexuals reports either no or minimal differences between the two groups; whatever differences do exist can only be attributed to the presence of laws criminalizing homosexual behavior.

While the existence of a direct effect of criminalizing laws on the self-attitudes of homosexuals may seem somewhat dubious, the existence of effects on the attitudes of homosexuals toward society and other people generally may be more plausible. Weinberg and Williams (1974, p. 152) found sizable attitudinal differences between male homosexuals and the general male population of the United States: 47 percent of the former versus 77 percent of the latter agreed that "most people can be trusted"; 52 percent versus 73 percent said that "human nature is cooperative"; 34 percent versus 23 percent agreed that "no one cares what happens to you"; and 69 percent versus 93 percent felt they were a "happy person." That gays have less sanguine views of human nature and society suggests that they are strongly alienated from the social order and are less willing than heterosexuals to grant it legitimacy. Through criminalizing the gay population, the moral ties of gays to society are weakened, and thereby, society itself is weakened. Being legally cast out of respectable society, many gays feel that the obtaining moral order is not their order and is not worthy of their support.

The effects of consenting adults laws on the behavior of homosexuals are much disputed. Advocates for retaining laws against homosexual sex believe that in the absence of such laws, the volume of proscribed acts would increase tremendously. This belief is based on the assumption that laws deter homosexuals from engaging in sexual acts. The doctrine that criminal laws deter persons from committing proscribed acts, as typically stated (Wilson 1975, pp. 181-201) assumes that the more severe the penalties and the greater the probability that a crime will be detected, the more people will be deterred. Advocates of deterrence typically place a greater emphasis on detection (certainty of punishment), since in order for the severity of the penalties to have any effect on people's behavior, there must be some nontrivial probability that their behavior will be detected. In the case of laws against homosexual behavior, it seems that the legal penalties are already quite harsh in many states, for example, sodomy in Idaho—mandatory five-year sentence, sodomy in Missouri—mandatory two-year sentence (Boggan et al. 1975, pp. 175, 187). Hence the question of the deterrent effects of such laws largely rests on the extent to which offenses may readily be detected.

It is widely accepted that only a minuscule percentage of the homosexual acts committed ever come to the attention of the agencies of law enforcement. The major study on arrests for homosexual behavior conducted by Gallo and his colleagues (1966) in Los Angeles during the early 1960s indicates fairly clearly the reasons for the nondetectability of such offenses. Of 968 persons arrested for sexual offenses in the Los Angeles area, only 3 percent were arrested in their homes or in a hotel/motel. The vast majority were arrested in public places. Restrooms, vehicles, parks, and theaters included 80 percent of the places of arrest. Accordingly it seems clear that the chances of arrest are nearly nonexistent when the parties confine their sexual encounters to private places. Since it is likely that the overwhelming majority of homosexual encounters occur in private places, it may reasonably be concluded that only a very small percentage of such acts receive official attention.

If the laws proscribing homosexual acts have any deterrent effect, it seems that the effect must largely be limited to acts committed in public places. The policing of public places frequented by homosexual men certainly does increase the risk of arrest; this is widely agreed upon by participants in restroom activity (Humphreys 1970, pp. 81-87). It seems likely that such risks may deter some segments of the homosexual population from availing themselves of the services to be found in public terminals. Most gays probably view such places as too risky and/or too sordid and prefer to acquire sexual partners in safer places, such as gay bars, steam baths, parties, and so forth. The segment of the male homosexual population for which detection has the least deterrent effect is that segment which chooses not to participate in gay society. This segment, which would include those who are heterosexually married and those who reject an explicitly gay identity, are likely to be those most in need of the sexual services of public places.

In light of the above, we suggest that to the extent that the purpose of laws criminalizing homosexual acts is to deter men from engaging in such acts, these laws have only a minimal effect. Those men who are deterred relocate their activities to the safer settings of the gay world and to private residences. Those individuals who frequent public terminals are the least likely to be deterred because they lack or refuse to participate in the gay world. In the study of arrests of homosexual men in the Los Angeles area, it was found that 28 percent had been arrested before for some sexual offense (Gallo et al. 1966, p. 803). Hence they are the most likely segment of the population of male homosexuals to bear the costs of detection. In consequence, it seems that the laws criminalizing homosexual acts function in a largely punitive, nondeterrent manner.

A more rational approach by legal authorities to homosexual behavior would be to decriminalize homosexual acts in private and to allow, even encourage, the development of explicitly gay settings, such as bars and baths. Such an approach is voiced by some of the more enlightened police officials, for example, former Sheriff Hongisto of San Francisco. This approach encourages homosexual men to relocate their sexual activities to the safer and more esthetic settings of the gay community. It provides alternatives to engaging in impersonal sex in public places. This policy would include a cessation of deploying plainclothes vice officers in gay bars. Such deployment clearly makes bars an unsafe place to negotiate sexual encounters and destroys their utility as alternative settings to public places. Fortunately it seems that such practices have been dying out in recent years in many cities, Los Angeles being a major exception.

One of the more difficult definitional problems in drafting a consenting adults law is to define in a nonarbitrary manner the age at which legal adulthood begins. Presently legal definitions of adulthood vary considerably between states and depend upon the particular activity under consideration—for example, marriage, voting, driving, or drinking. In order to approach the thorny problem of defining adulthood for sexual purposes, we take the indirect tack of asking what is feasible rather than what is desirable. Our intent here is to consider whether laws defining sexual adulthood at varying ages are enforceable. If we can determine that any, or all, definitions of sexual adulthood are unenforceable, we have grounds for rejecting such definitions.

The locale within which a sexual encounter occurs appears to be the major condition determining whether that encounter is noticed by others. As the Los Angeles arrest data show, only 3 percent of those arrested for homosexual offenses were arrested for acts occurring in private places. Saghir and Robins (1973, p. 71) found that age is strongly related to the locale within which sexual encounters occur. For example, the vast majority of teen-age homosexuals conduct their sexual relations "in private settings only": 91 percent for those under 15 years of age and 59 percent for those 15 to 19 (the figures for other age groups are 58 percent for those 20 to 29, 48 percent for those 30 to 39, and 68 percent for those 40 and older).* Because of the greater privateness of homosexual sex among teen-agers, it would appear that laws proscribing homosexual acts among teen-agers are even less enforceable than is their application to adults.

We believe that Saghir and Robins's data on age and locale of sexual encounters somewhat underrepresent the degree of privateness of the sexual encounters of male homosexuals during their middle teen-age years (15 to 17). Had they used a finer age breakdown, they might have found that the degree of privateness of those aged 15 through 17 would have been much closer to the 91 percent of those under 15 than to the 58 percent for those in their twenties. Our rationale for this belief is that it is probable that age of coming out relative to one's legal adulthood affects the setting in which one acquires sexual partners. Those who come our prior to their majority cannot avail themselves of the sexual marketplaces of the gay world. Hence if they have come out, they must utilize public settings. If they have not yet come out, their sexual encounters are likely to occur in the more private settings of teen-age friendships. Since such settings are almost completely beyond the surveillance of police or other authorities, any attempts by persons other than parents or relatives to regulate the sexual behavior of teen-agers would be doomed to failure.

Our Detroit data permit us to indirectly explore some of the sexual behavior of teen-age homosexual males. Table 11.1 shows the relationship between age of coming out and the locales utilized to acquire sex partners. The particular question was: "When you were first coming out, to what extent did you try to meet sex partners in each of the following places?" The responses of Table 11.1 have been dichotomized into "never" versus the combined categories of "occasionally," "often," and "very often." These data show that those male homosexuals who come out earlier tend to utilize public settings to acquire sexual partners more than do those who come out later. In particular, they are more likely to frequent beaches, parks, and restrooms. They also are more likely to utilize the school as a source of sexual partners, evidently because they are simply more likely to still be in school. They also utilize gay parties more. We are somewhat surprised that those who come out at younger ages are only slightly and nonsignificantly less likely to utilize gay bars as sexual marketplaces. Our suggested explanation for this lack of relationship is that some young gays may obtain entry to bars with falsified identification, while others may hang around the outside of, or parking lots adjacent to, such bars.

---

*The other categories of Saghir and Robins's table showing locale by age are "public places only" and mixed "public and private." For no age group is the number frequenting "public places only" greater than 5 percent.

TABLE 11.1

Cruising Locales During Coming Out, by Age of Coming Out* (percent)

Cruised at:	Age of Coming Out		
	Less than 16	16–20	21 and Over
Beaches	56	37	32
N	72	65	85
$X^2 = 9.75$; df = 2; $p < .01$; gamma = –.32			
Bars	83	91	87
N	70	67	87
$X^2 = 2.05$; df = 2; p = ns; gamma = 0.12			
Homophile organizations	46	44	30
N	68	63	82
$X^2 = 4.49$; df = 2; p = ns; gamma = –.22			
Parks	61	54	40
N	71	66	87
$X^2 = 6.97$; df = 2; $p < .04$; gamma = –.28			
Restrooms	47	41	23
N	72	64	84
$X^2 = 11.07$; df = 2; $p < .01$; gamma = –.36			
Baths	51	39	32
N	70	66	84
$X^2 = 5.93$; df = 2; p = ns; gamma = –.27			
Gay parties	74	79	58
N	68	67	81
$X^2 = 8.46$; df = 2; $p < .02$; gamma = –.26			
School	54	35	32
N	71	65	80
$X^2 = 7.83$; df = 2; $p < .02$; gamma = –.29			
Work	28	34	22
N	71	65	82
$X^2 = 2.59$; df = 2; p = ns; gamma = –.12			
Heterosexual parties	28	32	20
N	69	65	81
$X^2 = 3.07$; df = 2; p = ns; gamma = –.15			
Streets	59	42	43
N	70	64	82
$X^2 = 4.92$; df = 2; p = ns; gamma = –.21			

*Significance tests use a .05 level.

Source: Compiled by the authors.

These data suggest that for those young gays who have decided to assume their own sexual autonomy at an early age, their inability to gain entry to the sexual marketplaces of the adult gay world obliges them to utilize public settings. Through the use of such settings, they increase the risks of police attention. Yet such risks may not have a substantial deterrent effect if they lack alternative settings in which to negotiate sexual encounters. It seems that when adulthood comes unevenly, that is, when one becomes an adult in some spheres of one's life but not in others, problems of articulating the different spheres arise. Many of our subjects appear to have acquired sexual adulthood but have not yet been granted the legal license to pursue that adulthood. Thus laws defining adulthood may have had negative effects through propelling young gays into such unesthetic and unsafe settings as public restrooms.

Consenting adults laws should be eliminated in favor of consenting persons laws. That is, reference to adult status in such laws should either be deleted or else adulthood should, for sexual purposes, be drastically redefined to a much younger age, such as 14. We have two rationales for this suggestions. For those young gays who have not yet come out, and hence who pursue their sexual lives in private settings, any legal restrictions on their voluntary sexual encounters are almost totally unenforceable. For those young gays who have come out and have assumed sexual autonomy, it is undesirable that they, by virtue of their legal minority, should be obliged to resort to public settings for sexual purposes. Gay youth centers could possibly serve as alternative meeting grounds to public settings. They could also serve as places in which young gays could repair the damage to their self-esteem and self-image that they daily receive from their heterosexual peers. (For reasons that apply equally to homosexuals and heterosexuals, we do not suggest that teen-aged gays should have legal access to adult drinking establishments.)

There are a number of objections to a consenting persons law that must be considered. Sexual exchanges may occur between pairs of adults, pairs of minors, and between an adult and a minor. Voluntary exchanges between adults are, by common assumption, exchanges between competent persons acting with reasonable prudence to obtain their mutual satisfaction. Also, such exchanges are largely not capable of surveillance. Hence they are neither within the state's interest or competence to regulate. Voluntary exchanges between minors, while not necessarily exchanges between prudent and competent persons, are almost inaccessible to police surveillance due to the private settings in which they usually occur. Because both parties are of minor status, we may assume a lack of substantial exploitation in the relationship. Although the state may have some legitimate concern for such exchanges, it would seem that such exchanges, when they are brought to the attention of officials, could better be dealt with by trained counselors rather than by the courts and the police.

The case of sexual exchanges between adults and minors arouses the strongest objections in the general population. In consequence, all states have legal provisions on statutory rape or contributing to the delinquency of a minor or more specialized laws applying to homosexual acts between adults and minors. The concern here is that because of the age inequality between the parties, there is a presumed likelihood of the adult having used physical, economic, or psychological coercion on the minor. Also, it is felt that the minor is often not competent to understand or take into consideration the consequences (pregnancy or social stigma) arising from such sexual encounters and that the minor, because of inexperience, is subject to deception and/or manipulation. Further in the case of sexual relations between an adult and a minor of the same sex, it is often believed that the minor's sexual orientation is still sufficiently malleable that homosexual encounters during teen-age years can decide his adult sexual orientation. We consider these concerns below.

Concerning the view that sexual transactions between adults and minors are often based on some form of coercion, we cannot deny that such cases occur. Yet we note that the presumption of coercion is an *assumption* and need not be a necessary part of adult-minor transactions. To make an assumption of coercion solely on the basis of age inequality is to substitute popular opinion for evidence. Rather than making this questionable assumption, a superior legal approach would be to develop *direct* evidentiary criteria for the existence of some form of coercion. Such indicators of coercion could be threats, unfulfilled or unfulfillable promises, or the use of economic sanctions. Through such an approach, courts could render justice on an individual basis.

Instances of manipulation or attempted manipulation of adults by minors are sufficiently common to indicate that the assumption of adult exploitation is often dubious. For instance, many college teachers have been approached by flirtatious students hoping to better their grades.

There is some truth to the belief that teen-agers, because of diminished competence, are incapable or unwilling to take into consideration the consequences of their sexual actions. This seems particularly true for heterosexual encounters, in which teen-age girls risk the possibility of pregnancy due to a lack of foresight or simple planning (Fullerton 1977, pp. 144–47). Concerning the possibility of stigma resulting from having engaged in homosexual acts, this threat is largely independent of the adult or minor status of the parties to a transaction. Virtually all persons engaging in homosexual acts know that such acts are highly discredited and take actions to prevent them from becoming public knowledge.

The notion that the sexual orientations of teen-agers are flexible and that engaging in homosexual acts could permanently influence their sexual propensities is a much more difficult idea to assess. Evidence on the plasticity of human sexual orientations is far from conclusive. Also, it is not known which ages are most plastic and which least. We have suggested that at least among males, sexual orientation is very largely fixed during the first few years of life and not subject to substantial later modification. The work of Green (1973) and Whitam (1977) supports this. Sagarin (1975, p. 150) disagrees and points to many instances in Kinsey's data in which males had been homosexual—that is, engaged in homosexual acts—for relatively short periods of their lives but who had subsequently become heterosexual. We have questioned whether such converts to heterosexuality were really homosexual or were principally heterosexuals, who for reasons of curiosity, kicks, or money, were briefly dabbling in homosexual sexual acts.

Based substantially on Kinsey's data on the occurrence of homosexual acts among heterosexual teen-age males, the notion of plasticity of sexual orientation during the teen-age years has received much currency. Gays themselves have helped popularize these ideas by arguing that "we're all a little gay." In contrast, Tripp has argued that "certainly most adolescent homosexual activities are inconsequential. . . . Even homosexual males describe these experiences as having been impersonal and unimportant" (1975, p. 88). Such activities may be largely peripheral to a heterosexual's basic sexual orientation. There is by now considerable evidence that heterosexual males can and do engage in substantial homosexual activity without that activity affecting their self-identities as heterosexual persons. Reiss (1961) has documented how teen-age groups of males may repeatedly engage in sexual acts with adult homosexuals for money, while retaining strong identities as heterosexuals. Similarly it seems that in the majority of cases of teen-age males who prostitute themselves to adult men for money, their sexual orientations are heterosexual (Lloyd 1976). We also note that of the 50 participants in impersonal sex in public restrooms interviewed by Humphreys (1970, p. 112), 54 percent were heterosexually married. Accordingly we suggest that heterosexual males have an ability to engage in homosexual behavior in a relatively impersonal manner such that that behavior is not considered an expression of their basic sexual identity.

It seems that laws proscribing sexual encounters between adults and minors have been almost exclusively formulated with a view to preventing heterosexual adult-minor encounters. When the assumptions of the heterosexual model are applied to homosexual encounters, they are substantially misapplied. The dangers to minors envisioned under such laws are largely nonexistent. Teen-age males are less subject to coercion and deception than teen-age girls. Teen-age homosexual behavior is less indicative of sexual orientation among males than among females. Physical, or other forms of, coercion in adult-minor homosexual encounters are almost totally lacking. For instance, while rape of teen-age girls is relatively common, rape of teen-age boys is extremely rare except in those instances where a teen-age gay is raped by a male heterosexual in such settings as juvenile detention homes and correctional facilities. Through reformulation of the criminal codes, there can be formulated consenting persons laws or consenting persons laws appropriately modified to deal with the rather different phenomena of homosexual and heterosexual encounters. Such laws could deal directly with situations of coercion, threat or manipulation without making dubious and gratuitous assumptions of fact.

We do not believe that a consenting persons law would give rise to many adult homosexuals pursuing teen-age males. With the exception of teen-age males who engage in homosexual hustling, teen-agers and adult homosexuals live in separate social worlds. In the Los Angeles study of homosexual felony arrests, only 5 percent of the defendants and 4 percent of their sexual partners were under 20 years of age (Gallo et al. 1966, p. 803). In our chapter on sexual age preferences (Chapter 7), it was reported that only 4 percent of those 18 to 24 and 15 percent of those 25 to 29 were interested in a younger sexual partner. Since persons in their twenties are socially and culturally closest to teen-agers and, therefore, most likely to have contact with them, their disinterest in younger sexual partners suggests an absence of a realistic "threat" from the adult gay world. Further the general youth-orientedness and macho emphasis of teen-age male culture effectively serves to keep most adults, including parents, at some distance. Indeed it is principally adults in occupations requiring direct contact with teen-agers—teachers, counselors, ministers—who have most access to teen-age persons. Conceivably a consenting persons law could be formulated so as to proscribe sexual transactions between persons so employed and their *direct* charges.

PUBLIC SEX: THE "SEXUAL OUTLAWS"

One major component of the popular view of male homosexuals is that they are preoccupied with the indiscriminate solicitation of sexual partners in such public places as restrooms, parks, and streets. Underlying this view is the belief by a majority of heterosexuals that gay men are "oversexed" (Levitt and Klassen 1974). Often the belief is held among heterosexual males that all homosexual men are attracted to all heterosexual men no matter how psychologically or physically unappealing the latter may be. Such beliefs probably reveal more about the sexual psychology of heterosexual men than about the motivations of homosexuals. Such views may reflect the heterosexual man's conception of how he would behave if he were homosexual. Supporting this notion, we recall Humphreys' finding that 54 percent of his participants in sex in restrooms were heterosexually married (1970, p. 112). Since many heterosexual men are unable to conceive of a relationship between males that is both affectionate and erotic, they may, by extension, attribute to gay men only the most mechanical and impersonal of sexual motivations.

There is an element of truth in the popular view that homosexual males do acquire sexual partners in a variety of public places and engage in fleeting sexual encounters. This fact is attested to by a variety of authors (Humphreys 1970; Tripp 1975, pp. 157–59; Saghir and Robins 1973, pp. 68–71). Such sex in public places is viewed with abhorrence by a majority of heterosexuals and is disapproved of by many homosexuals. Very few writers of any sexual persuasion have defended public and promiscuous sex. The most eloquent advocate of such sexual behavior is John Rechy. In his autobiographical novels, *City of Night* (1962), *Numbers* (1967), and most recently *The Sexual Outlaw* (1977), he views such sex as a challenge to a stultifying morality of domesticity and praises the excitement and rewards of impersonal sex.

> Each moment of his outlaw existence (the sexual outlaw) . . . confronts repressive laws, repressive "morality." Parks, alleys, subway tunnels, garages, streets—these are the battlefields. To the sexhunt he brings a sense of choreography, ritual, and mystery—sex-cruising with an electrified instinct that sends and receives messages of orgy at any moment, any place (1977, p. 28).

In contrast to Rechy's view, the public condemns and prosecutes the public and quasi-public sexual acts of homosexual men. Instances of public heterosexual sex, by comparison, have received very little attention from police, from inquisitive social science researchers, or in the popular press. Perhaps only in the pornographic press has public heterosexual sex received any visibility. The relative absence of police raids on drive-in movies in college towns, as opposed to skid row movies frequented by homosexual men, or on the parked cars in "lovers' lanes," as opposed to the parked cars near homosexual "turfs," attests to the selective perception of, and attention to, the sexual acts of gay men. If male homosexuals detected by the police in public sexual acts are not prosecuted under the laws against sodomy or oral copulation, they are prosecuted under laws against disorderly conduct or offending public decency (Gallo et al. 1966).

We may ask which segments of the public, in fact, are subjected to such offenses against decency? The study of Los Angeles arrests provides a clear answer to this question. Out of 493 felony arrests dealt with in court, the testimony of offense was presented by the arresting officers in 459 cases. In only 12 cases was testimony presented by an independent observer. In the remaining cases, a variety of persons presented testimony, for example, a psychiatrist, the defendant, or the defendant's sexual partner (Gallo et al. 1966, p. 804). Similarly in 475 misdemeanor cases, there were only 29 instances where an independent observer testified (Gallo et al., p. 828). These data strongly suggest that the segment of the public whose sense of decency is offended by public and quasi-public homosexual acts are the police. The police in the course of their duty seek out situations where their tastes are likely to be offended. Searching behavior by the police includes such activities as sending plainclothes vice officers into gay bars, placing decoys in public parks and restrooms, and, in Los Angeles, flying at night over the wooded areas of a park in helicopters with searchlights.

It is clear that the number of offenses against public taste could be drastically reduced through discontinuing police searches for sexual transactions in public and quasi-public places. The problem of public sex is very largely a non-problem due to the fact that the parties to such encounters typically go to lengths to ensure privacy for their transactions. In consequence, there are rarely observers present whose tastes are likely to be offended (Humphreys 1970, pp. 78–80). Because of the general absence of outside observers and the absence of a complaining victim, the only way in which police may enforce laws against public sex is to assume the role of a secret police. As with other victimless crimes—for example, prostitution, drug taking, gambling—police must present themselves as "legitimate" participants in a legally proscribed behavior in order to detect evidence of offense (Skolnick 1966, pp. 115–16). The only meaningful sense in which there may be an offended party arising out of such situations is through there being present an *unwilling* observer to a sexual transaction. If the observer is present willingly, he becomes a "participant" in the transaction. In the case of the police, we presume their presence is willing, if not at the wishes of the individual officer, at least as a result of the will of the police department.

In light of the above, it would be reasonable to suggest that police largely withdraw their presence from those settings frequented by gay men for purposes of brief sexual encounters. Routine patrols could readily be maintained for purposes of maintaining general public order. Police intervention would be justifiable in situations where the volume of sexual transactions is sufficiently large that it is likely that visitors to the locale might become *unwilling* observers to such transactions. However, given the locations of such settings and the fact that the settings are typically occupied by gay men during the late evening, the likelihood of unwilling observers being present is much reduced. Indeed the general absence of heterosexual persons from such places during the late evening invites suspicion of the motives of the few heterosexuals who may be present. Such settings at times attract groups of young heterosexual males interested in robbing or assaulting gay men. Similarly police should generally absent themselves from gay bars and completely absent themselves as plainclothes officers. An occasional "walk through," as is done with many types of liquor establishments, would be sufficient to determine that licensing rules are being observed and that there is a modicum of public order present.*

In the above discussion, we have not relied on the data on homosexual offenders reported by Gebhard et al. (1965) for several reasons. The data are roughly 30 years old. More importantly, all of their "homosexual offenders versus adults" either are or have been inmates of institutions. Such persons are a highly selected group, who through mixtures of indiscretion, repeated pursuit of sexual partners in public places, and bad luck have ended up being incarcerated. Since the vast majority of adult homosexual offenders are given probation, incarcerated offenders are unrepresentative even of those arrested for such acts.

LEGAL GAY MARRIAGES

In a number of states, gay couples and organizations have attempted to gain legal recognition for same-sex marriages. To date, all of these efforts have been unsuccessful. The prospects for future success appear quite limited, with the possible exceptions of such liberal states as Oregon and Massachusetts. What would be the advantages of legal recognition of same-sex marriages? It might be pertinent to ask, "Why do the gays want legal marriages when so many straights now want out of them?" Upon analysis, the advantages of legal marriage may appear to be limited.

The tax advantages of legal marriages are modest to nonexistent for a heterosexual working couple without children. Hence for gay males, the tax benefits could not reasonably justify entering a marriage. For those gays who have children, there is currently available the tax status of unmarried head of household. This tax status has greater utility for lesbians than for gay men, since the former, not infrequently, have children in their households. Legal marriages would also benefit lesbians more than gay men, because the legality of a lesbian marriage could provide substantial legal support for lesbians fighting to retain custody of their children.

Legal marriages would be of benefit for purposes of inheritance. Legal status as spouse would ensure the transmission of a larger percentage of an estate to the surviving partner than is currently the case where the surviving partner simply has the status of "friend." Legal inheritance as a spouse would increase the now nonexistent inheritability of economic levels among gays. Legal marriages would also be of some benefit to gays for Social Security arrangements. Legal marriages would enable the surviving partner to obtain survivor's benefits. However, such benefits would be an advantage only in those few cases where one party had not acquired Social Security retirement benefits in his own right. Since in the vast majority of cases, both partners of both male homosexual and lesbian relationships have acquired their own benefits through many years of employment, the advantages of legal marriages through increased retirement benefits would be limited.

More substantial benefits could be expected from legal marriages in the area of housing. Numerous communities have ordinances proscribing residence in the same house by persons unrelated by blood or marriage. Occasionally these ordinances are enforced. Legal marriages for gays would largely nullify them. Material benefits could be obtained through lowered insurance rates. Currently many insurance companies will not provide insurance to persons they believe to be gay or will charge them higher insurance rates or rates for single persons even if they are homosexually linked. However, such insurance benefits do not have great applicability among gays, because most gays are reasonably confident that when they die they will have no one to whom they will care to provide for their future. The fairly general lack of life insurance among gays is related to the nonmarried condition of most older gays. If a larger percentage of gay men were married, legally or not, life insurance would be a more common phenomenon among gays. Thus in such places as San Francisco and New York, with their large concentrations of coupled gays, advertisements from insurance companies appear in the various gay media.

In the area of employment, legal gay marriages could have disastrous effects. If only for tax-withholding purposes, all employers must know one's marital status. This virtually requires that the potential or current gay employee reveal to his employer that he is married to a person of the same sex. In contrast, a single gay is permitted more freedom to conceal his sexual orientation, even though his single condition may arouse suspicion. Through being obliged to reveal that one's spouse is a person of the same sex, maximal opportunity is created for job discrimination. Even if hired, the gay employee would lose much of his ability to select those work associates to whom he would reveal or not reveal his sexual orientation. The freedom to so select would be even more sharply limited vis-a-vis superiors, since they would have access to personnel files.

Some of the negative effects on employment of legal marital status for gays could be eliminated by the passage and stringent enforcement of laws banning job discrimination on the basis of sexual orientation. However, it would still be debatable whether the protection provided by such laws could equal the protection presently provided gays by their ability to "pass" as heterosexual. Given the latitude employers, and particularly private employers, possess in the areas of hiring, firing, and promoting, it is questionable whether the gay person who had been discriminated against might ever know he or she was discriminated against. Further if he or she did learn of such discrimination, the time and effort required to pursue a discrimination case through the pertinent bureaucracies and courts could appear so formidable that the easier course of action would be to simply forget it. Consequently it seems that the existence of laws banning job discrimination on the basis of sexual orientation may be a prerequisite for legal gay marriages. Marital status has been so extensively articulated with employment structures that it seems very difficult to insulate the latter from changes in the former. (Of course, the negative effects of legal homosexual marriages on employment would be minimal in those occupations where there is substantial tolerance for gays, as well as among the self-employed.)

It is arguable what the effects of legalized same-sex marriages would be on the coupling relationships of gay men. It is clear that the imagery of an enduring romantic relationship with another man has substantial appeal among male homosexuals. In response to the question, "Do you hope to eventually acquire a long-term lover?" 52 percent of our 235 respondents said "yes," 14 percent responded "no," and 34 percent said they already had such a partner. Although some of their hopes for such a relationship may be destined to frustration, a substantial minority of gay males would at some time during their lives probably enter into a legal marriage if given the opportunity. The advent of such marriages, of course, would entail the subsequent phenomena of divorce and, probably, some bigamy.

Legal sanction for same-sex marriages could provide a measure of symbolic support for enduring relationships within the gay community. Such persons might even become role models for the rest of the community and thereby provide a cultural counterweight to the images of gay men as predominantly or exclusively being "sexual outlaws." However, as became apparent in our treatment of the coupling relationships of gay men, being a happily married gay man is not necessarily incompatible with sexual outlawry. The most enduring couple relationships had developed a permissive arrangement toward sexual encounters that were external to the marital relationship. Such an arrangement seemed to combine the benefits of an enduring affectionate relationship with the pleasures of a varied sexual life. An arrangement that combines the rewards of both married and nonmarried life-styles is rarely found in the heterosexual world, which prefers to consider the two life-styles as mutually exclusive. We venture that the advent of legal gay marriages providing greater symbolic support for enduring relationships in gay culture would widen their range of life-style options. New, but not necessarily incompatible, alternatives would be available within the gay community. The alternatives would range from legal monogamous marriage with sexual fidelity to a career of sexual outlawry. Through the selection of one such life-style (or a combination), the institutionally provided alternatives could be designed to meet the visions of individual happiness of most gay persons.

Given that the economic gains accruing from the legalization of same-sex marriages are rather modest, it seems that the symbolic advantages are the major issue. Many gays want legal equality with heterosexuals and rightly see that limiting legal sanctions to heterosexual unions implies that homosexual unions are morally inferior to heterosexual ones. Even in states that have removed the disapproval of homosexual relationships through passing consenting adults laws, the limitation of legal marriage to heterosexual unions implies that such unions are preferred by the state. Conservatives such as State Senator Briggs of California have "instinctively" realized that legal status for gay marriages implies the approval of the state, rather than simply providing a registration function, as in the cases of cars and pets. Hence such conservatives have bitterly opposed the legalization of same-sex marriages.

Logically legal equality of homosexual unions could be obtained in two ways. The first way, and the one advocated by most gays, would be the legalization of same-sex marriages on the same terms as for heterosexual unions. The second would be through the legal nonrecognition (delegalization) of heterosexual unions. Under the second approach, sexual unions of all kinds—other than coercive ones—would be matters of private concern, which would not be within the state's domain of interest. The marital union per se would not be a matter of state interest, while only the parental relationships would have legal status. As a voluntary relationship, the marital union would be a private matter. However, since the parental relationship is involuntary for the child, the state, acting in its capacity of parens patriae, could legitimately supervise that relationship. However, given the honored status of marriage and the family and the despised status of homosexual relationships, the legal inclusion of the latter within the former seems rather improbable for the foreseeable future. The advent of legal same-sex marriages, except perhaps in one or two very liberal states, will probably remain only a dream of gay activists. (If a few states did recognize homosexual unions, the question of reciprocal recognition of marriages between the states could raise some interesting legal points.)

NONDISCRIMINATION LAWS

While the benefits to gays and their culture that would result from the legalization of same-sex marriages are arguable, the benefits deriving from the passage of laws banning discrimination in employment on the basis of affectional or sexual preference are not. Only the practical means of implementing and enforcing such legislation are really open to dispute. As argued earlier, such legislation would permit gay men and women to become more widely diffused in the occupational structure rather than being concentrated in a variety of occupational "clumps." Through such diffusion, gays would be able to advance to higher occupational ranks that would be consistent with their own abilities.

Although approximately 40 municipalities have passed laws banning employment discrimination based on sexual preference, most of these laws were enacted only within the last five years. Hence there is very little evidence on how effective these laws are. Very few appeals have been based on such laws. There have accumulated a number of cases in which gay persons have appealed personnel actions taken against them and, in the course of those appeals, claimed that their sexual preference was legally irrelevant to their employment. However, almost all of these appeals have not been based on claims of illegal discrimination on the basis of sexual preference in jurisdictions that proscribe such discrimination. Hence there is not yet in existence a body of legal precedents through which such nondiscrimination laws may be analyzed. Below we discuss several difficulties in making such laws effective.

In order to avail oneself of the protection of a law banning discrimination in employment on the basis of sexual preference, the gay employee would have to be rather brave. It is almost inevitable that such cases would receive much publicity in the local media. Hence to avail oneself of this legal protection is to come out to one's heterosexual associates. Through using that legal recourse one would lose much of one's ability to "pass" as heterosexual. One also would invite the risk of receiving threatening and obscene phone calls from one's local community. Also, one's heterosexual friends might be sufficiently embarrassed by the publicity that they would discontinue any personal relationship.

Even if the gay complainant were to win his or her case and obtain reinstatement in a formerly occupied job, the occupational effectiveness of the individual could have been largely destroyed. A gay high school teacher might well find it difficult to relate to or control a class of students who were aware of his or her sexual preference. There have been some instances in which a college professor has come out to his classes. The responses in these cases were somewhat mixed. Perhaps a majority of the students were accepting, but a large minority were nonaccepting and either spent the semester resenting the teacher or withdrew from the class. In the case of a police officer who would be known to the public to be homosexual, one could readily imagine situations in which citizens would behave in a hostile manner to the officer. In the event that the gay complainant wins his or her suit but seeks a job elsewhere, the publicity surrounding the person could close the doors to many places of employment. In such a situation is he/she then to be advised to instigate yet another complaint or suit?

A number of the above-described effects on one's employment are illustrated in the case of seven female employees of the Boise Police Department who were fired for being lesbians.* One of these women was a regular patrol officer; there were only two on the police force. The rest were dispatchers, dog-catchers, or clerical workers. Their firings in early January 1977 were front-page news in the local newspaper and remained so for several months. After intense community publicity, petitions on their behalf, counterpetitions, and the establishment of a Women's Legal Defense Fund, the fired employees filed a civil suit against the city for several million dollars. Since neither Idaho nor Boise has legal provisions banning discrimination on the basis of one's sexual orientation, they were obliged to sue on other grounds. They claimed that there had been sex discrimination against them, since the police department had not investigated the sexual practices of its male employees. (Under Idaho law, *all* sexual transactions between persons not married to each other are illegal.) They also claimed that their rights to privacy had been violated. The information later surfaced that (1) the Police Department had staked out the women's houses at night in order to record comings and goings; (2) that the one telephone in the police station that was provided for personal employee use, and which the police manual described as the only telephone line that was not tapped, had been tapped and had been a principal source of information on which to base the women's firings.

---

*The information describing this case is to be found in the *Idaho Statesman* beginning January 3, 1977 and running for the next seven months. Some information is also based on conversations with a number of participants in the affair.

During the months following the firings, several of the women attempted to obtain employment in other police departments in the surrounding area, but none was successful. Although there may not have been any jobs currently available in the area, the great publicity the affair had received would have made it politically difficult for a police department to hire any of the women without provoking an outraged response from the community. During this period, several of the women received threatening and obscene phone calls and letters. In winning such a suit, it is difficult to imagine that the complainants would have been able to return to their former jobs and function there without great discomfort or relate effectively to a highly prejudiced community. Legal victories so obtained may be Pyrrhic ones.

Laws banning job discrimination on the basis of sexual preference typically contain provisions excepting certain occupations. These occupations include those of police employee, military personnel, intelligence persons, and occasionally, jobs entailing financial trust. The rationale for the exclusion of such jobs from nondiscrimination protection is that gays are viewed as subject to blackmail. It is felt that gay persons could be induced to violate their job responsibilities when threatened with public exposure. Occasional arguments also used to exclude these jobs from legal protection are that heterosexual employees would find it difficult to work with gay co-workers and that gay persons are too emotionally unstable to occupy these jobs. Since the latter two arguments are based purely on prejudice, we deal only with the blackmail argument.

Gay activists counter the "blackmailability" argument by saying that the gay person's vulnerability derives totally from his legally proscribed status. If homosexuality and homosexual acts were not matters that could result in discharge or prosecution, the gay person would not be subject to blackmail. In consequence, it is argued that the way to eliminate such vulnerability is to pass nondiscrimination laws that would apply to *all* occupations, including "sensitive" ones, and to decriminalize homosexual acts. While this argument has force, it does not follow that the passage of such legislation would *completely* remove all grounds for blackmail. Gay persons could be sufficiently averse to public exposure of their homosexuality that they might be willing to cooperate with their blackmailer. Exposure to one's family, to one's wife and children, or to one's friends and colleagues could be sufficiently painful to some gay persons that they could be susceptible to blackmail. This would be particularly true for those homosexual males who are heterosexually married or who otherwise lead "very heterosexual" life-styles. However, such susceptibility to blackmail cannot justify the categorical exclusion of all gay persons from "sensitive" jobs. The susceptibility-to-blackmail argument cuts two ways. If gays are susceptible to blackmail, only those gays should be hired for "sensitive" positions who are not susceptible to blackmail. Those gays who are not susceptible to blackmail are those who are most openly gay. By being open about their sexual orientation, they have removed the threat of blackmail. By such openness, gay employees might well be less susceptible to blackmail than their heterosexual colleagues, and certainly less so than a heterosexually married colleague who is also gay.

Rather than extending our arguments on the susceptibility to blackmail of gay persons, we turn to the evidence on the topic, which is sparse and somewhat contradictory. Tripp claims that "with the single possible, though very doubtful, exception of Austria's Alfred Redl (who handed over entirely false military information to Russia in 1912), there is no case on record of any person in any government ever having been blackmailed into disloyalty or anything else" (1975, p. 213). This claim is somewhat contradicted by two *New York Times* (March 3, 1966 and May 17, 1967) articles, in which it was reported that several dozen occupationally prominent gay men (including a professor, dean, congressman, an admiral, and several businessmen) had been subject to continuing blackmail and had been forced to pay many thousands of dollars to their heterosexual blackmailers. The organized group executing the blackmail had carried out its operations during the early and mid-1960s. It is difficult to understand the actual conditions making blackmail effective in these cases and, hence, the extent to which one could generalize from these cases. Since little information was given about the victims, it is not known what percentage of them were heterosexually married. Such a marital condition would, of course, substantially have increased the victims' vulnerability to blackmail. The modus operandi adopted by the blackmailers in this case was to represent themselves as police officers and to threaten the victim either during or shortly after the victim had a sexual encounter with a confederate of the blackmailers. This strongly suggests that the basic threat in these cases was not one of exposure but one of arrest and possible conviction under the rather savage sodomy laws of the period. To the extent that the threat was one of arrest rather than exposure, it seems likely that the passage of consenting adults laws would go a long way toward undercutting the possibility of blackmail.

On the topic of blackmail, Humphreys says

> (1) most blackmailing is done by law enforcement personnel and as a result of decoy operations; (2) some blackmailing is practiced by those who pose as police officers; (3) a small amount is attempted (seldom with success) by close friends of the victims . . . most men involved for any length of time in homosexual activities have had experience with police blackmail (1970, pp. 89–90).

Also, "Every respondent over the age of thirty whom I interviewed extensively had at least one story of police payoffs amounting to blackmail" (Humphreys 1970, p. 89). We disagree with the last two sentences quoted because they are grossly misleading and are either flatly untrue or equivocal. The assertion that "most men . . . have had experience with police blackmail" is equivocal in that it suggests that most gay men have been blackmailed, when a more reasonable interpretation is that most men have either known someone who was blackmailed or heard stories of such blackmail. Also, such stories, or even a single story, tend to acquire great notoriety among gay persons. Hence despite the probable rarity of blackmail, it is quite likely that "every respondent over thirty . . . had at least one story of police payoffs amounting to blackmail." The expression "amounting to blackmail" is also an equivocation in that it does not distinguish a situation of continuing payments by the victim—as in the *New York Times* articles cited above—from a situation of one-payment extortion by a police officer. That the latter is the case for most or all of Humphreys' respondents is suggested by his reference to a man who had "'bought off' decoys for amounts ranging from sixty to three hundred dollars" in eight separate instances (1970, p. 89). These rather modest amounts suggest one-time extortions, as compared with the very large amounts involved in the classical blackmail situations described in the *New York Times* articles.

We suggest that instances of true blackmail were rather rare among Humphreys' respondents. It should be noted that among the various types of male homosexuals, those studied by Humphreys underwent the greatest risks of extortion or blackmail due to their habit of visiting restrooms (with consequent exposure to apprehension by the police). Also, because more than half were heterosexually married, they had the least ability to resist police extortion. It is clear that it is impossible to generalize estimates of the incidence of blackmail from Humphreys' data to the broader gay world. We do not here quarrel with Humphreys' claim that most blackmail is done either by police or by persons representing themselves as police officers.

In analyzing the Kinsey data, Simon and Gagnon (1967) reported that 12 percent of their sample of homosexual men (exclusively homosexual plus mixed homosexual and heterosexual) had been blackmailed. Since our principal concern is with the extent to which a gay person's vulnerability to blackmail could affect his job performance, we again raise the question of whether these cases of blackmail were one-shot situations of extortion or whether there was a continuing relationship between exploiter and victim. Only in the latter situation does there seem to be the possibility that the victim might be induced to engage in actions contrary to his employer's policies. Simon and Gagnon provide no evidence on the nature of the "blackmail"; hence our question remains unanswered.

The incidence of blackmail of whatever nature among contemporary gays is probably somewhat less than 30 years ago, when Kinsey was collecting his data. Since that time, many states have either repealed their laws against homosexual acts or have allowed them to fall into disuse. Also, as the numbers of openly gay bars, baths, and other establishments have grown, the need for homosexual men to frequent high-risk places, such as restrooms, has probably lessened. Further many contemporary gays would simply refuse an attempted blackmailer's demands. Thus Saghir and Robins reported that of those gay men who had been subjected to "attack, robbery, or blackmail," 43 percent "informed police, or lawyer or stood up to the robber" (1973, p. 164).

Data provided by Saghir and Robins (1973, pp. 163-65) strongly suggest that what is sometimes reported as blackmail by either researchers or respondents is almost always either simple one-shot extortion or robbery. Of their 89 male homosexual respondents, 34 had at some time been "attacked, robbed, threatened, or blackmailed." In at least 28 of these cases, it seems clear from the nature of the victim's losses that there was no true blackmail involved; they were cases of simple robbery. The losses consisted of "cash money, possessions, e.g., TV, watch, possessions were vandalized." In the remaining cases, there had been threats only. Accordingly with the possible exception of the Kinsey data, the evidence for the existence of true blackmail of homosexuals is extremely sparse. There is no evidence at all of blackmail designed to get the victim to violate his employment responsibilities. Even in the *New York Times* reports of blackmail, the goals of the exploiters were solely monetary and had no evident effect on the victims' job performance. As an attempt to determine whether blackmail of homosexuals exists, we attended a meeting of the Sociologists' Gay Caucus at the 1977 annual meeting of the American Sociological Association and asked the group there if anyone had ever known anyone who had been blackmailed. Of the approximately 20 men present, most of whom were involved in research on homosexuality and all of whom had extensive knowledge of gays, only 1 responded affirmatively; his data on the topic have been discussed above.

The evidence for homosexuals being poor risks in responsible or sensitive jobs because they are vulnerable to blackmail seems almost nonexistent. It may even be true that as Tripp claims, there are no recorded cases of blackmail influencing the job performance of gay persons. While it is true that male homosexuals have been subjected to extensive extortion—particularly from police—and simple robbery, all of this seems irrelevant to their ability to perform on the job. It seems that most of the extortions based on threat of arrest could be eliminated through the passage of consenting adults (or persons) laws and through the removal of police officers from sites frequented by gays. It is less likely that the volume of incidents of threat, assault, and robbery would be reduced through these changes. Many of these incidents seem based on threats of violence, or actual violence, received from sexual partners, who assume that most gay men can be physically intimidated or abused with impunity (Saghir and Robins 1973, p. 164). Most of these sexual partners seem to be basically heterosexual men or bisexual men who do not define themselves as "gay" or even homosexual (Reiss 1961).

It would seem that the vulnerability of homosexuals to true blackmail has been blown up into a full-scale myth. Gay persons themselves may have contributed to the development of this myth by indiscriminately calling robberies and one-shot extortions instances of blackmail. Yet even if homosexuals are subject to blackmail, this would not justify their exclusion from sensitive positions. It would only imply that gay persons who were the most open about their sexual orientations would be desirable employees due to their invulnerability.

THE BEGINNING

The evolution of the questions asked about homosexuality during the post-World War II era has shown evidence of a beginning of sanity in this area. Both the topics discussed by persons of informed opinion and the issues faced by policy-making bodies have drifted, though much more slowly for the latter, away from a nearly exclusive preoccupation with the sexual techniques and assumed psychopathology of gays. Until the advent of Hooker's (1957, 1965) seminal works, the questions most asked about homosexuals dealt with the particular ways in which they could best be categorized as psychopathological and what would be the best means of cure. Only in the post-Hooker years was the question considered worth discussing of whether homosexuals were, in fact, sick or whether they were simply being different.

Slightly later, there occurred such investigations as that of Gallo et al. (1966) and the Wolfenden Report (1957), showing that there appeared to be no visible social harm resulting from homosexual acts. Such acts were gradually recognized by informed opinion as constituting voluntary transactions between mentally competent adults. It was realized that the policing of such acts was both beyond the state's competence and legitimate sphere of interest. Hence homosexual acts became recognized as victimless crimes, and there began the passage of a number of consenting adults laws.

In the later 1960s, there began explorations of aspects of the lives of homosexuals other than their sex lives or their psychopathological conditions. Hence there arose interests in aging processes among gay men, the coming-out stage, and how gays managed to articulate their stigmatized status with their jobs (Simon and Gagnon 1967; Dank 1971; Humphreys 1970). The realization dawned on interested persons that gays are not "gay" all of the time and that they wash dishes, get promoted, have friends, and discriminate in ways very similar to heterosexuals.

As the preoccupation with the sex lives of gays diminished and an interest in other aspects of their lives expanded, it became apparent that very little was known about these other aspects. Although popular prejudice attempted to fill in these research gaps with stereotypical information, sufficient information became available to indicate that such stereotypes and information based on them were simply untrue. Since the vast majority of gay persons hold down jobs and perform them satisfactorily, it has become clear to many informed persons that job discrimination based on sexual orientation is palpably unjust. Hence in recent years, there has been a measure of support for the passage of bans on such discrimination.

Even more recently, attention has broadened to include discussions of gays as marital partners and as parents. Questions of current interest are: "Will being raised by gay adults make an offspring gay?" "What is the gay family like, and how does it differ between lesbians and gay men?" "How do the parents of gay persons react to the knowledge that their children are gay?" Slowly some of the answers to these newer questions have seeped into the minds of the educated public and even, though more slowly, into the minds of legislators. We hope in the above work to have contributed to this process.

APPENDIX: GLOSSARY OF STATISTICAL TERMINOLOGY

Alpha Reliability Coefficient. This coefficient, which can vary from 0.0 to 1.0, is often computed for scales consisting of several items or questions. Its purpose is to measure the extent to which the constituent items of a composite scale all measure the same underlying variable or trait. If they do measure the same trait the total score on the composite scale is considered a more accurate measure of the variable of interest. By convention alpha coefficients should be at least 0.6 in magnitude, and preferably greater than 0.7, although research workers—as opposed to diagnosticians of individual persons—often settle for slightly lower reliabilities.

Beta. Beta is a coefficient which can be positive or negative and usually is in the range from 1.0 to -1.0. A positive sign indicates a direct relationship between two variables; a negative sign indicates an inverse relationship. Its special utility is that it indicates the relative strength and direction of association between a dependent variable and a given independent variable *after the effects of a specific set of other independent variables have been controlled.*

Chi-Squared (X^2). This statistic is commonly computed of percentage tables to estimate the likelihood that the relationship in a given table could be due to such chance phenomena as sampling error or measurement error. For small values of chi-squared, roughly less than 3.84, one may assume that the results in a table are likely to be due to chance. However, how great a value of chi-squared is needed to decide that one's result is non-chance depends on the number of rows and columns in a given table.

Degrees of Freedom (df). Since it is almost impossible to define degrees of freedom without having to employ other statistical terminology, suffice it to say that, for cases other than percentage tables, degrees of freedom is very near to sample or subsample size, In general, larger samples permit more accurate or stable findings.

Eta. This coefficient varies from 0.0 to 1.0 and measures the strength of relationship between a categorical variable such as race or sex and some other more continuous variables like income or an attitude. Higher values indicate stronger degrees of relationship between two variables.

F. This statistic serves the same function as chi-squared in letting the researcher know whether a particular relationship is likely to be a chance one. Higher values of F are more likely to be non-chance although the value needed to make a decision of a non-chance finding depends on the sample sizes of the groups being examined and on the number of groups or variables being examined at the time.

Gamma. Gamma coefficients vary from -1.0 to 1.0 and indicate, like beta above, the strength and direction of the relationship between two variables.

Monotonic. A relationship between two variables is monotonic when there is not a direct relationship for one segment of the "curve" and an inverse one for another segment. That is, the relationship never reverses direction.

N. N simply stands for the number of persons in any given group or category.

ns. This expression means that a particular relationship was not found to be statistically significant. A finding of statistical nonsignificance means that the relationship is likely to be a chance finding.

One-Way Analysis of Variance. This statistical procedure, which produces an F value, compares groups of persons who differ on one variable such as religious denomination to see if they are statistically significantly different on some other variable.

p. P is the probability that a particular finding is due to chance factors. Conventionally, social scientists agree that p values must be equal to or less than .05—one in twenty—before a finding is accepted as non-chance or "real." P is determined from the obtained values of chi-squared, F, and t.

r. The Pearsonian correlation coefficient (r), like gamma, measures the strength and direction of a relationship between two variables. It varies from -1.0 to 1.0. One can compare different r's to see if variable A has a stronger relationship with variable B than it does with variable C.

$r_{12.3}$. This is called the partial correlation coefficient and varies from -1.0 to 1.0. It shows the strength and direction of association between—in this case—variables 1 and 2 after the effect of variable 3 has been statistically controlled or adjusted.

$R_{1.23\ldots}$. The multiple correlation coefficient, varying from 0.0 to 1.0, indicates the strength of relationship between a given dependent variable and a *collective* set of other variables. In this case the dependent variable is variable number 1 and the set has the two variables 2 and 3 although it could have more. Associated beta values—defined above—indicate the relative strengths of the variables within the set of other variables as predictors of the dependent variable.

Reproducibility and Scalability Coefficients. It is impossible to briefly and simply define these. However, they are only mentioned briefly and in a footnote above.

Standard Deviation (s.d.). Standard deviations are measures of the amount of heterogeneity or inequality in the scores on a given variable. Their values depend completely on the given variable.

t. This statistic serves an identical function as F. It is used to determine whether a given result is likely to be due to chance. It is used when one is comparing two groups on a dependent variable.

Two-Way Analysis of Variance. A two-way analysis of variance computes the mean values of a dependent variable for each combination of the values of two independent variables and then assesses the extent to which differences between the means are due to chance by computing several F values. It also enables one to know if there is an effect of only one independent variable, of both, of neither, or whether the effect of one depends on the value of the other.

V. Cramer's V is, like gamma, a measure of the strength of relationship between two variables in a percentage table. Unlike gamma, it varies only from 0.0 to 1.0 and can measure curvilinear and nonmonotonic relationships.

BIBLIOGRAPHY

Achilles, Nancy. 1967. "The Development of the Homosexual Bar as an Institution." In *Sexual Deviance*, ed. John Gagnon and William Simon, pp. 228–94. New York: Harper & Row.

Altman, Dennis. 1971. *Homosexual: Oppression and Liberation*. New York: Outerbridge and Dienstfrey.

Arnstein, Robert L. 1971. "Homosexual Concerns of College Students." *Sexual Behavior* 1 (December): 24–31.

Barr, R. F., B. Raphael, and Norma Hennessey. 1974. "Apparent Heterosexuality in Two Male Patients Requesting Change-of-Sex Operations." *Archives of Sexual Behavior* 3 (July): 325–30.

Bartell, Gilbert. 1971. *Group Sex*. New York: Peter Wyden.

Becker, Howard S. 1963. *Outsiders: Studies in the Sociology of Deviance*. Glencoe, Ill.: Free Press of Glencoe.

Bell, Arthur. 1971. *Dancing the Gay Lib Blues*. New York: Simon and Schuster.

Benjamin, Harry, and R. E. L. Masters. 1964. *Prostitution and Morality*. New York: Julian Press.

Bertelson, David. 1970. "A Comparative Approach to the Meaning of Gay Liberation." Mimeographed. Berkeley, Calif.: Berkeley Gay Switchboard.

Bieber, Irving. 1976. "A Discussion of Homosexuality: The Ethical Challenge." *Journal of Consulting and Clinical Psychology* 44 (April): 163–66.

———, H. J. Dain, P. R. Dince, M. G. Dreelich, H. G. Grand, R. H. Gundlach, M. W. Kremer, A. H. Rifkin, C. W. Wilber, and T. B. Bieber. 1962. *Homosexuality: A Psychoanalytic Study*. New York: Basic Books.

Blau, Peter, and Otis Dudley Duncan. 1967. *The American Occupational Structure*. New York: Wiley.

Blood, Robert. 1972. *The Family*. New York: Free Press.

———, and Donald M. Wolfe. 1960. *Husbands and Wives*. New York: Free Press.

Blumstein, Phil, and Pepper Schwartz. 1976. "Bisexuality in Men." *Urban Life* 5 (October): 339–58.

Boggan, E. Garrington, Marilyn Haft, Charles Lister, and John Rupp. 1975. *The Rights of Gay People*. New York: Avon Books.

Brain, Robert. 1976. *Friends and Lovers*. London: Hart-Davis, MacGibbon.

Breton, Raymond. 1964. "Institutional Completeness of Ethnic Communities and the Personal Relations of Immigrants." *American Journal of Sociology* 70 (September): 192–203.

Brown, Howard. 1976. *Familiar Faces, Hidden Lives: The Story of Homosexual Men in America Today*. New York: Harcourt Brace Jovanovich.

Brownmiller, Susan. 1975. *Against Our Will: Men, Women and Rape*. New York: Simon and Schuster.

Bryan, James. 1966. "Occupational Ideologies and Individual Attitudes of Call Girls." *Social Problems* 13 (Spring): 441–50.

Bryant, Anita. 1977. *The Anita Bryant Story: The Survival of Our Nation's Families and the Threat of Militant Homosexuality*. Old Tappan, N.J.: Fleming Revell.

Carrier, Joseph. 1977. "Sex-Role Preferences as an Explanatory Variable in Homosexual Behavior." *Archives of Sexual Behavior* 6 (January): 53–65.

———. 1971. "Participants in Urban Mexican Male Homosexual Encounters." *Archives of Sexual Behavior* 1, no. 4, 279–91.

Cavan, Sherri. 1966. *Liquor License: An Ethnography of Bar Behavior*. Chicago: Aldine.

Clark, Don. 1977. *Loving Someone Gay*. Milbrae, Calif.: Celestial Arts.

Collier, John, Jr. 1967. *Visual Anthropology: Photography as a Research Method*. New York: Holt, Rinehart and Winston.

Cory, Donald Webster. 1951. *The Homosexual in America: A Subjective Approach*. New York: Greenberg.

Cotton, Wayne L. 1972. "Role-Playing Substitutions among Male Homosexuals." *Journal of Sex Research* 8 (November): 310–23.

Cunnison, Foster, Jr. 1969. "The Homophile Movement in America." In *The Same Sex*, ed. Ralph Weltge, pp. 113–28. Philadelphia: United Church Press.

Dank, Barry. 1971. "Coming Out in the Gay World." *Psychiatry* 34 (May): 180–97.

Davis, Kingsley. 1971. "Sexual Problems." In *Contemporary Social Problems*, ed. Robert Merton and Robert Nisbet, pp. 351–60. New York: Harcourt Brace Jovanovich.

Dawson, Kipp. 1975. *Gay Liberation: A Socialist Perspective*. New York: Pathfinder Press.

D'Emelio, John. 1974. "Introduction." In *Universities and the Gay Experience*, pp. 9–18. Proceedings of the Conference of the Gay Academic Union, November 23, 1973, New York.

DeVall, William. 1976. "Social Research on Support for Civil Liberties." In *Comparative Human Rights*, ed. Richard P. Claude, pp. 326-52. Baltimore: Johns Hopkins.

———. 1973. "Gay Liberation: An Overview." *Journal of Voluntary Action Research* 2 (Winter): 24-35.

Drew, Dennis, and Jonathan Drake. 1969. *Boys For Sale*. New York: Brown Book.

Dubin, Robert. 1956. "Industrial Workers' Worlds." *Social Problems* 3 (January): 131-42.

Edwards, Harry. 1973. *The Sociology of Sport*. Homewood, Ill.: Dorsey Press.

Ellis, Albert. 1968. "Homosexuality: The Right to Be Wrong." *Journal of Sex Research* 4 (May): 96-107.

Epstein, Joseph. 1970. "Homo-Hetero: The Struggle for Sexual Identity." *Harper's Magazine* 241 (September): 37-51.

Farrell, Ronald, and Clay Hardin. 1974. "Legal Stigma and Homosexual Career Deviance." In *Crime and Delinquency: Dimensions of Deviance*, ed. Marc Riedel and Terence Thornberry, pp. 128-40. New York: Praeger.

Farrell, Ronald A., and James F. Nelson. 1976. "A Causal Model of Secondary Deviance: The Case of Homosexuality." *Sociological Quarterly* 17 (Winter): 109-20.

Fenichel, Otto. 1945. *The Psychoanalytic Theory of Neurosis*. New York: Norton.

Ferenczi, S. 1914. *Sex in Psychoanalysis*. New York: Basic Books.

Field, Mervin. 1977. "Sharp Split on Gay Issues." *San Francisco Chronicle*, August 12, pp. 10 ff.

Fisher, Peter. 1972. *The Gay Mystique: Myth and Reality of Male Homosexuality*. New York: Stein and Day.

Frazier, E. Franklin. 1957. *Black Bourgeoisie*. Glencoe, Ill.: Free Press of Glencoe.

Freedman, Ronald. 1957. "Migration Differentials in the City as a Whole." In *Cities and Society*, ed. Paul Hatt and Albert Reiss, pp. 367-81. 2d ed. New York: Free Press.

Freund, Kurt, Ernest Nagler, Ronald Langevin, Andrew Zajac, and Betty Steiner. 1974. "Measuring Feminine Gender Identity in Homosexual Males." *Archives of Sexual Behavior* 3 (May): 249-60.

Fullerton, Gail. 1977. *Survival in Marriage*. Hinsdale, Ill.: Dryden Press.

Gagnon, John. 1967. "Sexuality and Sexual Learning in the Child." In *Sexual Deviance*, ed. John Gagnon and William Simon, pp. 15-42. New York: Harper & Row.

———, and William Simon. 1973. *Sexual Conduct*. Chicago: Aldine.

Gallo, Jon, Stefan Mason, Louis Meisinger, Kenneth Robin, Gary Stabile, and Robert Wynne. 1966. "The Consenting Adult Homosexual and the Law: An Empirical Study of Enforcement and Administration in Los Angeles County." *UCLA Law Review* 13 (August): 643–832.

Gebhard, Paul, John Gagnon, Wardell Pomeroy, and Cornelia Christenson. 1965. *Sex Offenders*. New York: Harper & Row.

Geis, Gilbert. 1974. *One-Eyed Justice*. New York: Drake.

———. 1972. *Not the Law's Business?* Washington, D.C.: National Institute of Mental Health.

Gerassi, John. 1966. *The Boys of Boise*. New York: Macmillan.

Gerlach, Luther, and Virginia H. Hine. 1970. *People, Power, Change: Movements of Social Transformation*. New York: Macmillan.

———. 1970. "The Social Organization of a Movement of Revolutionary Change: Case Study, Black Power." Mimeographed. Minneapolis: University of Minnesota.

Goffman, Erving. 1963. *Stigma*. Englewood Cliffs, N.J.: Prentice-Hall.

Green, Richard. 1976. "One-Hundred Ten Feminine and Masculine Boys: Behavioral Contrasts and Demographic Similarities." *Archives of Sexual Behavior* 5 (September): 425–46.

———. 1975. "Sexual Identity: Research Strategies." *Archives of Sexual Behavior* 4, no. 4: 337–52.

———. 1974. *Sexual Identity Conflict in Children and Adults*. New York: Basic Books.

———. 1973. "Twenty-Five Boys with a Typical Gender Identity." In *Contemporary Sexual Behavior: Critical Issues in the 1970's*, ed. Joseph Zubin and John Money, pp. 351–59. Baltimore: Johns Hopkins.

Guild Publishers. 1972. *The Guild Guide*. Washington, D.C.: Guild.

Gusfield, Joseph. 1968. "The Study of Social Movements." In *International Encyclopedia of the Social Sciences*, ed. David Sills, pp. 445–52. New York: Macmillan.

———. 1963. *Symbolic Crusade: Status Politics and the American Temperance Movement*. Urbana: University of Illinois Press.

Haist, Mark, and Jay Hewitt. 1974. "The Butch–Fem Dichotomy in Male Homosexual Behavior." *Journal of Sex Research* 10 (February): 68–75.

Hall, Richard. 1969. *Occupations and Social Structure*. Englewood Cliffs, N.J.: Prentice-Hall.

Harris, L., and Associates. 1975. *The Myth and Reality of Aging in America*. Washington, D.C.: National Council on Aging.

Harry, Joseph. 1977. "Marriage among Gay Males: The Separation of Intimacy and Sex." In *The Sociological Perspective*, ed. S. McNall. 4th ed., pp. 330–40. Boston: Little, Brown.

———. 1976a. "Age and Sexual Culture among Gay Males." Paper presented at the meeting of the Society for the Study of Social Problems, New York City. Mimeographed.

———. 1976b. "On the Validity of Typologies of Gay Males." Paper presented at meeting of the American Sociological Association, New York City, August. Mimeographed.

———. 1974. "Urbanization and the Gay Life." *Journal of Sex Research* 10 (August): 238–47.

———. 1970. "A By-Product Theory of Primary Behavior." *Pacific Sociological Review* 13 (Spring): 121-26.

Hencken, Joel, and William O'Dowd. 1977. "Coming Out as an Aspect of Identity Formation." *GAI Saber* 1 (Spring): 18–22.

Heron, Alastair. 1963. *Towards a Quaker View of Sex: An Essay by a Group of Friends*. London: Friends Home Services Committee.

Hirschi, Travis. 1969. *Causes of Delinquency*. Berkeley: University of California Press.

Hoffman, Martin. 1968. *The Gay World: Male Homosexuality and the Social Creation of Evil*. New York: Bantam Books.

Hooker, Evelyn. 1967. "The Homosexual Community." In *Sexual Deviance*, ed. John Gagnon and William Simon, pp. 167–84. New York: Harper & Row.

———. 1965. "Male Homosexuals and Their Worlds." In *Sexual Inversion: The Multiple Roots of Homosexuality*, ed. Judd Marmor, pp. 83–107. New York: Basic Books.

———. 1957. "The Adjustment of the Male Overt Homosexual." *Journal of Projective Techniques* 21 (March): 17–31.

Horowitz, Irving, and James Katz. 1975. *Social Science and Public Policy in the United States*. New York: Praeger.

Horowitz, Irving, and Martin Liebowitz. 1968. "Social Deviance and Political Marginality: Toward a Redefinition of the Relation between Sociology and Politics." *Social Problems* 15 (Winter): 280-96.

Howard, John. 1974. *The Cutting Edge: Social Movements and Social Change in America*. Philadelphia: Lippincott.

Humphreys, L. 1972. *Out of the Closets*. Englewood Cliffs, N.J.: Prentice-Hall.

———. 1970. *Tearoom Trade*. Chicago: Aldine.

Hunt, Morton. 1974. *Sexual Behavior in the 1970's*. New York: Dell.

Inciardi, James. 1975. *Careers in Crime*. Chicago: Rand McNally.

"Interview with a Homosexual Spokesman." 1971. *Sexual Behavior* 1 (November): 18.

Irwin, John. 1970. *The Felon*. Englewood Cliffs, N.J.: Prentice-Hall.

Karlen, Arno. 1971. *Sexuality and Homosexuality*. New York: Norton.

Katz, Jonathan. 1976. *Gay American History, Lesbians and Gay Men in the U.S.A.* New York: Crowell.

Killian, Lewis. 1964. "Social Movements." In *The Handbook of Modern Sociology*, ed. Robert Faris, pp. 426–55. Chicago: Rand McNally.

Kinsey, Alfred, Wardell B. Pomeroy, and Clyde E. Martin. 1948. *Sexual Behavior in the Human Male*. Philadelphia: W. B. Saunders.

Kitsuse, J. 1962. "Societal Reaction to Deviant Behavior." *Social Problems* 9 (Winter): 247–56.

Komarovsky, Mirra. 1975. *Sociology and Social Policy: The Case of the Presidential Commissions*. New York: Elsevier.

———. 1964. *Blue-Collar Marriage*. New York: Random House.

Kopay, David, and Perry Deane Yourn. 1977. *The David Kopay Story*. New York: Arbor House.

Lehne, Gregory. 1976. "Homophobia Among Men." In *The Forty-Nine Percent Majority: The Male Sex Role*, ed. Deborah David and Robert Brannon, pp. 66–68. Reading, Mass.: Addison-Wesley.

Lemert, Edwin. 1967. *Human Deviance, Social Problems, and Social Control*. Englewood Cliffs, N.J.: Prentice-Hall.

Levine, Martin. 1977. "The Gay Ghetto." Paper presented at meeting of the American Sociological Association, Chicago, August. Mimeographed.

Levitt, E. E., and A. D. Klassen. 1974. "Public Attitudes toward Homosexuality." *Journal of Homosexuality* 1, no. 1: 29–43.

Leznoff, Maurice, and William Westley. 1956. "The Homosexual Community." *Social Problems* 3 (April): 257–63.

Lipset, S. M., and Everett Ladd. 1976. "The Aging Professoriate." *Chronicle of Higher Education* 12 (May 24): 16.

Lipset, S. M., Martin Trow, and James Coleman. 1956. *Union Democracy*. Glencoe, Ill.: Free Press of Glencoe.

Lloyd, Robin. 1976. *For Money or Love: Boy Prostitution in America*. New York: Ballantine Books.

Lofland, John. 1969. *Deviance and Identity*. Englewood Cliffs, N.J.: Prentice-Hall.

Lubeck, Steven, and Vern Bengston. 1977. "Tolerance for Deviance: Generational Contrasts and Continuities." Paper presented at meeting of the American Sociological Association, Chicago, September. Mimeographed.

McCaffrey, Joseph. 1972. *The Homosexual Dialectic*. Englewood Cliffs, N.J.: Prentice-Hall.

Maccoby, Eleanor, and Carol Jacklin. 1974. *The Psychology of Sex Differences*. Stanford, Calif.: Stanford Press.

McConnell, Jon P., and J. David Martin. 1969. "Judicial Attitudes and Public Morals." *American Bar Association Journal* 55 (December): 1129–33.

MacDonald, A. P., and Richard G. Games. 1974. "Some Characteristics of Those Who Hold Positive and Negative Attitudes toward Homosexuals." *Journal of Homosexuality* 1, no. 1: 9–27.

McIntosh, Mary. 1968. "The Homosexual Role." *Social Problems* 16 (Fall): 182–92.

McNeill, John. 1976. *The Church and the Homosexual*. Kansas City, Missouri: Sheed, Andrews, and McNeill.

Madge, John. 1962. *The Origins of Scientific Sociology*. New York: Free Press.

Matza, David. 1964. *Delinquency and Drift*. New York: Wiley.

Miller, Marie. 1971. *On Being Different*. New York: Random House.

Miller, Walter. 1958. "Lower-Class Culture as a Generating Milieu of Gang Delinquency." *Journal of Social Issues* 14 (March): 5–19.

Mills, C. Wright. 1959. *The Sociological Imagination*. New York: Oxford.

Money, John, and Patricia Tucker. 1975. *Sexual Signatures*. Boston: Little, Brown.

Murray, John. 1971. *Homosexual Liberation: A Personal View*. New York: Praeger.

Myrick, F. 1974. "Attitudinal Differences between Heterosexuality and Homosexually Oriented Males and between Covert and Overt Male Homosexuals." *Journal of Abnormal Psychology* 83 (February): 81–88.

National Institute of Mental Health. 1969. *Final Report of the Task Force on Homosexuality*. Evelyn Hooker, Chairman. Bethesda, Md.: NIMH.

National Opinion Research Center. 1973. *General Social Survey*. Chicago: National Opinion Research Center.

Nunnally, Jum. 1967. *Psychometric Theory*. New York: McGraw-Hill.

Nyberg, Kenneth, and Jon Alston. 1977. "Analysis of Public Attitudes toward Homosexual Behavior." *Journal of Homosexuality* 2 (Winter): 99–108.

Ovesey, Lionel. 1965. "Pseudohomosexuality and Homosexuality in Men." In *Sexual Inversion: The Multiple Roots of Homosexuality*, ed. Judd Mormor, pp. 211–33. New York: Basic Books.

Perrucci, Robert. 1974. *Circles of Madness: On Being Insane and Institutionalized in America*. Englewood Cliffs, N.J.: Prentice-Hall.

Perry, Troy. 1972. *The Lord Is My Shepherd and He Knows I'm Gay*. New York: Bantam Books.

Pihlblad, P. T., and C. L. Gregory. 1957. "Occupations and Patterns of Migration." *Social Forces* 36 (October): 56–64.

Plummer, Kenneth. 1975. *Sexual Stigma: An Interactionist Perspective*. London: Routledge and Kegan Paul.

Pomeroy, Wardell. 1972. *Dr. Kinsey and the Institute for Sex Research*. New York: Harper & Row.

Rechy, John. 1977. *The Sexual Outlaw*. New York: Grove Press.

———. 1967. *Numbers*. New York: Grove Press.

———. 1962. *City of Night*. New York: Grove Press.

Reichert, Reimut, and Martin Dannecker. 1977. "Male Homosexuality in West Germany." *Journal of Sex Research* 13 (February): 35–53.

Reiss, Albert. 1961. "The Social Integration of Queers and Peers." *Social Problems* 9 (Fall): 102–19.

Remlinger, Gaston. 1969. "The Legitimation of Protest: A Comparative Study of Labor History." In *Protest, Reform, and Revolt: A Reader in Social Movements and Collective Action*, ed. Joseph Gusfield, pp. 363–76. New York: Wiley.

Rodman, Hyman. 1971. *Lower-Class Families: The Culture of Poverty in Negro Trinidad*. New York: Oxford.

Rooney, Elizabeth, and Don Gibbons. 1966. "Social Reactions to 'Crimes without Victims'." *Social Problems* 13 (Spring): 400–410.

Rubington, Earl. 1973. "Variations in Bottle-Gang Controls." In *Deviance: The Interactionist Perspective*, ed. Earl Rubington and Martin Weinberg, pp. 338–47. New York: Macmillan.

Safilios-Rothschild, Constantina. 1970. "The Study of Family Power Structure: A Review of 1960–1969." *Journal of Marriage and the Family* 32 (November): 539–52.

Sagarin, Edward. 1975. *Deviants and Deviance*. New York: Praeger.

———. 1969. *Odd Man In: Societies of Deviants in America*. Chicago: Quadrangle Books.

Saghir, Marcel, and Eli Robins. 1973. *Male and Female Homosexuality*. Baltimore: Williams and Wilkins.

San Francisco Chronicle. October 10, 1977. "Gallup Polls on Gay Job Rights Issue," p. 8.

Schatzman, Leonard, and Anselm Strauss. 1973. *Field Research: Strategies for a Natural Sociology*. Englewood Cliffs, N.J.: Prentice-Hall.

Schofield, Michael. 1965. *Sociological Aspects of Homosexuality*. Boston: Little, Brown.

Schur, Edwin. 1971. *Labeling Deviant Behavior*. New York: Harper & Row.

Sherrill, Kenneth. 1977. "Homophobia: Illness or Disease?" *GAI Saber* 1 (Spring): 27–40.

Shibutani, Tamotsu. 1955. "Reference Groups as Perspectives." *American Journal of Sociology* 60 (May): 562–69.

Siegelman, Marvin. 1972. "Adjustment of Male Homosexuals and Heterosexuals." *Archives of Sexual Behavior* 2 (June): 9–25.

Simmons, J. L. 1965. "Public Stereotypes of Deviants." *Social Problems* 13 (Fall): 223–32.

Simon, William, and John A. Gagnon. 1969. "On Psychosexual Development." In *Handbook of Socialization Theory and Research*, ed. David A. Goslin, pp. 733–52. Chicago: Rand McNally.

———. 1967a. "Homosexuality: The Formulation of a Sociological Perspective." *Journal of Health and Social Behavior* 8 (September): 177–85.

———. 1967b. "The Lesbians: A Preliminary Overview." In *Sexual Deviance*, ed. John Gagnon and William Simon, pp. 247–82. New York: Harper & Row.

Sjaastad, Larry. 1962. "The Costs and Returns of Human Migration." *Journal of Political Economy* 70 (October): 80–93.

Skolnick, Jerome. 1966. *Justice Without Trial*. New York: Wiley.

Smith, Richard, and Brian Garner. 1977. "Are There Really Any Gay Athletes?" *Journal of Sex Research* 13 (February): 22–34.

Socarides, Charles. 1968. *The Overt Homosexual*. New York: Grune and Stratton.

Spector, Malcolm. 1977. "Legitimizing Homosexuality." *Society* 14 (July): 52–56.

Stoller, Robert, Judd Marmor, Irving Bieber, Ronald Gold, Charles Socarides, Richard Green, and Robert Spitzer. 1973. "A Symposium: Should Homosexuality Be in the APA Nomenclature?" *American Journal of Psychiatry* 130 (November): 1207–16.

Stouffer, Samuel. 1955. *Communism, Conformity, and Civil Liberties*. New York: Peter Smith.

Sykes, Gresham, and David Matza. 1957. "Techniques of Neutralization: A Theory of Delinquency." *American Sociological Review* 22 (December): 664–70.

Teal, Donn. 1971. *The Gay Militants*. New York: Stein and Day.

Tobin, Kay, and Randy Wicker. 1972. *The Gay Crusaders, In-Depth Interviews With Fifteen Homosexuals*. New York: Paperback Library.

Tripp, C. A. 1975. *The Homosexual Matrix*. New York: McGraw-Hill.

Udry, Richard J. 1974. *The Social Context of Marriage*. 2d ed. Philadelphia: Lippincott.

U.S. Bureau of the Census. 1975. *Statistical Abstract of the United States*. Washington, D.C.: Government Printing Office.

———. *The 1970 Census of Population: Characteristics of the Population–Michigan*. Washington, D.C.: Government Printing Office.

Warren, Carol. 1974. *Identity and Community in the Gay World*. New York: Wiley.

Weinberg, Martin. 1974. *Male Homosexuals: Their Problems and Adaptations*. New York: Oxford.

———. 1971. *Homosexuals and the Military*. New York: Harper and Row.

———. 1970. "The Male Homosexual: Age-Related Variations in Social and Psychological Characteristics." *Social Problems* 17 (Spring): 527–38.

———. 1966. "Becoming a Nudist." *Psychiatry* 29 (February): 15–24.

———, and Colin J. Williams. 1975. "Gay Baths and the Social Organization of Impersonal Sex." *Social Problems* 23 (December): 124–36.

Weltge, R. W. 1969. *The Same Sex: An Appraisal of Homosexuality*. Boston: Pilgrim Press.

West, Donald J. 1967. *Homosexuality*. Chicago: Aldine.

Westwood, Gordon. 1960. *A Minority: A Report on the Life of the Male Homosexual in Great Britain*. London: Longmans.

Whitam, Fred. 1977. "Childhood Indicators of Male Homosexuality." *Archives of Sexual Behavior* 6 (March): 89–96.

Williams, Colin J., and Martin S. Weinberg. 1971. *Homosexuals and the Military: A Study of Less Than Honorable Discharge*. New York: Harper & Row.

Wilson, James Q. 1975. *Thinking About Crime*. New York: Vintage Books.

Wittman, Carl. 1972. "Refugees from America: A Gay Manifesto." In *The Homosexual Dialectic*, ed. Joseph McCaffrey, pp. 157–71. Englewood Cliffs, N.J.: Prentice-Hall.

Wolfenden, Sir John. 1957. Report of the Departmental Committee on Homosexual Offenses and Prostitution. London: Her Majesty's Stationery Office.

Yearwood, Lennox, and Thomas S. Weinberg. 1977. "Black Organizations; Gay Organizations: Sociological Parallels." Paper presented at Americal Sociological Meeting, Chicago. Mimeographed.

Young, Allen. 1971. "Out of the Closet: A Gay Manifesto." *Ramparts* 10 (November): 52–59.

Zurcher, Louis, Jr., R. George Kirkpatrick, Robert Cushing, and Charles Bowman. 1971. "The Anti-Pornography Campaign: A Symbolic Crusade." *Social Problems* 19 (Fall): 217–37.

ABOUT THE AUTHORS

Joseph Harry received his B.A. from Reed College in 1961 and his Ph.D. from the University of Oregon in 1968. He has taught at Wayne State University, the University of Nebraska at Omaha, the College of Idaho, and is currently in the sociology department at Northern Illinois University. His principal areas of sociological interest are deviance, criminology, and the sociology of leisure. He has published widely in most of the sociological journals.

William B. DeVall received his B.A. from the University of Kansas in 1960 and his Ph.D. from the University of Oregon in 1970. He has taught at the University of Alberta, the College of Idaho, Simon Frasier University, and is Professor of Sociology at Humboldt State University. His major areas of sociological interest are social movements, the sociology of leisure, and environmental sociology. He has published numerous articles in these areas.

RELATED TITLES
Published by
Praeger Special Studies

*THE AGED IN THE COMMUNITY: Managing Senility and Deviance

Dwight G. Frankfather

ALIENATION IN CONTEMPORARY SOCIETY: A Multi-disciplinary Examination

edited by Roy S. Bryce-Laporte
and Claudewell Thomas

THE CYCLE OF VIOLENCE: Assertive, Aggressive, and Abusive Interaction

Suzanne K. Steinmetz

*DEVIANCE AND SOCIAL CONTROL IN CHINESE SOCIETY

edited by Amy Auerbacher Wilson,
Sidney L. Greenblatt, and
Richard W. Wilson

PASSAGE THROUGH ABORTION: The Personal and Social Reality of Women's Experience

Mary K. Zimmerman

WOMEN AND MEN: Changing Roles, Relationships, and Perceptions

Libby A. Cater,
Anne Firor Scott,
with Wendy Martyna

*Also available in paperback.